# A LIBRARIAN'S WAR

Books by Molly Guptill Manning

*The War of Words*
*When Books Went to War*
*The Myth of Ephraim Tutt*

# A LIBRARIAN'S WAR

## THE MAN WHO FOUGHT WORLD WAR II WITH BOOKS AND BROUGHT THE JOY OF READING TO MILLIONS

MOLLY GUPTILL MANNING

OXFORD
UNIVERSITY PRESS

OXFORD
UNIVERSITY PRESS

Oxford University Press is a department of the University of Oxford.
It furthers the University's objective of excellence in research, scholarship,
and education by publishing worldwide. Oxford is a registered trade mark of
Oxford University Press in the UK and in certain other countries.

Published in the United States of America by Oxford University Press
546 Fifth Avenue, New York, NY 10036, United States of America.



CIP data is on file at the Library of Congress.

ISBN 9780197861240

DOI: 10.1093/oso/9780197861240.001.0001

Printed by Marquis Book Printing, Canada

The manufacturer's authorized representative in the EU for product safety is
Oxford University Press España S.A. of Parque Empresarial San Fernando de Henares,
Avenida de Castilla, 2 – 28830 Madrid (www.oup.es/en or product.safety@oup.com).
OUP España S.A. also acts as importer into Spain of products made by the manufacturer.

MIX
Paper | Supporting responsible forestry
FSC® C103567
FSC www.fsc.org

*To Eric,*
*whose kindness and encouragement*
*made this book possible*

# *Contents*

If anyone thinks the armed forces don't want books, I have created a nice special hell of my own for them and can command the services of a heavily armed squad of help-mates to put them there.

—Anonymous soldier, 1943[1]

# Introduction

The foot soldiers of World War II said there were three types of infantrymen—"the quick, the lucky, and the dead."[1] Each foray into battle was a gamble. As the roar of artillery and staccato of gunfire began, a soldier was giving war's roulette wheel a spin.

In early December 1944, fate seemed to smile on the American troops stationed along the borders of France, Belgium, and Germany. Flare-ups of fighting were so uncommon that some GIs joked that their surroundings were as peaceful as a ski resort, and nearly as picturesque.[2] Before them stretched the Ardennes forest, a pristine landscape that looked like a scene from a postcard, with enormous fir trees lightly powdered by fresh snow and ice-kissed streams carving through undulating hills.[3] Rumor had it that the war would be over by Christmas.[4]

Before dawn on December 16, 1944, American troops were startled awake by the thunder of enemy artillery and rockets. Red, green, amber, and white flares lit up the dark sky as shells sailed toward their foxholes. The deranged melody of battle swelled as the rumble of tanks and percussion of mortars joined the requiem, enveloping troops in deafening sound.

For over an hour, the earth pulsated. And then it stopped.[5] The sudden silence was made eerier by the thick blanket of fog that had settled across the area, enveloping the Americans in a "white darkness" that gave the sensation of blindness.[6] Troops awaited orders. None came. Some men sensed movement ahead and stared into the void. Making their way through the opaque cloud clutching the earth were packs of German soldiers dressed in white, blending with the fog and snow,[7] like ghostly wolves sneaking up on their prey. Gunfire erupted at the harried Americans. They had two options: die or make what the military called a "strategic retreat." Many ran for shelter in the trees as a hail of bullets chased them. The quicker ones made it.

They were clearly outnumbered by the enemy—some of Germany's finest troops. Their hopes for survival dimmed by the minute.[8] If they could figure out where the American lines were, perhaps they could make it out alive. The woods were laced with snow-covered lanes and firebreak roads. Which to take, and in what direction?[9] As dusk descended, they heard the muffled purr of an engine on a nearby road. They could make out the silhouette of a car crawling through the woods, headlights dimmed by blackout patches.[10] American or German? Were they lucky or dead? One brave soul stepped onto the road and flagged down the car. He figured his odds were fifty-fifty.

Lieutenant Colonel Ray Love Trautman ordered his American driver to stop as soldiers poured out of the woods and surrounded his car. Just by looking at them, Trautman could guess what they had been through. Their gray faces and bloodshot eyes betrayed their ordeal, tattered uniforms bore the markings of battle, and hollowed expressions spoke of trauma. A man was holding a bloody stump wrapped in fabric, where his hand had been.[11]

The highest-ranking member of the group, Trautman took charge. He needed to reconnect these men with their units while facing the possibility of fighting the Germans. However, the men had abandoned their weapons in their hasty retreat, and Trautman did not have specialized training in drawing battle plans or leading troops in combat. He was the Army's chief librarian and was on a fact-finding assignment for General Eisenhower, who had assured him that the sector was quiet. Trautman's expertise involved keeping soldier morale high, mainly by arming them with reading material—magazines, books, and comics.[12] Under different circumstances, troops would flock to Trautman as though he was a celebrity at a United Service Organizations (USO) show, except that instead of asking for an autograph they would shout out the titles of books they hoped he would add to the list of pocket-sized paperbacks he had invented for troops, known as the Armed Services Editions (ASEs). Some might ask if Trautman had any ASEs to spare.

The stranded soldiers standing before Trautman were not looking for things to read. They were seeking survival. It seemed unlikely that a librarian's skillset would be of much use.[13]

In the coming days, Trautman would prove them wrong. As it turned out, a well-read officer and librarian could concoct a battle plan to fend off a column of German tanks with improvised weaponry. And he was certainly the only commanding officer to treat his men to books if they survived.

# 1

# Children of the Night

They say that we are children of the night.
My wife and I can neither read nor write.
Though my son Paul—he's going off to school,
I do not want my son to be a fool—
I want my Paul to learn to read and write.
I want my son to learn to figure right.
I don't want him to be a child of night.

—Jesse Stuart[1]

From a young age, Ray Trautman learned that opportunities did not come knocking; they had to be made. Growing up in a rural farming community in Ohio, fortuity ran in short supply and hardship was abundant. Through struggle, sheer willpower, and an unshakeable desire to make the most of himself, Trautman grew undaunted by difficulties, strengthened by the challenges he faced, and steadfast in his drive to pave his own path. He succeeded. Before reaching the age of forty, he revolutionized the literary universe, transforming the book and magazine industries forever.[2]

He entered the world on July 22, 1907, in the sleepy village of Mowrystown, Ohio, which boasted a population of around 200 people.[3] Hailing from France and Germany, Trautman's great-grandparents were lured to Ohio in the 1830s by the promise of cheap land and good farming. For decades, they and their children tilled and harvested.[4] However, Trautman's father, George, was not interested in following the family tradition. A free spirit, he wanted to explore careers outside of farming and spent much of his life cycling through different types of employment. First he tried his hand at business, working as a salesman with the Diehl Brothers, the owners of Mowrystown's general store and flour mill.[5] A music lover, he spent evenings and weekends drumming in his local band.[6] After his marriage to Bertha May Parrot in 1903, George founded his own stock breeding outfit, focusing primarily on horses.[7] By 1914, he had four children—Wilson "Ford," Ray, Emma, and Huldah—and decided that cultivating the land might provide a more reliable paycheck. As a "truck farmer," George grew a variety of crops to sell at market, with his children assisting with farm chores before and after school.[8] Corn, potatoes, and other vegetables were staples. But the real money came from tobacco. Though a poor season would result in sales at only three cents per pound, when the weather cooperated, tobacco commanded a whopping ten cents per pound.[9] After welcoming his and his wife's fifth child, Madalie, in 1921, George lost his appetite for leaving his earnings to the whims of Mother Nature.[10] Giving up farming, he found work as a building contractor; he remained with this profession until he retired in the early 1940s.[11]

George and Bertha Trautman modeled a strong work ethic and encouraged their children to discover their own interests. They took pride in ensuring that all of them attended school, learning to read and write as young as six years old.[12] This was no small feat. The local school, Whiteoak Rural School, served all of the children in the community and was underfunded. It struggled to maintain a library of donated materials.[13] Mowrystown itself did not have its own community library.[14] Being so scarce, books were precious. Perhaps this is what made them so enticing to Ray. Curious about the world beyond his small community, Ray turned to books to explore new frontiers. He had an insatiable appetite for learning, and reading was the main way he could feed this hunger. Whenever he could get his hands on a new volume, he dove between two covers and spent hours soaking up every detail. From a desk in a crowded classroom or in the embrace of a shade tree on his family farm, books allowed Trautman to go on vacations his family could never afford, learn history and science that would never be covered in his classes, and imagine possibilities for himself that did not exist in his small town.

The more he read, the more books he wanted to read. If only they were not so hard to find.

Trautman's love of reading would guide him down a different path than what his siblings chose for themselves. Ray's older brother, Ford, ultimately took an interest in working alongside his father in the construction business; Huldah worked in retail stores; Emma became a clerk at a bank;[15] and Madalie worked in a store before marrying. Ray set his sights on college. In the 1920s, the average cost for one year of tuition was $700.[16] The average salary for a farmer in Mowrystown was around $450 per year.[17] Although his parents would lend moral support, Ray would have to find a way to pay for his aspirations. Meanwhile, he would also have to figure out what, exactly, he aimed to do with his life.

At sixteen years old, Ray had almost no savings. Somehow, he needed to finish high school while also earning an income that would pay for college. At first it seemed hopeless. Most businesses employed workers from 9 to 5, but Ray had to attend school during those hours. In 1921, his family moved to Newport, Kentucky,[18] located across the Ohio River from Cincinnati. There, in the big city, the East Night High School offered courses in the evening so students could work by day. Ray immediately applied for admission to the school and sent job applications to businesses across the city.

His diligence paid off. Not only was he granted a seat in East Night's five-year program, but he also secured a clerk position at the Union Central Life Insurance Company.[19] Making around $20 per week, Ray saved his earnings.[20] Union Central's offices were located in what was, at 495 feet, the tallest building in the world outside of New York City.[21] On lunch breaks, Ray could not resist riding the elevator to the thirty-fourth floor.[22] On a clear day, he could see Cincinnati's sprawl of buildings give way to the Kentucky Hills.[23] A world of potential seemed to unfurl at such a height; Ray would gaze into the distance and dream of his future. On other days, he walked to the Cincinnati Public Library's central branch, just five blocks from work, where a different world was revealed to him through its 50,000 books, plus countless magazines and newspapers. After having had virtually no library before, Trautman felt as though he had discovered a cache of lost treasure. Though he did not live in Cincinnati, all nonresidents employed in the county were eligible to register for a library card and have free access to all branches in the Cincinnati Library system.[24] Ray took full and frequent advantage of his borrowing privileges, becoming a familiar face amongst the stacks. Here, Ray began to grapple with his future. He read articles in local newspapers about the aviation breakthroughs of the nearby Dayton-Wright Company.[25] Maybe he could pilot planes and explore the world? He read classics like Charles Dickens's *David Copperfield*, finding inspiration to reach beyond his humble origins and make the most of himself. Like David, he believed an education would enable him to thrive in his life's calling.[26] There was T. S. Eliot's *The Waste Land and Other Poems*, with haunting words of admonition to strive upwards and resist the quicksand of inertia.[27] Reading filled his mind with ideas, while also stirring fears of failure. College would be difficult and expensive, and whether he could succeed and finance this dream was uncertain.

In 1924, after two years of working and studying full-time, Ray was accepted for admission to the 1925 freshman class at the University of Kentucky. After graduating from East Night High School in June 1925, he spent the summer saving every penny he earned while searching for employment opportunities that would be conducive to his college schedule.[28] As Ray made inquiries, he learned about the Reserve Officers Training Corps (ROTC) program. By agreeing to undergo basic and advanced military training and spending two weeks each summer in the Army, he would receive subsistence money and the possibility of a future in the military.[29] Unsure what profession he might ultimately join, Ray believed a military background would only help him. He would receive training, build discipline, and might be able to pursue his burgeoning interest in aviation if he pursued flying school after graduation. At the very least, he needed money for tuition, and the ROTC would pay him. He signed up.

In July 1925, Trautman arrived at the University of Kentucky for his first two-week Army summer camp. Among the college-bound students was a six-foot-tall, 110-pound lanky individual who, like most rural farm boys in the summertime, was not wearing shoes.[30] Knowing this young man would be chewed out by an officer, Trautman gave away the only spare pair of shoes he owned.[31] This was how Trautman became a lifelong friend to Jesse Stuart, a native of Kentucky who also had big dreams and no money to pay for them. Stuart would later become a bestselling author and Pulitzer Prize finalist, but what bonded the two men that day—besides their shoe size—was their mutual love of books.[32] Stuart had packed the handful of tomes that composed his personal library and, at night, the two read, talked, and built hope for their futures.[33]

Over the next two weeks, Stuart and Trautman trained and shared how badly they wanted to go to college and see the world. Though kindred spirits in many ways, they could not have been more different in their attitudes towards the military. While Trautman managed to adjust to the Army's regimentation, Stuart did not. He refused to salute, failed inspection (he left books on his bunk), and was caught sneaking out at night.[34] When the two weeks were up, by some miracle Stuart managed to be honorably discharged and left the Army for good. Trautman, in contrast, was just beginning decades of service.[35]

In the fall of 1925, Trautman began his studies at the University of Kentucky while also taking every odd job he could get. His savings, and the meager pay from the ROTC, were not enough to cover four years of tuition and expenses. He worked as a barber, switchboard operator, and private tutor.[36] Meanwhile, he balanced a full schedule of classes while auditing as many courses as he could. In narrowing his focus to a single major, Trautman leaned toward the sciences. Originally an agricultural college, the University of Kentucky prided itself on providing students a mixture of hands-on experience in a field of study and a general liberal arts education.[37] Having grown up without bookstores, and largely without libraries, Trautman did not yet consider the possibility of a career working with books. It would take several years, and some experimentation and soul-searching, before Trautman would gravitate in that direction. During his first year of college, geology won his heart. Its frequent field work appealed to his love of the outdoors, and he was fascinated how the mere observation of a creek bed or rockface gave clues to what geological marvels might lie beneath.[38] As he earned his degree, Trautman explored the limestone outcroppings of nearby Elk Lick Falls;[39] a magnetite mine in Cranberry, North Carolina; the unique rocks of Roan Mountain in Virginia; and many other places.[40] Just as it seemed he was finding his way, he discovered he was running out of money. After two years of college, his finances failed him and he could not pay for a third year of tuition. Forced to take a temporary leave and pursue full-time employment, he hit a low point.

Trautman found work in the fall of 1927 in the advertising department of the *Cincinnati Post*.[41] The following April, he left the newspaper to take a position at the nearby Kroger Grocery and Baking Company. His work ethic and professionalism earned him a raise, and within a month he was promoted to store manager. For the next year and a half, Trautman worked long hours and saved as much money as he could. He made tentative plans to return to the University of Kentucky in September 1929, and in preparation asked his geology professors whether they knew of any paid positions within the school. It turned out that there was an opening for a job cataloging mineral and fossil specimens.[42] Confident that he could now afford a third year of college by spending his savings while earning money from his new geology job, Trautman resigned from Kroger and returned to school full-time, including resuming his ROTC training. After completing his junior year in 1930, Trautman worked as a student instructor in the university's geology laboratory for his senior year. He graduated in 1931 with a Bachelor of Science degree.[43] Having completed four years of ROTC, he earned a commission as second lieutenant.[44]

He had achieved his goal of earning a college degree, yet Trautman felt directionless. The nation was fully in the grip of the Great Depression and facing staggering unemployment rates. Geologists were not in high demand. When the University of Kentucky offered him the opportunity to be a paid graduate assistant while earning a master's degree, he leapt at the chance.[45] He hoped another year of study would help him crystallize a plan for his life. After spending part of his summer as an instructing officer at the Citizens' Military Training Camp at Fort Thomas,

Kentucky, Trautman commenced his graduate studies and completed his master's degree in geology in August 1932.[46]

Trautman now had two degrees and a commission, but no job prospects. Leaning on his ROTC experience and strong interest in aviation, Trautman tested his luck by applying to the Army Air Corps, one of the most elite and selective branches of the Army. Trautman asked his ROTC supervisor, Captain William Cunningham, for a required reference and received a strong endorsement. Cunningham stated that Trautman was an individual of "exemplary character," who was "splendidly adapted for the service," and "the best man to have graduated from the University during the past two years." Cunningham closed by noting that Trautman was "of the type and character that are needed in our regular establishment."[47] With his application complete, all Trautman could do was wait for an answer.

In the meantime, Trautman searched for a job. Serendipitously, Trautman saw an advertisement for a management position at the local Ex Libris Book Shop in downtown Lexington, Kentucky.[48] It was a small shop, across from the bus depot, and received a steady stream of customers from near and far.[49] Trautman immediately fell in love with the work. Surrounded by shelves of books, each day Trautman spent hours in the company of people searching for something that only a book could provide. He prided himself on his ability to connect readers with the tales that would deliver whatever sort of adventure, escape, knowledge, or inspiration they were seeking. Book collectors also frequented the shop, and Trautman began to learn how to hunt for rare volumes and turn a profit when selling them to bibliophiles and hobbyists. Trautman was so content managing the Ex Libris that when the owner announced a desire to close, Trautman somehow arranged to purchase the store.[50] Many years later, reflecting on the joys of running a small bookstore, Trautman said:

> A bookshop is the natural habitat of authors, collectors, local historians, readers, and all those with such related artistic interests; it draws them irresistibly as a magnet [to] bits of iron. These booklovers, in the presence of the great literary minds of the past, are apt to unbend to a degree

> impossible elsewhere. The bookman . . . is the unobtrusive center of this rare society, gaining bibliographic skill from his many teachers and passing back to the stream of habitues and visitors bits of wisdom or curious fact gleaned from his contacts with the great and the obscure.[51]

For six months, Trautman contentedly felt he had found his calling. Then, in early 1933, the rug was pulled from beneath him when he received the astonishing news that he had qualified for appointment as a flying cadet at Randolph Field, Texas,[52] being one of the 175 men selected for the March 1933 class.[53] When he had applied, this news would have elated him. Now, it made him sick. He would have to leave his beloved bookstore. Yet he could not bring himself to forgo this once-in-a-lifetime opportunity to learn to fly. Aviation still fascinated him, and he could not ignore that he had beaten incredible odds by earning a seat as a flying cadet. Uncertain if he was making the right move, Trautman nevertheless sold the Ex Libris Book Shop[54] and reported to Fort Thomas, Kentucky, on February 21, to formally enlist. "Carry only a change of underclothing and toilet articles when you report," the Army instructed. Cadets would be leaving their civilian lives and individuality behind.[55]

Eighteen miles northeast of San Antonio, Randolph Field had opened in 1931 and immediately earned the distinction of being the Army's "West Point of the Air."[56] While airplanes played a significant role in World War I, the Army did not maintain a centralized program in military aviation after that war; flying schools were small and scattered, from March Field in Riverside, California, to Brooks, Duncan, and Kelly Fields, as well as Fort Sam Houston in Texas.[57] Randolph Field would consolidate the Army's flying program, realizing the Army Air Corps' long-term aim of building a modern, innovative campus to train the finest young men with the best equipment and instruction available.[58]

New cadets (called "dodos" by upperclassmen) faced one of the most rigorous training programs in the country. Each day, they devoted six hours to some combination of flight training and ground school. On average, new students would spend the bulk of their first two months in a classroom and only thirty minutes in the air each day. As they gained competency and textbook training, their flight time increased.[59] Students were warned that the program was so difficult that getting "washed out" should not be considered a failure. Between 1932 and 1939, more than 50 percent of flying cadets were dismissed before completing the thirty-week program.[60] Trautman heeded these warnings but remained steadfast. After weathering years of adversity to achieve his goal of graduating college, he had developed confidence in himself. If he was determined to accomplish something, he would find a way to do it.

Trautman's "hell month"—as he and the other dodos called it—began on March 2, 1933, replete with constant drills, surprise inspections, and abuse from upperclassmen. As described by Beirne Lay, a cadet in the 1932 class, each day "we all stood there at cramped attention and absorbed an oral punishment that was calculated to goad the most placid individual into a state of mental chaos."[61] As if the instructors did not produce sufficient angst, hazing rituals added an additional layer. When walking down a hallway and turning into a new corridor, for the amusement of their seniors, a dodo had to mimic the wings of a plane by "lift[ing] his arms and stretch[ing] them out with the one on the side toward which he was turning slanting down, the other slanting up." While eating breakfast, a dodo was obligated to wear flight goggles. This eyewear severely limited vision at certain angles, and upperclassmen were kept entertained by watching dodos try to shovel food into their mouths and miss. While these rituals had some basis in training—the arm movements helped reinforce how to bank a plane and eating with goggles helped familiarize cadets with blind spots they would encounter while flying—they were mainly exercises in humiliation.[62]

All the indignities slipped away when Trautman eased into a cockpit. As his plane steadily climbed into the air, he watched as Randolph Field grew small and the world opened up; sprawled out before him was a quilt of cotton patches, cornfields, and thickets of green-gray mesquite.[63] The clouds greeted him and the air grew crisp and cool the higher he rose. After all the barking instructors and upperclassmen abuse on the ground, flying brought a sense of peace. Every hour in the air only confirmed that this was exactly what Trautman wanted to do. He was a model student in the classroom, operated with admirable attitude and skill during drills, and made sure to keep his room and equipment inspection-ready. But his instructors noticed a possible weakness in Trautman's vision. Even the slightest infirmity was enough to prompt the dreaded washout.[64] When Trautman underwent additional visual examinations, he failed them.[65]

On April 15, 1933, barely six weeks in, Trautman was dismissed from the Army Air Corps due to imperfect eyesight. Despite knowing that at least half of his class would share the same fate—if for other reasons—the news was devastating. Nothing compared to being at the controls and steadying a ship as it gained altitude. Floating across the sky reminded him of being atop the Union Central Life Insurance Building—it was invigorating to feel that possibilities stretched infinitely in all directions. Now, Trautman only saw defeat.

When two of Trautman's friends—Bill Yeakley, a former Princeton University football captain, and another cadet whose name has been lost to time—received word that they were also being dismissed from Randolph Field, the three met in San Antonio to bemoan their circumstances.[66] With their futures dashed, they wallowed in dejection and a sense of aimlessness. What now? As they spitballed and halfheartedly tried to hatch new dreams, the group considered pooling their meager funds and cashing in on Trautman's geology knowledge by setting out for the west and prospecting for gold. It seemed plausible enough and nothing was holding them back. They packed their things, clambered into an old Model T Ford, and motored their way across 2,200 miles to the headwaters of the Columbia River in Canada. From there, they ditched their car and rafted down the river in search of a place to camp and pan for riches.[67]

They spent much of the month of May 1933 not far from Donald Station, British Columbia. As Trautman explained in a letter home, "The Rocky Mountains are on our East and the Selkirks on our West. Between them flows the mighty Columbia, a treacherous stream." They set up camp surrounded by evergreens, pines, cedars, spruce, balsam, and the occasional birch and white poplar. With the nearest store thirty miles away, they lived off the land, fishing and hunting for food. Most days, weather depending, Trautman and his friends went on exploration hikes, often trekking more than twenty miles as they searched for the most promising signs of gold deposits. "Have seen some of the most beautiful scenery in the world," Trautman wrote his sister Huldah. He and his friends slept on the ground, tolerated squirrels "running over our faces as we sleep," and were forced to grow beards to keep the bloodthirsty mosquitoes from assaulting their faces. In the process, Trautman's depression from being washed out had lifted. "I never felt better in my life," Trautman confided to Huldah.[68]

After weeks of exploring, the group of twenty-five-year-olds believed they found a likely spot for gold and decided to relocate. Trautman and his friends broke down their camp, loaded their possessions onto rafts, and floated down the river. After several miles, they spotted a group of Native Americans on the shore. As the rafts glided by, the Native Americans waved their arms and yelled; for what reason, Trautman and his friends were unsure. Soon, however, they realized the rafts were picking up speed; waterfalls were ahead. They leapt into the water and fought the strong current to shore. Their lives were saved, but their rafts and belongings were gone.

Another adventure had come to an unceremonious end. Over the next several days, Trautman and his friends hiked back to where they had parked their Model T, sleeping on blankets of balsam and hunting for food along the way. They drove the 2,200 miles back to San Antonio with a few nuggets of gold in their pockets and their spirits revived.[69]

Unsure of what to do next, Trautman noticed a sign advertising a store manager vacancy at the H. A. Moos Bookstore in downtown San Antonio. Again, as he would his entire life, he gravitated to books. Thanks to his experience at the Ex Libris Book Shop, Trautman was hired.[70] After spending the rest of 1933 and several months of 1934 in San Antonio, he decided to return to Kentucky and his family.

Once again, Trautman searched for a job, but the Great Depression lingered and openings were scarce. As many young men did, Trautman considered employment opportunities under President Franklin Roosevelt's New Deal programs. Of them all, the Civilian Conservation

Corps (CCC) struck a chord with Trautman. Formed in 1933, the CCC provided employment to out-of-work men, ages eighteen to twenty-five, who were in good health and had no criminal record. A man could enlist for a six-month stint (that could be extended) of work that would pay $30 per month.[71] Work included "preventing fires, floods, and soil erosion" as well as building, maintaining, or repairing "paths, trails, and fire-lanes in the national parks and national forests."[72] Spending his days outside and working with the land were appealing to Trautman. Between his geology field trips at the University of Kentucky and the weeks he had spent in the wilderness of British Columbia, Trautman craved the sense of well-being he felt in nature; the CCC offered him an outlet with a paycheck. The Army was responsible for building CCC camps, as well as transporting, feeding, clothing, and caring for enrollees, who numbered 300,000 by July 1933 and would grow to three million by the program's end in 1942.[73] Regular Army officers, usually with a rank of first lieutenant, were placed in charge of each CCC camp.[74] This is what Trautman wanted to do, though as a second lieutenant, he was one notch too low. Taking matters into his own hands, Trautman campaigned for a promotion, and in August 1934 became a first lieutenant in the infantry reserves. He applied for active duty with the CCC and in 1935 joined up.[75]

His time there was short-lived. In July, Trautman was assigned work that required a lengthy hike, and he seemed to contract a severe cold. Days later, he began to experience acute chest pain and was admitted to the post hospital for observation. X-rays revealed a buildup of fluid, which was periodically aspirated only to return. Chest pains and fevers were intermittent over the course of six weeks, and though tuberculosis was suspected, Trautman tested negative.[76] A medical mystery, Trautman was transferred to the Walter Reed General Hospital in Washington, DC, where he spent the next five months receiving treatment.[77] Throughout his convalescence, Trautman dreamed of returning to his post at the CCC in Kentucky. However, in October 1935, he received a letter informing him that he was relieved from active duty. Though he applied from his hospital bed for a six-month extension, his request was denied. He was informed that the CCC had reduced its use of active-duty officers. The cause for this change was growing criticism that the CCC was simply a back-door method to increase the size and strength of the Army.[78] Civilians began to replace Army officers for many CCC leadership positions.

During his stay at Walter Reed, Trautman managed to secure a job with the Library of Congress, one that involved preparing bibliographies of first editions of Kentucky authors.[79] When he was well enough, Trautman left his bed and worked in the nation's greatest library. When his symptoms kept him bedridden, Trautman retreated into a world of books, using stories to distract him from the pain and uncertainty. In December 1935, Trautman fully recovered—to his doctor's surprise—and was discharged from Walter Reed. Once again, he had no job prospects and would have to build himself up from scratch.

Returning to Cincinnati, Trautman found employment as an adult education counselor at the Cincinnati Public Library.[80] As always, he found solace being surrounded by books. Having been an avid patron of the library when he worked at the Union Central Life Insurance Company, he found it a comfort to return to a place he knew and loved. In a matter of months, Trautman's passion for library work drew the attention of Pauline Fihe, a seasoned librarian,[81] and Chalmers Hadley, the head librarian.[82] Both saw that Trautman was a natural at working in the orbits of books and education, and, though they would be sorry to see him go, encouraged him to explore a career that would help him develop that gift. But he was a college-educated geologist with no credentials in education or librarianship. He could not imagine returning to school at this point to pursue another degree, this time in library science. Instead, Trautman decided to apply for a new job with the CCC, which had recently expanded its commitment to provide educational opportunities for its enrollees. Trautman discovered that the CCC was hiring college-educated civilians to serve as "educational advisers." Each adviser would be able to fashion their own brand of educational programming for their assigned camp. Having already worked with the CCC, gained experience educating adults at the Cincinnati Public Library, and witnessed the obstacles to education facing young farmhands from places like Kentucky and Ohio, Trautman believed this job would be a good fit for him.

In April 1936, Trautman received a letter from the United States Commissioner of Education, informing him to again report for work with the CCC.[83] Initially, Trautman worked as the assistant to the district educational adviser for the CCC post at Fort Thomas, Kentucky. There he happened to meet an Army medical clerk who would change his life.[84] Her name was Jane MacDonald, and Trautman was immediately taken by her love of books, electric smile, and kind heart. They began to date, and after a year's courtship, they married in Elkhart, Indiana, in August 1937.[85]

Shortly after marrying, Trautman was assigned to CCC Company 3541 in Walton, Kentucky. With wide latitude to transform the company's educational offerings, Trautman was determined to provide a comprehensive array of activities that had something for every enrollee. Walton was not fertile ground for an educational program. The area consisted primarily of small farms, and the majority of enrollees had stopped attending school around the fifth grade, mainly in order to work.[86] Trautman learned that most residents had no access to books, and even those who attended the local high school found only "an assortment of discarded and gift books kept in the principal's office" and "several mail bags full of old government reports and publications" that a local congressman donated.[87] While the community needed a good library, it was "too poor to support [one] of its own."[88]

Trautman wanted to use his position at the local CCC to benefit the whole community. For starters, he aimed to cure the widespread illiteracy at the camp; many enrollees reported that neither they, nor anyone in their family, could read or write. They were what Trautman's friend, Jesse Stuart, called "children of the night," whose hands were educated in working the soil, but whose minds had not been sharpened in the classroom. Trautman did not judge them; he understood them. When he was an adolescent, Trautman noticed his classmates disappear from school—often for weeks at a time, sometimes never to return—because they were expected to help their parents with planting, tending, and harvesting fields as well as assisting with everything from breeding to preparing animals for market. Although Trautman's parents kept their children in school, Trautman and his siblings were well versed in physically demanding agricultural work because they grew up breeding horses and raising crops to sell. Rather than view the development of the mind and body as mutually exclusive, Trautman believed there was merit to nurturing both. So he taught illiterate CCC enrollees how to read and write, breaking, as one of Trautman's colleagues put it, "a family tradition."[89]

After ensuring everyone in his orbit could navigate the written word, Trautman filled the camp library with books for them to read. Not just any books would do. Like he did at Ex Libris and the H. A. Moos Bookstore, Trautman endeavored to learn the reading tastes of his "customers" in the CCC so that he had titles they would enjoy. He stretched his funding to purchase a variety of books, including reference, nonfiction, and fiction.[90] He also spearheaded a program to get popular books without having to pay for them, using the library system. While working at the Cincinnati Public Library, he had learned that the library loaned books to rural communities in the county to create small borrowing libraries. For example, the general store for the tiny enclave of Sharonville proudly hung a shingle announcing that it doubled as a library; 250 books from the Cincinnati Public Library were available for borrowing, and every three months a new set of 250 books replaced the last batch to ensure a fresh selection.[91] Inspired by this concept, Trautman partnered with local Kentucky libraries so that Company 3541 could periodically borrow collections of the public library's recent acquisitions.[92] He also helped develop sets of "traveling libraries" that rotated among several camps every three to four months.[93] Because most of the enrollees at Company 3541—which numbered around 200 men[94]—were local, when they visited home each weekend, they often brought a book to read to their family.[95] In this way, Trautman's CCC library managed to serve not only the enrollees, but the larger community.

Trautman did not stop with books. Since some clamored for periodicals, Trautman scrounged up enough money to subscribe to fifty-six magazines per month.[96] He also ordered educational movies for the post, led and sponsored several hobby groups, and personally administered aptitude tests to help connect young men with post-CCC jobs that would suit their interests.[97] He turned to his friends at the Cincinnati Public Library when he needed help developing a curriculum and best teaching practices.[98] It was a dizzying array of activities, but they made an unmistakable difference in the quality of life for the men in camp. For those who had entered the CCC reluctantly or bristled at the notion of menial work, Trautman's ambitious program of education, recreation, and entertainment infused them with a sense of pride and accomplishment. Not only did these young men develop vocational skills, but they also gained the ability to use books to better themselves.

In late 1938, when Trautman submitted his activities report to Howard Oxley, the director of CCC camp education at the US Office of Education,[99] he received a personal letter in response. Oxley praised Trautman's innovative program and said it would influence the development of programming in all camps.[100] This meant that Trautman's ideas would reach beyond the 200 men in Company 3541, possibly extending to millions across the country.[101]

The CCC was a turning point for Trautman. It made him realize that helping people foster a love of books was the most rewarding career he could imagine. Whenever he worked with books, Trautman felt a sense of fulfillment that was unmatched by anything else he did. And he couldn't seem to leave them alone. Since college, he managed bookstores, worked at the Library of Congress, gained employment at the Cincinnati Public Library, and built a library and education program for CCC enrollees. By 1939, he felt sure his life's calling involved books and he was willing to take a risk to seal this fate. Trautman believed he needed one more credential to make this new dream a reality, and he set his sights on pursuing a master's degree at Columbia University's School of Library Service, then considered the country's preeminent institution in the field. With a degree from it in hand, Trautman believed the doors to the world of books would swing wide open.

Yet Trautman did not feel overly confident when he submitted his application. He had never been to a city as large as New York nor seen a college campus as grand as Columbia's. He wondered if other students would have a huge advantage over him if they had undergraduate degrees in education, library science, or any other major more suitable to librarianship than geology. Would they perceive him as a "child of the night," a rural simpleton who had no place in a top-tier graduate program? And what if yet another disappointment was in store for him? He had already endured so many setbacks, from running out of money for tuition as an undergraduate, to washing out from the Air Corps, to losing almost everything on his gold mining trip, and to being discharged from the CCC while he was at Walter Reed. Each time he faltered, Trautman regained his footing, but the stakes felt higher than ever before. He was in his thirties, and soon there would be pressure to start a family. The window for him to start over again was closing. In Trautman's view, if he did not earn a library degree immediately, he might never have the chance again.

# 2

# Now or Never

> Whether I shall turn out to be the hero of my own life, or whether that station will be held by anybody else, these pages must show.
>
> —*David Copperfield*, Charles Dickens[1]

In August 1939, Jane and Ray Trautman marked two years of marriage. They did not have much, but they had created a happy life together in Walton, Kentucky, a town of under 1,000 people, about twenty miles south of Cincinnati. After saving their earnings for a year, they purchased a "new" secondhand bedroom set, a rug, a chair, and a trunk.[2] When they brought this haul home, they spent days arranging and rearranging *their* furniture. As the seasons shifted and the wind carried a chill, they would read the nights away nestled around a roaring fire, its glow creating a sense of cheer against the gloom of the long, dark winter. The summers in Walton were lovely. Jane recalled summer afternoons spent walking through the fields and pastures under a canopy of deep blue sky and billowing clouds, talking about their future as she loaded her arms with goldenrod and asters. They divided household chores; when Jane cooked, Trautman washed the dishes.[3] They were happy with their life in the Kentucky hills, which Jane described in her diary as "glorious."[4] Kentucky, and the life she built with Trautman, felt like home to her.

When a letter arrived that summer offering Trautman admission to the Columbia University School of Library Service, the news was bittersweet. Trautman was a step closer to achieving his next big goal—status conferred by one of the world's most prestigious institutions and certification in the world of books—but this came at the cost of leaving the happiness he and Jane had in hand.

Whether Trautman could accept Columbia's offer hinged on the usual complication: money. Worry over it practically bled from sheets of paper covered in calculations estimating the cost of tuition, books, rent, food, and necessary incidentals. With rent in New York easily commanding $8 or $9 per week, and tuition totaling several hundred dollars, by Trautman's arithmetic, he and Jane would need at least $900 to sustain them for one year after depleting their meager savings.[5] Yet again, Trautman nurtured a dream that felt prohibitively expensive. He inquired whether Columbia offered any sort of financial assistance by way of teaching, assistantships, scholarships, or stipends. He learned that many library students applied for fellowships with local libraries, which provided practical work experience and a salary. Whether Trautman would be sitting in a Columbia University classroom in September or behind his desk at the CCC in Kentucky depended on whether he could secure such a fellowship. Columbia offered to circulate Trautman's name and credentials to institutions in New York that were hiring.

In mid-July, a letter from the College of the City of New York arrived, informing Trautman that he had been considered for a part-time assistant position but that all fellowships were filled. He would be placed on a waiting list for a job that would likely pay around $500 per year.[6]

Trautman was crestfallen. School was scheduled to begin within weeks, and all he had been offered was a place on a waiting list for a position that would cover only half of his expenses. The situation looked bleak. He realized that if the College of the City of New York had already completed its hiring, the same was likely true of the other fellowships. He felt he had no choice but to forfeit his seat at Columbia. From his desk at the CCC, Trautman reluctantly fed a fresh sheet of paper into his typewriter and began to hammer the keys, responding to the College of the City of New York. "It is with regret that I will not be in a position to attend the School of Library Service at Columbia University even if I should be so fortunate as to secure such employment as is provided in your fellowship."[7]

Then he grabbed another piece of paper, crammed it through the typewriter's rollers, and addressed a letter to the dean of the School of

Library Service. He thanked the dean for forwarding his name to City College but regretted he "would be unable to attend Columbia even with the assistance which might be offered."[8]

Before mailing these letters, Trautman wrote a third one, to his friend at the Cincinnati Public Library, Pauline Fihe. Trautman had asked Fihe for a letter of recommendation for his Columbia application and felt he owed her an explanation for why he could not attend. "If there is anything in the world I should like to do it is to go and take Library training," Trautman confided to Fihe. "In fact I feel so deeply about it that I perhaps expressed some of my discontent in the attached letters. You are the only person with whom I feel free to express my reactions in this matter." Trautman sent the drafts of his letters to Fihe and asked for her honest opinion as to whether they should be rewritten or left unmailed. He was worried they might seem "too impertinent" and he did not want "to imply that I consider myself so important that special consideration should be shown to me."[9]

Just as Trautman had given up hope, a letter arrived from Charles Gosnell, the assistant librarian at Queens College, inviting Trautman to apply for a fellowship at the rate of $750 per year.[10] Queens College was a newly founded part of the City University of New York system, first opening its doors in October 1937 with the enthusiastic support of Mayor Fiorello La Guardia.[11] Its library boasted 30,000 volumes; but Gosnell admitted that "much of the organization is yet to be completed, and we feel that we can offer experience beyond the usual routine assigned to the beginner in library work."[12] The opportunity seemed too good to be true—Trautman could earn almost all the money needed for his expenses while learning his new trade. Trautman immediately mailed his completed application, and on August 2, received a reply inviting him for an interview on August 7 at 2 p.m. in New York City. "You are one of the leading candidates for the position," the letter confirmed. However, it also warned that a final decision might not be made until after the new school year began.[13] This was Trautman's only chance at gaining a fellowship and attending Columbia. He had to take this leap of faith.

Trautman requested leave from the CCC and purchased train tickets. To avoid the cost of a hotel, Trautman took an overnight train, arriving in New York on Monday morning, August 7. Bleary-eyed, he emerged onto the streets of the city and was immediately dazzled. He had never been to New York City, and the energy pulsating from its streets was captivating. He zipped across the city in a subway, joined the throngs of people bobbing up and down to the ebb and flow of the sidewalk's tide, and became part of the metropolis's glorious cacophony. Once he arrived at the Queens College Library in Flushing, he roamed the halls and stacks, met with library staff, and was introduced to Dr. Paul Klapper, the president of the college.[14] Leaving a favorable impression on everyone he met, before Trautman left the campus to return to Kentucky, a small piece of blue notepaper was handed to him. On it was a handwritten message from Dr. Klapper: "I shall be glad to recommend your appointment as fellow to be assigned to the College Library at a salary of $750.00 per annum, effective Sept. 1, 1939."[15] This slip of paper felt like a winning lottery ticket. It meant Trautman could fulfill his dream of attending Columbia and earning a library degree. The salary was just shy of what he needed, but Trautman knew he could make up the difference using the book-buying and -selling skills he had acquired managing the Ex Libris and H. A. Moos Bookstores.[16]

Back in Kentucky, Trautman chipperly reported to his desk at the CCC on August 8 and once again took to his typewriter. "The undersigned requests that he be relieved from assignment and duties of Camp Educational Adviser.... The reason for submission of this request is to enable the undersigned to attend Columbia University where he will pursue a course in graduate instruction."[17] Having gotten this formality out of the way, Trautman next wrote to Fihe. He had last written her on the verge of giving up and could hardly wait to tell her the good news. She could disregard his last letter and those he had enclosed, for, as he wrote, he had "just returned from New York" after interviewing for a fellowship at the Queens College Library. "The appointment as 'Fellow' has been made, and the lucky person is Ray L. Trautman by the grace of God and certain good friends." As for earning additional income to cover all expenses, Trautman added that he was looking forward to "browsing around the old bookstores of New York and selling the books" to collectors.[18]

With less than one month before courses began, Ray and Jane frantically prepared for their move to New York. Their beloved furniture was shipped to relatives in Louisville, Trautman's books were carefully packed into cartons, and their personal effects were crated. On August 31, 1939, the couple's friends and family organized a goodbye dinner, and the following day, Ray and Jane boarded a train. The magnitude of this moment—leaving everything they knew to start a new life in a strange city so Ray could chase his dream of becoming a librarian—weighed on them both. Ray did not have a backup plan; he felt enormous pressure to thrive in the classroom and at his fellowship. Jane expressed a similar sentiment in her diary, "Hope Ray likes his job as Fellow at Queen's College Library. It's his one chance to make a success of his life!!!"[19]

* * *

On the morning of September 2, Trautman and Jane arrived in New York and checked into the Belvedere Hotel on 48th Street in Midtown. They immediately began their search for an apartment. After scanning newspapers and making numerous inquiries, they came up empty-handed.[20] The next day, they found a temporary room in an apartment at 500 West 122nd Street, a few blocks from Columbia. It was small, expensive, and on the first floor—in full view of all passersby. Jane recorded in her diary, "we are still dazed & don't like N.Y."[21] She hoped they would adjust.

The first outing the couple took after moving to New York was to see one of the greatest attractions on the globe, the World's Fair in Queens. Opening on April 30, 1939, the fair had already attracted millions of visitors by the time the Trautmans walked through its storied entrance and found themselves awestruck by the incredible range of novelties on display. Almost immediately, they understood why it was considered one of the great wonders of New York. Joining the 100,000 people who walked through Corona Gate that day in September 1939, the Trautmans were, like so many others, soon spellbound by the creativity, ingenuity, and novelty that met them at every turn.[22] They marveled at all they experienced—the General Motors Futurama, a Technicolor film, taste-testing Brazilian and Turkish coffees, an aerial ballet, bands and operas, art and sculpture. They toured the world's nations through the various pavilions, including Norway, Australia, New Zealand, Belgium, France, Venezuela, Peru, Ecuador, and Japan.[23] They saw the largest and fastest roller coaster built to date, glass blowing, bobsledding, skating, and trapshooting.[24] The gates opened at 9 a.m. and the lights went dark at 2 a.m.[25] Jane and Ray walked until their legs gave out.[26] In her diary, Jane wished they could have spent days touring the "stupendous" and "beautiful" displays. She had a different assessment of her first subway ride. It had been a fearsome experience—the speeding train snaking through pitch-black tunnels, barreling along with its thundering wheels, only to be punctuated by shrieking brakes at every stop. "Was relieved to get back home alive," she wrote.[27] Still, the World's Fair provided a glimpse of what the city had to offer—museums, art, theater, music, new technology, fashion, and enterprise. It was a place where people arrived with suitcases of dreams that they dared to unpack and explore. To Jane, the World's Fair felt like a microcosm of the city; it could overwhelm, but it also offered opportunities that could not be found anywhere else. In her diary, she confidently predicted that they would "get oriented" and give the city their best shot.[28]

There was little time for adjustment. Immediately, Ray began to settle into his responsibilities as a fellow and student. On Monday, September 4, 1939, he took the subway to the campus of Queens College, where he began the tasks of organizing its nascent library and managing circulation.[29] It seemed nothing less than herculean. Tens of thousands of books needed to be cataloged and shelved, and it was Trautman's job not only to cure this lack of organization but also to assist Queens College students as they used their new library.[30] Three days each week, Trautman worked from morning to night combing through mountains of books and painstakingly updating records, pasting circulation labels inside each tome, adding protective covers, and assigning call numbers.[31] While he gained practical experience, the monotony of the work caused Trautman to develop a lifelong contempt for certain tasks. In fact, when he began his search for post-graduation employment, he stated that he would happily fulfill practically any role but would "NOT consider cataloging work."[32]

Between his three long days at Queens College, Trautman spent another three days each week proudly rambling across the campus of Columbia University as one of its newest graduate students. The curriculum was rigorous and often highly technical, causing Trautman to feel distant from the experiences that fueled his desire to attend library school; when he worked in bookstores and with CCC enrollees, he felt like his work was making a difference in people's lives.[33] Learning the mechanics of librarianship, while necessary, felt impersonal and several steps removed from the thrill of connecting people to the titles they would most enjoy. However, Trautman found ways to make his schoolwork more satisfying. When he took a course on the preparation of bibliographies, he nursed his continued interest in aviation by preparing a comprehensive reference list on "Metal Airplane Construction."[34] He also found a sense of awe as he wandered Columbia's South Hall (now Butler Library), where the School of Library Service was housed under the same roof as the university's magnificent library.[35] Constructed in 1934 to replace Columbia's previous library, Trautman found inspiration in what he described as South Hall's "rich resources" of books and students dedicated to working with them.[36]

Operating on a schedule as syncopated as a Scott Joplin rag, Trautman teeter-tottered between his library work and his coursework while stealing moments to spend with Jane, who was struggling to find her own routine. Having worked as a medical clerk with the CCC, Jane initially hoped to find employment in a government hospital in New York City.[37] If she was successful, her diary makes no mention of it. Instead, it seems Jane supported Ray's demanding schedule by undertaking all household responsibilities—from managing their finances to shopping, cooking, and even finding a more suitable apartment. She also read voraciously. With Ray having access to both the library at Columbia University and the Queens College Library, he cared for Jane by borrowing any book she desired. Jane's diary shows that she sometimes read a book a day, with favorite authors including Willa Cather, D. H. Lawrence, Jane Austen,

Sherwood Anderson, and Ellen Glasgow; she went through a phase of reading many works by Russian authors: Gogol, Chekhov, Tolstoy, Turgenev, and Dostoyevsky.[38] Ray may have been preparing for a life working with books, but it seems Jane was spending just as much time with them.

Each week, Ray tried to devote one day to spending quality time with Jane. They would explore the city together, visiting stores like Macy's or Lord & Taylor, splurging on the occasional Broadway show, or enjoying a special meal at a restaurant.[39] Still, Jane's diary reveals that Ray never really took a full day off. After enjoying time with Jane, he would stay up to study as she fell asleep.[40] Jane admired Ray's work ethic and determination. Though she was initially unsure of uprooting their lives so Ray could study librarianship, he had won her confidence before his first semester was complete. As she wrote in her diary, "He's getting along swell in school. I knew he would."[41]

Meanwhile, Trautman faced the pesky problem of not having quite enough money to pay for rent, food, incidentals, and tuition. Like many New Yorkers, he had to practice the art of the side hustle. His took the form of operating his own book business, "Americana Trautman," which he ran out of the new tiny apartment that Jane had rented for them on the third floor of 434 West 120th Street.[42] Using contacts he had made in Kentucky and Texas through the bookstores he operated, Trautman communicated with customers and dealers by postcard; he would receive "want lists" from clients, libraries, and institutions and maintained a "search-and-report service for them."[43] To find the titles he needed, Trautman scoured used bookstores across New York City, attended book auctions, and bought rare editions at low prices. Book Row, the secondhand and antiquarian bookshops lining Fourth Avenue from 8th to 13th Streets, felt like a second home.[44] "From narrow, hole-in-the-wall crannies to multistory buildings with sagging floors creaking under the weight of their volumes," the wares of the Fourth Avenue shops, as one historian described, "bloomed across sidewalks, with stalls and bins of bargain books edging storefronts."[45] Trautman got to know many of the proprietors and which "notoriously scruffy book caves" might be hiding prized first editions and elusive titles.[46] It was an art unto itself to navigate the idiosyncrasies of each bookman's sales policies—some penciled prices inside the covers of their books, while others had to be asked and a price came out of thin air; negotiating was acceptable practice in some shops, a sin in others.[47]

Trautman loved everything about the hunt for titles, persnickety personalities, knowledgeable shopkeepers and clientele, and streets packed with an embarrassment of bookstores and untold millions of books. He scavenged for specific tomes, carrying a small notepad where he kept track of book requests and purchases.[48] It reveals his search for a variety of works, including those of Carl Sandburg, Rudyard Kipling, Louisa May Alcott, Balzac, and William Wesley Woollen.[49] Besides a broad gamut of books, Trautman also tracked down rare maps and sheet music for his customers.[50] Trautman savored the thrill of the hunt, the reward of spotting a treasured title and scoring a low price for it, and then connecting an eager buyer with a book they long wished to have. As his expertise grew, he not only sold to collectors and institutions but also consigned rare editions to the Parke-Bernet Galleries, a highly respected Fifth Avenue establishment.[51] In this manner, Trautman not only studied the art of librarianship and book stewardship in school but also had the time of his life exploring New York's book scene and working within it.[52]

Though Americana Trautman specialized in antiquarian books, Trautman made an exception when it came to new books by his Kentucky friend, Jesse Stuart.[53] Since their friendship began with their two-week Army crash course in 1925, Trautman watched Stuart doggedly pursue a writing career while choking back a sense of inferiority due to his backwoods roots, average education, and unpolished demeanor. When Stuart's first book of poetry was published in 1934, *Man with a Bull-Tongue Plow*, some critics found fault with it. One reviewer bemoaned a "narcissistic tendency" that tainted each verse.[54] Another described the poems as "orthodox sonnets,"[55] and yet another said the poems were "diffuse, sometimes a bit soft, sometimes a bit over-colloquial."[56] Trautman knew the feeling of a bruised dream, as well as the combination of desperation and sheer will that fueled Stuart. To show his support, Trautman purchased as many copies of *Man with a Bull-Tongue Plow* as his meager savings allowed and loudly recommended it to anyone who would listen. Stuart was deeply moved and sustained by Trautman's confidence. "If all men bought this book as you have bought it, the book would be a financial success. If all men prophesized its merits as you have prophesized them, it would be more than a financial success. It would live, perhaps, a very long life," Stuart wrote to Trautman in 1934.[57]

In 1939, Stuart turned to Trautman when his first novel, *Trees of Heaven*, was initially rejected for publication. "I [am] down and out and lonely as hell," Stuart admitted.[58] Since childhood, Stuart was certain he would be a writer who would tell *his* tales of Kentucky and the colorful creatures who might have been impoverished financially, but not in spirit or determination.[59] Trautman saw himself in Stuart's stories. For Stuart to succeed meant other "children of the night" could, too. When E. P. Dutton published *Trees of Heaven* in 1940, Trautman became a one-man publicity firm, preparing favorable reviews and sending them to major publications;[60] he also designed a mail-order postcard advertising *Trees of Heaven* and sent it to his entire Americana Trautman mailing list.[61] The book sealed Stuart's reputation as a gifted writer. *Trees of Heaven* earned a glowing front-page rave in the *New York Times Book Review*; the book was described as infused with "freshness and vigor and human warmth; it has sensitivity and strength.... [It] wells up as freely as a hill-country spring."[62] Stuart would never forget how Trautman believed in him before the reviewers did.

As fate would have it, the two friends were reunited in early 1940 when Stuart was invited to speak at Columbia University.[63] Though Stuart's packed schedule allowed for little time to visit, the two marveled over how far they had come—from barefoot kids working Kentucky farms to young men making their marks in the world of books—one by writing them, and the other by connecting them to readers. Both were the stronger for their friendship. Stuart was buoyed by Trautman's unyielding support, and Trautman saw Stuart's success as evidence that if he pursued his dreams with diligence, persistence, and commitment, they might also come to fruition.

* * *

The year 1940 was perhaps Trautman's most formative. He was becoming more cosmopolitan, gaining confidence in himself, and steadily moving closer to earning a master's degree in library science. He threw himself into his studies, work at the Queens College Library, side hustle across Fourth Avenue's kinetic book scene, and supporting the literary success of his longtime friend. As busy as Trautman kept himself, news of war brewing and expanding across Europe cast a pall over his life, just as it did everyone else's. On the day he left Kentucky for New York, September 1, 1939, Germany had invaded Poland.[64] By the end of the month, Warsaw had surrendered unconditionally.[65] Because they were treaty-bound to come to Poland's aid, France and Britain were dragged into the war.[66] In the spring of 1940, Germany invaded Denmark and Norway.[67] The bad news just kept coming—Denmark immediately surrendered, Norway faced inevitable defeat, and Nazi flags began to appear on the streets of occupied Paris after the unthinkable had occurred and France fell to Germany.[68] On the heels of France's defeat, the German Army pressed on, invading the Netherlands, Belgium, and Luxembourg in May.[69] By month's end, all three had surrendered and were occupied.[70] In June, a jubilant Adolf Hitler broadcast a special announcement, declaring that his string of military successes "will go down in history as the most glorious victory of all time."[71]

Despite the swift spread of war across Europe, and Nazi Germany's by-now unmistakable assault on freedom, democracy, and liberty, the United States clutched its cloak of neutrality, operating under the comforting delusion that it would not become involved. Even as he campaigned for reelection in the fall of 1940, President Franklin Roosevelt stated, "I hate war now more than ever," and it was his "supreme determination" that the United States "will not participate in foreign wars, and we will not send our army, naval, or air forces to fight in foreign lands outside of the Americas, except in case of attack."[72] Yet, in May 1940, President Roosevelt requested that Congress provide funding for the nation's defense to the tune of 50,000 military planes by the end of the year, a massive surge in armament considering the Army Air Corps only had 1,200 planes in 1939.[73] Additionally, President Roosevelt was doing everything he could to support Britain through Lend-Lease, arguing the best way to stay out of the war was by providing Britain with military aid so it could fight and defeat Germany.[74] While President Roosevelt's words opposed war, pundits argued his actions would drag America into it.

Working and studying full-time for at least six days each week, Trautman kept his focus, or tried to, on earning his library degree and finding a job. As he neared graduation, Trautman completed an employment questionnaire supplied by Columbia, detailing his background in geology, education, and what he described as "military science." He listed his experience working with books—from running bookstores to working at the Library of Congress, building libraries for the CCC, and cataloging thousands of volumes at Queens College. Trautman stated the work that excited him the most was connecting CCC enrollees with books and magazines that sparked a joy of reading. "I am vitally interested in work with books and found their use to be the greatest single factor in the success of... the CCC," Trautman wrote in his cover note to one library.[75] He believed that books were a way to democratize opportunity, and he could do his part by improving literacy and access to libraries.

In the summer of 1940, Trautman received an invitation to interview at the Enoch Pratt Library. A gift to Baltimore from millionaire and philanthropist Enoch Pratt, the library was completed in the 1880s to fulfill Pratt's personal wish to make books available to all the residents of his city. It maintained liberal policies, allowing any person from the age of fourteen to borrow books while resisting rigorous rules that would deter people from using the library.[76] According to the *Baltimore Sun*, the Enoch Pratt Library considered itself a "people's university,... serving... all kinds of people, irrespective of race, color, condition or creed," and it was the library's policy to hire staff members who had library expertise and the "ability to make the patron feel 'at home.'"[77] Not only did the library's mission and ethos match Trautman's, but its vacancy for an assistant director of the department of industry and science was a good fit for him given his background in geology. When Trautman visited the library for his interview, he was impressed by the facilities and the friendliness of the staff and was thrilled to be offered the job. He accepted it, writing to Pauline Fihe at the Cincinnati Public Library, "It is a wonderful library building and the staff works together in perfect harmony."[78]

Trautman and Jane moved to Baltimore just as the US Congress passed the Selective Training and Service Act, which required all male citizens between the ages of twenty-one and thirty-six to register for the first peacetime draft in the nation's history.[79] On October 16, 1940, over sixteen million men registered for possible military service. That morning, President Roosevelt took to the airwaves to acknowledge his appreciation for registrants' demonstration of their commitment to democracy. He also assured the nation that the draft was in "defensive preparation and defensive preparation only," and that it was "those who have dared to threaten the whole world with war" that "have imposed upon us and upon all free peoples the necessity of preparation for total defense."[80]

Despite Roosevelt's assurances, it was becoming difficult to fathom how the United States would be able to stay out of the war. If democracy itself was under attack, the country would be a target. Trautman felt deeply divided. On the one hand, he felt some duty to help his country at a moment of global crisis and request active-duty service. He had been in the military, after all, and knew how badly it needed experienced soldiers. On the other hand, he had finally completed his library degree and had secured a job that matched his ambitions and vision of libraries as centers of information and community. He bemoaned his bad luck. As Trautman said in a letter to Fihe, just as he was getting "started in my life work... the war hysteria might prevent me from getting into my new profession."[81]

Somehow it seemed that every time Trautman was ready to take one step forward, events had a way of taking him two steps back. Since childhood, towering obstacles always seemed to stand in his way—his lack of finances made his educational dreams feel impossible, his eyesight destroyed his goal of flying, and now a world war threatened his ability to settle into a job that felt perfect for him. There was also Jane to consider. She had already willingly left her life in Kentucky to move to New York so Ray could go to Columbia; now she moved from New York to Baltimore so Ray could work at the Enoch Pratt Library. If Ray joined the Army, he would likely abandon her as he would have to go wherever the Army sent him. He felt duties to his new job, his country, and his wife, and the three did not point in one direction.

# 3

# Books Are What We Want

No man should have to walk more than a mile for a book.

—Ray Love Trautman[1]

After wrestling with his dilemma—to work in a library *or* serve in the military—for several weeks, Trautman landed on a compromise. What if he volunteered to serve as an Army librarian?

Trautman knew the Army had experimented with providing libraries for troops during World War I, and that the program was a resounding success thanks to the sweeping vision of the American Library Association (ALA). Founded in 1876, the ALA's aims were "promoting the library interests of the country and... increasing reciprocity of intelligence and good will among librarians."[2] For several decades, the group's main activities included an annual conference, forming special committees to address niche topics, and issuing publications.[3] However, in 1917, the US government turned to civilian groups to provide entertainment and recreation to troops, and the ALA was designated as the agency responsible for providing library facilities to military training sites in the United States, and later, to troops overseas.[4] The ALA established the Library War Service to fundraise and organize the development of military libraries.[5] It hosted book drives, solicited financial donations for the purchase of books, and secured Carnegie Corporation grants of $10,000 for each of the Army's proposed camp libraries and a library building at the Great Lakes Naval Training Station.[6] In Paris, the ALA established an outpost at 10 Rue de L'Élysée and ran a book service for American troops in France. As it advertised in *The Stars and Stripes*, troops could mail a book request to the ALA (asking for up to two books at a time) and the ALA would ship the requested titles; when a soldier finished reading, he was asked to mail them back. There was no charge for this service.[7] By the end of 1919, the Library War Service had expended six million dollars on books and library facilities and distributed seven million books to US troops.[8] It built dozens of camp library buildings in the United States, supplied nearly 100 military hospitals with books, and collaborated with other aid groups like the YMCA to establish over 1,000 small library outposts across the United States and in France.[9] By the end of 1919, the Army and Navy relieved all civilian aid organizations from their wartime welfare work and announced that they would be developing permanent military morale departments.[10] In 1921, the Army Library Service was established as an arm of, what became known as, the Morale Branch of the Adjutant General's Office in the War Department; it was run by Army personnel rather than the ALA's librarians.[11]

Knowing how books improved the lives of troops during World War I, and experiencing how transformative literacy and books were for CCC enrollees during the 1930s, Trautman felt sure that books would play a critical role in World War II. He believed that military training would be most effective if it did more than teach troops to follow orders and prepare them to be combat-ready. Troops needed a sense of purpose for their service. An Army of citizen-soldiers fighting for democracy needed supplies that empowered them to think, learn, and form their own beliefs and ideas. Books could serve double duty by informing and educating troops while also providing a mental and emotional escape from the stress of military training and war.[12] Did anyone in the new Morale Branch of the Army feel this way?

On November 1, 1940, from his desk at the Enoch Pratt Library, Trautman drafted a letter to the Adjutant General's Office in Washington, DC. "The undersigned is interested in extended active duty with a library assignment."[13] With his record of military service, being swept into the Army seemed inevitable. Though he was reluctant to leave Enoch Pratt and a job that closely fit his interests and ethos, Trautman hoped by requesting an Army library job, he might take some control over his destiny.

Fatefully, at the time Trautman mailed his letter, the War Department was scouring its officer pool to select someone to lead the Morale Branch's library program.[14] Since 1924, the highest position in the Army Library Service, library specialist, had been left vacant, causing years of stagnancy across the nation's military libraries.[15] With plans for swift mobilization of hundreds of thousands of citizen-soldiers beginning in 1940, the Army needed a new leader for its libraries. It turned to two prominent experts for help. The first was Luther Dickerson, who had served during World War I as librarian at Camp Doniphan in Oklahoma; a camp library supervisor for the southeastern states; librarian of the American Expeditionary Force's university in the Cote d'Or, France; director of libraries for occupation troops after the Armistice; and he was the first and only library specialist to lead the Army Library Service after the war.[16] Upon discharge from the Army, he became head librarian of the Indianapolis Public Library, which he built into one of the top four libraries in the United States.[17] Perhaps no one better understood the unique challenges military libraries faced or the world of good they provided soldiers. The Army's second consultant was Carl Milam, who served as executive secretary (a position now called executive director) at the ALA beginning in 1920 and was a vocal champion of libraries.[18] He started his career as a student assistant at the University of Oklahoma Library and quickly developed a passion for bringing libraries into close contact with the public. Believing that books "should be made more readily accessible to everyone," Milam campaigned to educate the public about library service and worked to expand the reach of libraries through the development of small branches in rural communities and the outskirts of high-population areas.[19]

In assisting the Army, Dickerson and Milam were given "mobilization regulations" for library provisions, which consisted of a vague description of the need to expand peacetime library service.[20] With this minimal guidance, the duo recommended that the War Department create a position called chief librarian, select a professional librarian for the post, and assign a rank equal to the other leaders in the Morale Branch.[21] The War Department initially insisted that a professional librarian would not be needed, but Dickerson and Milam pushed back, expressing disbelief that the Army would entrust a library budget of $250,000 to someone with no specialized training in book selection and acquisition.[22] The War Department surrendered to their expertise and asked them to find the right man for the job.

Using a machine designed by IBM, the Army processed over 12,000 officer cards in search of all men who had credentials in librarianship. Trautman was culled from this pool, and he ultimately made the shortlist, one of five candidates selected to interview with Dickerson and Milam.[23] According to their records, Dickerson and Milam liked Trautman because he had "enough knowledge of library work to understand the philosophy, and little enough to be impatient with unnecessary routines."[24] Trautman's diverse experience—having managed bookstores, developed libraries for young men as an educational adviser with the CCC, and worked in public libraries—was a credit to him. In addition, they knew the War Department would look favorably on his long relationship with the Army—ROTC, a flying cadet at Randolph Field, and five years in the CCC (the CCC being jointly operated by the Army and the Department of the Interior).[25] Trautman would be familiar with Army organization and administration as well as procedures for acquiring and handling books in a library setting.[26]

What he lacked, however, was experience planning large-scale library programs, a high military rank, and—perhaps most significant—clout in the library world. Trautman was only beginning his career and virtually no one knew who he was. The Enoch Pratt Library, for all its prestige and sense of mission, was not as impressive as, for example, managing a large city system.

As Dickerson and Milam deliberated, Trautman checked his mailbox each day, awaiting the envelope from the Army deciding his fate. When it finally arrived, it was in the form of orders—standard Army practice. "First Lieutenant Ray Love Trautman…, Infantry Reserve, is ordered to active duty with the Adjutant General's Department, effective

20 November, 1940," it said. The orders were silent as to whether he had been chosen for the librarian role for which he had interviewed, or if he would be assigned the usual work of a first lieutenant, commanding a contingent of green infantrymen and drilling them in the ways of combat at a training facility somewhere in the United States.[27]

On November 20, Trautman left for Washington and reported for duty. To his great relief, he learned that he had been selected to serve in the Morale Branch as the Army chief librarian, a title that he would be the first to wear.[28] He called Jane to share the good news that he would be continuing his library work. Perhaps less exciting for Jane was that they would need to move closer to Washington, DC—it would be their fourth home in fourteen months.[29]

* * *

Trautman wasn't sure at first whether he had been given the chance of a lifetime or a fool's errand. He was tasked with building a comprehensive library system for the entire US Army, but because the ALA had fund-raised and purchased books for the Army's libraries in World War I, there was no precedent for how an officer would obtain congressional funding to do this work.[30] At the age of thirty-three, he was now in nominal charge of a patchwork of outdated libraries spanning the United States. While the Army was on pace to swell to 1.5 million draftees in 1941,[31] Trautman had 500,000 books and a staff of two civilian clerks.[32] In reality, he had far fewer books to work with. The Army's bookshelves were filled with tattered relics from the previous war, such as forgotten best-sellers from twenty years earlier and few books that might help troops understand recent history and why the world was at war. If military libraries were supposed to entertain and educate, they would need to be stocked with modern titles.

Meanwhile, the Army was rapidly constructing new training posts to accommodate the huge influx of soldiers being drafted. Over 100 new facilities were being built, and each would require the purchase of an entire library's worth of books.[33] The magnitude of the job was daunting. Trautman had to deal with endless paperwork and the phlegmatic attitude many of his superiors felt for libraries.[34] Making matters worse, the War Department had disregarded Dickerson and Milam's advice to assign the chief librarian a rank commensurate with other supervisors in the Morale Branch. As historian John Jamieson said of Trautman, "He was placed at the bottom of the pyramid."[35]

Dickerson and Milam, at least, were aware of the obstacles and did what they could to help him. They knew from hard experience in the previous war that Trautman would need allies, and they hoped to supply some. Within weeks of Trautman's appointment as chief librarian, Milam sent a telegram to the head of the Army's Morale Branch. "The interest of librarians in plans for camp library service is so intense and wide-spread that I urge you to arrange for Lieutenant Trautman to attend the midwinter conference of the ALA in Chicago Dec. 27–30."[36] Milam knew this would be an important networking opportunity—over 1,000 librarians and library representatives attended the conference, from institutions large and small, from all corners of the country.[37] Since its origins, the ALA had grown to the largest and most powerful organization devoted to books and libraries in the United States, and perhaps the world. If World War I was any indicator, Army libraries would have sufficient books only because civilian librarians labored to get them there.

Milam's telegram produced results; Trautman received travel orders from the Army to go to Chicago for the ALA conference.[38] In the meantime, Dickerson and Milam, knowing too well what Trautman would be facing, continued to strategize. Dickerson, who was going to be attending the conference, wrote Milam that though the schedule was already finalized with programs and speakers, perhaps they could squeeze in a short speech by Trautman so he could "'trot [his] stuff'" and "get acquainted with all the big as well as little wigs in [the] A.L.A?"[39] Milam agreed and wrote Dickerson, "spend as much time with [him] as you can," making introductions and ensuring Trautman made connections with all the people he needed to know.[40]

The midwinter conference helped place Trautman on a national footing in the world of librarianship. Trautman gave a brief speech and participated in a Q&A session on the needs of Army libraries.[41] When one librarian asked him whether the Army would rely on public book drives to fill Army library shelves as it did during World War I, Trautman hesitated before answering. Army regulations did not allow any personnel to "solicit material for the Army," forcing him to respond that all books would have to be purchased using congressional funding.[42] He nonetheless knew—as did Dickerson and Milam—that book drives were his only hope of getting enough books for troops because he would not have the budget to purchase what was needed.

The data Trautman had on library funding painted a depressing picture. While large posts with thousands of draftees were allocated a budget for books, smaller facilities and outposts were not.[43] This meant that, of the approximately 230 Army libraries in the United States in 1941, only 77 of them received government funds. Though 46 additional libraries were expected to eventually receive book budgets, that still left over 100 libraries unfunded.[44] And even when funding was provided, posts usually received an average of $1 for reading material per soldier.[45] Considering that, at the time, hardcover fiction typically cost around $2 to $3 per book, and hardcover nonfiction could run as high as $4, government funds would barely cover one book for every three men.[46] Army libraries also needed to buy subscriptions to popular periodicals and newspapers. Exacerbating matters, each post individually purchased the reading materials it needed, making it difficult to take advantage of savings from bulk orders. Trautman began to wonder whether the system was rigged for failure. A book drive would have been incredibly helpful, but the decision to allow one had to be made by someone above Trautman's rank. In the end, while his trip to the ALA's midwinter conference helped broaden Trautman's contacts, he was not sure how he could use them to the Army's advantage.

He suspected that it would take more than librarians to direct a spotlight on the limitations of Army libraries, and in early 1941, Eleanor Roosevelt happened to illuminate the issue. An unusually active First Lady, Eleanor had earned a reputation for frequent participation in public affairs and politics.[47] Because Franklin Roosevelt's paralysis prevented him from traveling to places that were inaccessible, Eleanor served as his "eyes and ears," touring all corners of the United States and reporting back to him.[48] Eleanor often met with ordinary Americans and learned about their problems and concerns. She developed a keen sensitivity to their social struggles and hardships and received hundreds of letters daily from people imploring her to use her position to help them.[49] As the Selective Training and Service Act began to take effect in 1940, and young men were drafted into the military, Eleanor received letters from concerned parents and draftees about the poor conditions and inadequate facilities in the Army.[50] With four sons—all of whom would serve in the armed forces during World War II—as well as a daughter, Eleanor felt a nearly parental obligation to ensure that the nation properly support and care for those who had left their families to serve.[51]

In early 1941, it came to Eleanor Roosevelt's attention that the Army's racially segregated training facilities were woefully unequal, and this included recreation and libraries.[52] The Army was on pace to enlist approximately 400,000 Black soldiers by the end of 1941, and this number would double by war's end.[53] The First Lady personally disagreed with the armed services' insistence that racial segregation was necessary,[54] and pushed her husband to create equal opportunities for Black troops to serve in all capacities and to secure the same benefits for their service as white soldiers.[55] And sometimes she did the pushing herself.

It was Eleanor's habit to forward letters about Army conditions to Chief of Staff George Marshall. Marshall, in turn, required that all her concerns be investigated, and when there was a basis to the complaint, that a report detail what corrective measures were taken. Following this protocol, when she complained that Black service clubs had empty bookshelves, her inquiry was passed through Army channels until it reached the chief librarian's desk.[56] Just as he had done with customers in his bookstores and CCC enrollees, Trautman aimed to provide books the audience reading them most wanted. Accordingly, Trautman reached out to Howard University, founded in 1867 for the purpose of providing a first-rate college education to Black students (at the time, most colleges denied admission to Black applicants).[57] Trautman asked if he could be supplied with a list of the most sought-after reading materials circulating within the Howard community. In response, the Howard University Library prepared a lengthy list "for the possible assistance of those charged with the selection of books for colored service clubs."[58] Book titles spanned all genres—literature, poetry, drama, fiction, biography, art, music, education, religion, sports, sociology, and history. Many titles are still read today. There was Langston Hughes's *Weary Blues* and *The Ways of White Folks*; Zora Neale Hurston's *Their Eyes Were Watching God*; Booker T. Washington's *Up from Slavery*; Frederick Douglass's autobiography, *Life and Times of Frederick Douglass from 1817-1882*; and W. E. B. Du Bois's *The Negro.* There was also *Jazzmen* by Frederic Ramsey, Jr., and Charles Edward Smith; *Brown Bomber: The Story of Joe Louis* by John G. Van Deusen; *The American Race Problem* by Edward Reuter, and a legion of other titles. Howard University also recommended periodicals, including the NAACP's *The Crisis* and the National Urban League's magazine, *Opportunity.*[59]

When Eleanor Roosevelt learned that Black service clubs would be stocked with books recommended by Howard, she was so pleased with Trautman's solution that she invited him to meet with her in May 1941 at the White House.[60] Although the details of their meeting have been lost to history, Trautman seemed to win over the First Lady, securing her continued support and attention to the plight of Army libraries for years to come.

* * *

While Trautman could fulfill the First Lady's request for adequate books in at least some facilities, the problem remained that he could not fill *all* Army library shelves by relying exclusively on congressional funding. Trautman needed the War Department to change its stance on book drives. However, when he attended the Morale Branch's four-day conference in February 1941, it became painfully clear that books and libraries were not a priority. Chief of Staff George Marshall opened the conference by expressing his belief that morale was essential to training the best fighting force in the world. He quoted Napoleon's adage that "Morale is to matériel as three is to one," and added that the ratio now is "nearer five to one, or possibly even ten to one in some instances."[61] Marshall spoke about the importance of the conference, and how the information provided by representatives of different branches of morale work would guide future plans. Yet, libraries were never mentioned. After Marshall, Trautman listened to the leaders of the division's various branches (all of whom were generals, brigadier generals, colonels, lieutenant colonels, and majors) discuss movies, post exchanges, radio broadcasts, athletics, and dramatics.[62]

Although feeling slighted, Trautman did all he could to improve library service with the limited funding and support he was provided. By mid-1941, he made plans for traveling libraries (as he had used in the CCC), negotiated with publishers to provide the Army with special discounts, and secured free subscriptions to the Book of the Month Club for Army libraries.[63] He also campaigned for his own promotion, writing to the Adjutant General in the spring of 1941 that he had completed all the courses and credits required for captaincy and was "becoming increasingly embarrassed" by his rank of first lieutenant, which placed him as one of the lowest-ranking officers in the Morale Branch.[64] One month later, he became Captain Trautman.

* * *

Trautman thought it strange that the Army seemed indifferent to the important role of books in this war. The freedom of information was one of the foremost principles at stake. Beginning in the fall of 1933, Nazi Germany began to impose restrictions on books, producing lists of authors, subject matters, and titles that were considered so dangerous that they were banned and burned.[65] To ensure compliance by the German public, the Nazis hosted elaborate book-burning ceremonies across Germany in the spring of 1933.[66] The most theatrical was the first and largest, in Berlin. On May 10, 1933, over 40,000 people gathered to watch as 5,000 university students, carrying torches and singing Nazi songs, threw tens of thousands of books into an enormous bonfire.[67] Spectators listened as students took turns charging authors with literary sins against Germany and justifying the destruction of their books.[68]

Interrupting this dirge of names and crimes was a speech by Paul Joseph Goebbels, the minister of propaganda. Standing behind a rostrum skirted in swastika flags, Goebbels praised the book purge as essential to strengthening Germany.[69] Calculated to achieve the maximum effect, Goebbels's speech was broadcast live over the radio and was filmed and made into a newsreel to be replayed in movie theaters across the Reich. For the Nazis, the publicity and fanfare achieved the desired result. Ninety-three book burnings were held across Germany replicating the formula exhibited in Berlin: enormous bonfires, tens of thousands of books destroyed, large cheering crowds, and more media attention.[70]

What started as a ban on a few hundred titles in 1933 grew to restrictions on thousands of titles and authors by 1938.[71] As the German Army overtook nations across Europe—Poland, Denmark, Czechoslovakia, France, Belgium, the Netherlands—libraries in these occupied nations were entirely closed or "reorganized" to "Germanize" them. In this colossal effort for thought control, the Nazi Germans removed millions of volumes that did not align with their beliefs. By 1945, it is estimated that over 100 million books were destroyed across Europe by the Nazis.[72]

American librarians—including Trautman—felt a duty to fight Germany's censorship by guarding the freedom to read. As Flora Ludington, librarian of Williston Memorial Library at Mount Holyoke College, said in an article she wrote for the *American Library Association Bulletin*, "We who can go to our libraries and secure almost any book on almost any subject are living in a privileged society." "With us," Ludington added, "except for rare, sporadic, and isolated instances, censorship of books is nonexistent." She pointed out that *Mein Kampf* was on library shelves next to books denouncing it. By culling library collections and warping the selection of books to produce a singular ideology, Germany had weaponized libraries. It had distorted these temples of free thought and ideas into "agencies for indoctrination along National Socialist lines." The best way to fight this censorship spreading across Europe was to fill library shelves with diverse ideas, enabling Americans to exercise their democratic "freedom of access to the printed word."[73]

Under these conditions, Trautman wondered how the Army could *not* stock its bookshelves to overflowing so that the young men training for possible war would not only be outfitted in uniforms, but armed with knowledge and ideas.

Serendipitously, between 1940 and 1941, national periodicals published articles pleading for books in the Army. At the time, a severe morale crisis was taking root, as the Army lacked basic equipment and facilities for the 1.5 million men that had been drafted. A December 1940 piece in *Life* magazine described resentful draftees who were swept into uniforms and dragged through training. Awakened before the sun came up, draftees spent hours marching and maneuvering, following the orders of barking officers, and being assigned back-breaking jobs they hated. At the end of each long day, instead of relaxing, they pitched tents, twiddled their thumbs until their eyelids drooped, and then slept outside with snoring strangers. "There is more to making good fighters... than merely working them hard. Above all, their morale must be kept high," the article said. If crates of books and magazines were left in high-traffic areas, men could at least grab a story and mentally escape the Army each night. "If soldiers are given plenty of adventure books and detective magazines... they will be reasonably happy," *Life* predicted.[74]

In August 1941, a *Time* magazine exposé confirmed that morale had not improved. "I'll tell you what morale is," it began. "It is when a soldier thinks his army is the best in the world, his regiment the best in the army, his company the best in the regiment, his squad the best in the company, and that he himself is the best damn soldier-man in the outfit." These qualities were something "a large part of the U.S. Army conspicuously has not got," *Time* reported. "The great bulk of civilian soldiers had little pride of outfit [and] little joy of service," it added. They lacked rudimentary equipment, the food was "sloppy" and "unappetizing," and they suffered from a severe case of nightly boredom as they whittled away empty hours staring into the blank darkness with no amusements or activities to help pass the time.[75] A box of books and a pile of magazines would make a huge difference. Unless soldiers were provided entertainment that would keep them satisfied and engaged, training would be futile, *Time* predicted.

One month later, in September 1941, the *Saturday Review of Literature* delivered a history lesson about the popularity of books in World War I. It recalled how Army libraries from 1917 to 1919 had their chairs "full every night," with soldiers even sitting "on windowsills or on the floor" just to have a place to read. At small or isolated posts where the Army did not keep books or libraries, soldiers took matters into their own hands. One soldier in 1918 "appealed to the Newark Public Library. 'Can't you send us something to read? We are . . . lonesome,'" he pleaded. The Newark Public Library felt duty-bound to mail a box with books, cigarettes, and candy. Within days, a heartfelt reply was received. "Thanks for the box. If you ever did good to anybody you did it to me, but please don't bother to send the eats. Use all the space for books. Books are what we want."[76]

According to the *Saturday Review*, nothing had changed over the course of two decades. Troops still wanted "the whole works, from Homer to 'Heart Throbs,'" and reading material was needed for all tastes and abilities, from "the man of culture" to the "illiterate private." Everyone flocked to the library because it was "the one place . . . where a man could evade the discipline, noise, and enforced companionship that were everywhere else." Had the Army learned nothing from the success of its libraries during the Great War? "The therapeutic value of such psychological escape seems so clear that the present [attitude towards] libraries . . . is hard to understand," the article declared.

Reaching the same conclusion as *Time* and *Life*, the *Saturday Review of Literature* pleaded for the military to ramp up its libraries and book programs. "Most of the million and a half American soldiers [who had been drafted] are going to read, and the better the camp libraries provided for them, the more they will read to advantage." At a time when morale was "none too high," supplying *good* books and libraries would make a huge difference. Giving them things to read "will make better soldiers and eventually, better civilians."[77]

* * *

When civilian librarians read about the Army's need for books, they took matters into their own hands. Since the Army could not solicit donations, civilian librarians gave books without being asked. They conducted rogue book drives and routed boxes of books to Army library doorsteps. There was no reason to let good books go to waste; Army librarians put them into circulation. For example, when a newspaper reported in 1941 that Camp Edwards—with 35,000 men, it was one of the largest posts in New England—failed to receive its book order due to a shipping snafu, the Massachusetts Division of Libraries commanded the immediate assistance of all civilian librarians in the state. Overnight, they were asked to launch book drives and rally their communities to give reading material to their local troops.[78] Publicity campaigns were hatched to spread the word.[79] Within one week, 4,000 books had been collected, loaded onto trucks, and transported to Camp Edwards.[80] A steady flow of books continued to arrive thereafter.

Camp Edwards was hardly the exception. Unauthorized book drives for the Army spread across the country. In Chicago, "10,000 good books" were collected when newspapers reported that the Sixth Service Command (covering Illinois, Michigan, and Wisconsin) had more requests for books than they had on their shelves.[81] In Modesto, California, a "Service Men's Book Week" was declared and the public was asked to donate their "novels and detective stories" along with any other "good reading" for local army camps.[82] Camp Upton on Long Island received 1,700 gift books and 1,500 magazines after a community collection was hosted by the nearby Freeport Library.[83] When the paperback publisher Pocket Books suggested readers could mail their books to the Fourth Service Command (in Atlanta, Georgia) once they finished reading, so many donations were made that a warehouse had to be rented to provide temporary storage.[84] Local drives intensified over the summer of 1941 as women's clubs, social groups, and community libraries hosted book-collection campaigns and the public eagerly answered the call for books.[85] As one librarian said, "By the summer of 1941, two facts were very clear: the army did need books, and whether invited to do so or not, the American people—from school boys to club women—urgently desired to give them."[86]

Each day, the War Department received a fresh batch of letters from concerned citizens and organizations eager to assist the Army in its bookless plight, attracting the attention of the newly appointed chief of the Morale Branch, Brigadier General Frederick Osborn. Whether Osborn was qualified for this role is questionable. He had no military experience, retired at the age of forty after a lucrative career in business, and then devoted himself to the study of eugenics and what he described as "racial preventative medicine."[87] In the 1930s, Osborn had even spoken favorably about Hitler's eugenics program in Germany.[88] His appointment was likely due to his friendships with President Roosevelt and Secretary of War Henry Stimson, for his background does not suggest expertise in military affairs or developing esprit de corps.[89] Trautman's personal feelings about Osborn were never documented, and records suggest Osborn's interest in Trautman extended to a single encounter.

In October 1941, Trautman was called into Osborn's office and asked for his opinion about whether there would be any merit to a single, nationwide book drive instead of the myriad slapdash, homespun campaigns he kept reading about. Trautman knew that he had his moment. A large-scale effort to collect gift books would be incredibly useful, he told General Osborn, and recommended that the Army collaborate with the ALA as it had done in World War I.[90] Osborn seemed to accept the wisdom of this. Trautman was told to draft a letter for Osborn's signature to alert the ALA that the Army was receptive to receiving gift books.[91] Trautman did so. He also sent a separate letter to Milam, the ALA's executive secretary, letting him know that Army approval for a national book drive was forthcoming.[92]

Thanks to Trautman's early warning, Milam was prepared to hit the ground running once he received Osborn's letter. During October 1941, on behalf of the ALA, he reached out to two of the foremost aid organizations, the American Red Cross and the USO, to collaborate on hosting a national book drive.[93] In November 1941, Milam went to Washington to secure government approval from the President's Committee on War Relief Agencies, the Morale Branch of the Army, and the Bureau of Navigation of the Navy.[94] As expected, the green light was given.

It is no exaggeration to say that the role of books in American life would never be the same. Not only would this campaign, in the end, secure millions of books for the Army, but it would also provide librarians a platform to educate the American public about the importance of books, both in this war specifically and in the quality of their lives as citizens. The free flow of ideas was pitted against censorship and book bans, principles of equality were contrasted with the mythology of Aryan racial superiority, and truth countered propaganda. Democracy meant being exposed to the widest array of information. And this was true for troops and civilians alike. Language and ideas were being weaponized on all fronts. They could also serve as protective armor. People needed to read.

Trautman could rest assured knowing that beginning January 12, 1942, civilian librarians would be launching a nationwide book campaign with a goal of collecting ten million books for troops.[95] At long last, the days of half-filled shelves were over. If war came, a stockpile of books would be ready to play their part.

# 4

# Moving Literary Mountains

If you were far away from home, books would be the things that would mean the most to you in your leisure time. So, think of those who defend us in camps, on ships and on fighting fronts all over the world, and let's get busy today and provide the biggest collection of victory books we have ever had in this country.

—Eleanor Roosevelt[1]

The war began for the United States on a Sunday morning in early December 1941. Early risers on the island of Oahu were already fishing, surfing, or heading to church, while others still slept. A faint buzz was in the air, as a swarm of humming planes skimmed the horizon. This was not unusual; there were two Army airfields nearby, Wheeler and Hickam. However, as these aircraft approached Oahu, some bystanders observed peculiar red circles painted on their wingtips and fuselage. The planes then swooped low over the naval base at Pearl Harbor, where the United States Pacific Fleet was located, taking turns releasing bomb loads. A trail of explosions followed in their wake. Around the same time, lurking submarines unleashed torpedoes at idle ships moored in the harbor, along Battleship Row. The vessels were soon engulfed in black smoke as flames gnawed at them until some descended into watery graves. To ensure that the United States would be thoroughly immobilized from launching a meaningful counterattack, dive-bombers paid a visit to Hickam and Wheeler Airfields, strafing American airplanes and leveling barracks and hangars. "Within one tragic hour . . . the U.S. appeared to have suffered greater naval losses than in the whole of World War I," *Time* magazine reported.[2] When the total damage was tallied, the United States had 10 fewer warships, 177 wrecked airplanes, over 2,300 fatalities, and 1,272 wounded personnel.[3]

The following day, Congress overwhelmingly voted in favor of a declaration of war on Japan.[4] On December 11, the United States declared war on Germany and Italy.[5] Given the pace at which Germany had steamrolled over much of Europe, and the years of preparation favoring the Axis nations, the US military had some catching up to do. Everything needed to be intensified—the conscription rate, pace of training, and production of war matériel.

President Roosevelt had campaigned in 1940 on the promise to the American public, "Your boys are not going to be sent into any foreign wars."[6] Now, Roosevelt was going to be sending them, bolstered by the nation's overwhelming support. Polls established the public's willingness to work longer hours to produce war supplies, adopt a system of rationing to curb home-front consumption and maximize the flow of goods to troops, and give women the opportunity to volunteer for military service.[7] Roosevelt's popularity rate soared; one month after Pearl Harbor, 84 percent of Americans expressed confidence in his ability as president.[8]

Roosevelt was aware that he was now asking the nation to make painful sacrifices. He knew precisely how important it was to convey as forcefully and personally as he could the meaning of each man's service to the nation, to identify what values were at stake and were worth fighting for, and to express his confidence that democracy would be victorious over tyranny. He determined to do this in a letter to the troops. For inspiration, Roosevelt decided to consult the most compelling wartime speeches given over the ages.

When Trautman received a request from the White House to gather these addresses, he threw himself into the task.[9] There was Napoleon's 1796 speech to French troops, imploring them to fight for freedom and to bring honor to their country.[10] Most Americans had heard the appeal of King George VI in 1939, as he dedicated England to the task of spreading security, justice, and liberty to the world.[11] There was the speech—recorded by Roman historian Tacitus—of Caledonian leader Calgacus addressing his troops in AD 85 as they faced the Roman Army, equating victory with freedom from oppression: "Whenever I consider the origin of this war and the necessities of our position, I have a sure confidence that this day, and this union of yours, will be the beginning of freedom to the whole of Britain."[12] After combing through these and other speeches, Trautman seized upon their spirit and took the liberty of drafting a letter,[13] which he sent to the White House along with his compilation of addresses. He was deeply flattered to learn that the president liked his version so much that it was being adopted with only minor revisions and polishing. It was printed on White House letterhead, signed by President Roosevelt, and copies were immediately dispatched to troops already overseas; it was also reprinted in domestic newspapers for all to read.[14] Through 1944, as millions of US troops sailed from American shores, they would read Trautman's ghostwritten words:[15]

> TO MEMBERS OF THE UNITED STATES EXPEDITIONARY FORCES:
>
> You are a soldier of the United States Army.
>
> You have embarked for distant places where the war is being fought.
>
> Upon the outcome depends the freedom of your lives: the freedom of the lives of those you love—your fellow-citizens—your people.
>
> Never were the enemies of freedom more tyrannical, more arrogant, more brutal.
>
> Yours is a God-fearing, proud, courageous people, which, throughout its history, has put its freedom under God before all other purposes.
>
> We who stay at home have our duties to perform—duties owed in many parts to you. You will be supported by the whole force and power of this Nation. The victory you win will be a victory of all the people—common to them all.
>
> You bear with you the hope, the confidence, the gratitude and the prayers of your family, fellow-citizens, and your President—[16]

For most soldiers, the letter offered a tangible reminder of home, and of all that was at stake. Many saved their copy, sometimes mailing it to their family for safekeeping.

It was a contribution of which Trautman remained justifiably proud his whole life. For years, as a bookseller and a librarian, he had matched readers and books. Here he had helped a president find the words to embody what democracy represented for the men who would be fighting with their lives for it. Given that in the coming years Trautman would supply these men with millions of books, it was an appropriate start. Few would ever know his name or meet him, yet Trautman would profoundly influence their lives.[17]

* * *

Now that the nation was at war, the rate of conscription skyrocketed, compounding the Army's shortage of books. Trautman was relieved that plans had already been laid for the January 1942 commencement of a national book drive called the Victory Book Campaign (VBC). And he was thrilled that Althea Warren, the head librarian of the Los Angeles Public Library, had been chosen to lead the charge for book donations. Warren intuitively understood what the VBC needed to achieve based on her experience serving Camp Kearny, near San Diego, during World War I.[18] She observed how "some printed pages are medical plasters to extract pain, others are tourists' tickets out of boredom or loneliness to exhilarating adventures, still others are diplomas for getting promotion and drilling ideas into a quick-step."[19] To lead a new generation of librarians on a quest to collect "more books than are contained in any existing library in the world," was a great honor. As Warren put it, "It will be a satisfaction to scramble to get the books for [troops] which they will genuinely enjoy."[20]

The campaign was launched on a frigid January morning at the New York Public Library's home branch on 42nd Street in Manhattan. All day, streams of New Yorkers trudged up the grand staircase of this literary temple, clutching books to deposit into the VBC's coffers. It was expected that fifty miles of books would be processed in New York City and transported to wherever troops were going.[21] Meanwhile, librarians across the country, in towns large and small, advertised the VBC and ensured that book drops were located across grocery stores, schools, public transportation depots, libraries, department stores, movie theaters, gas stations, and any business willing to provide space for a book collection bin.[22]

In the five weeks following Pearl Harbor, 600,000 US soldiers were in transit.[23] Some rode the rails to begin training, while others who had completed it were headed to San Francisco to ship out to Hawaii, Australia, and the Philippines. Tens of thousands arrived at New York's Port of Embarkation and boarded transports headed for Iceland and Northern Ireland. Still others were sent to outposts in the Panama Canal Zone, air bases in South and Central America, or Alaska.[24] Wherever they were headed, travel meant downtime with nothing to do. During the weeks spent on transports, wondering where they were going and what they would face, idle minds were ripe with forebodings, and any distraction was welcomed. Knowing this, Trautman issued a "hurry-up call" for the VBC to immediately provide books.[25]

Within two weeks, 300,000 volumes had been collected in New York. To publicize the campaign, Hollywood stars, musicians, and politicians gave rallies and publicly donated their own books. Katharine Hepburn autographed a stack of titles inside the New York Public Library, as did former presidential candidate Wendell Willkie.[26] Meanwhile, stories of troops' demand for reading materials further stressed the need for a swift and effective campaign. The *New York Times* interviewed Major William R. Bolton, who stated that on a recent visit to "a northern outpost where there were twenty hours of darkness," he watched men "avidly reading by candlelight."[27] In the *American Library Association Bulletin*, Margaret Gilbert, the librarian at Camp Davis, located north of Wilmington, North Carolina, begged for more books. Every day, "crowds . . . come and select arm loads of books to carry back to the barracks," and groups "come each evening and sit buried for four hours behind the covers of books and magazines, stirring only when another soldier stumbles over some foot in the floor space so full of readers that another chair cannot be squeezed in." Troops devoured anything that involved printed words on a page. She said her "limited . . . book collection" was not enough and pleaded for "victory books."[28]

Heeding this call, America's librarians advertised the need for donations, and civilians—individually and through organizations—pitched in and did their part by giving them. As Althea Warren's biographer put it, there was "solicitation and packing by Boy Scouts, Camp Fire Girls; free transportation of books by passenger buses, trucking companies, newspaper delivery cars, milk companies, American Red Cross Motor Corps, American Women's Voluntary Services, and individuals."[29] By the third week of January, one million books had been donated nationwide;[30] however, it became clear that some quality control was needed. Many were donating books that they simply wanted to get rid of, including, in the words of one librarian, "worthless stuff collected from attic or cellar."[31] In some areas, up to 80 percent of donated books were unusable.[32] Newspapers had a field day educating the public that, in the words of the *Bangor Daily News* of Maine, "The Victory Book Campaign is not a substitute for the trash-can."[33] "'Equestrianism for Women' or 'Crawford County, East Minnesota' are books, all right, but hardly books that boys in the armed services want to read," a Vermont newspaper commented on recent donations collected in the area.[34] Imagine "how an army sergeant stationed in Iceland would greet a copy of 'Grandmother's Cookbook, 1890 edition,'" one columnist noted to her readers in St. Louis.[35] Trautman needed books, but not books like these.

Eleanor Roosevelt—again—came to the rescue. Perhaps because of her meeting with Trautman, she maintained an interest in the state of military libraries, and that included the work of the VBC. In her popular newspaper column, "My Day," she provided updates about its progress and her own repeated donation of books.[36] The First Lady was so committed to the cause that she joined the executive board of the VBC, serving on the Advisory Committee.[37] As she read the newspapers and saw the countless articles about the Army receiving outdated encyclopedia volumes, children's story books, knitting guides, and dog-eared volumes better suited for the wastepaper drive, she reached out to Norman Cousins, a friend who was the editor of the *Saturday Review of Literature* and a cochairman on the VBC's National Campaign Board. Cousins became the editor of the *Saturday Review* at the age of twenty-five,[38] and his love of books and reading resulted in a precipitous rise in the magazine's popularity—from 20,000 in 1940 to over 600,000 subscribers.[39] Cousins's editorials created a warm sense of kinship between the *Review* and its readers. "What emerges from my mailbag each day is the sense that I'm not just dealing with customers but with members of the family," Cousins said.[40] When Eleanor Roosevelt wanted to ensure the greatest impact was being made by the VBC, she knew Cousins would know how.

It was Cousins's belief that ten million books should have been raised within weeks—not a fraction of this number after two months—and that the caliber of books—in desirability and physical condition—needed to be much higher.[41] Because there was no end date for the campaign, Cousins believed the VBC needed a deadline, of sorts, to create a sense of urgency.[42] Eleanor Roosevelt offered to ask her husband to publicly designate a "Victory Book Day" to encourage a one-day surge of donations.[43]

Apparently, the First Lady was very persuasive. On April 14, 1942, President Roosevelt held a press conference, declaring that, by presidential proclamation, April 17 was "Victory Book Day." He joked with reporters that troops wanted to read "anything but algebra," but then, taking a more serious tone, said the public should give only those books that they personally enjoyed.[44] On the same day, the VBC disclosed that it had distributed around 2.4 million books, far short of its goal.[45] A bookish sense of emergency swept the nation. Suddenly book drops scattered across the country overflowed with reading material.[46] When the final tally of donations was made, the target of ten million books was met.[47]

There had to be an easier way than conducting a prolonged public campaign and begging for quality book donations. Eleanor Roosevelt decided to write Brigadier General Frederick Osborn, urging the Morale Branch to pledge its resources to support a library program that would "provide books for . . . all the men." Reliance on random book donations was no way to run "a real department," she said. Soldiers deserved better.[48]

Osborn replied to the First Lady, expressing confidence in the "officer in charge of the Army Library Service," whom he had met six months earlier.[49] Eleanor hoped her letter made a difference, for she also had confidence in Trautman's abilities and was eager to see what literary mountains he could move if granted more power and flexibility.

* * *

As the VBC endeavored to collect books, Trautman was sent on a tour of domestic Army facilities so he could see firsthand the reading habits and needs of the soldiers he was serving. From April to May 1942, he underwent a grueling itinerary. From Washington, Trautman proceeded to a brief stopover at Key Field in Meridian, Mississippi, and then traveled to Monroe, Louisiana, to speak at the Louisiana State Library Convention.[50] He then visited Louisiana's Camp Livingston, Camp Claiborne, and Camp Polk, and proceeded to Texas, where Trautman visited his old stomping ground at Randolph Field as well as Kelly Field, Brooks Field, Midland Field, and Sheppard Field. He circled into Oklahoma to visit the Enid Army Flying School and then proceeded east to visit Camp Shelby in Mississippi.[51] Across the South, Trautman found soldiers parched for reading materials while stationed in book deserts. The cause of this was rationing. Because use of rubber tires and gasoline was restricted, the VBC was forced to minimize how far books were transported by truck. The vast majority of books were donated to the VBC in the North, yet two-thirds of the men in Army training were in the South.[52] Trautman successfully coordinated with the Office of Price Administration, which curbed consumption of a variety of goods, so that the VBC could haul books over greater distances.[53] Librarians with empty shelves rejoiced when boxes of donated books finally arrived at bases in the South and Midwest. "It is hard for me to express my deep thanks for the very wonderful collection of books that the Book Campaign donated to our Post Library," one librarian from Kansas said. "Our library here is starting from scratch [and] I had spent days trying to figure out how I could get my shelves partly filled."[54] She would still have to sort, catalog, and shelve the books so troops could find the titles they wanted, but at least she would have a good selection for them to borrow.

Before he had a chance to get settled back in Washington, Trautman's superiors had another trip in mind for him—this one involved traveling overseas, visiting generals and privates alike, to see how the Army's library system could best serve troops in the various combat theaters. After all, if discontent ran rampant at home during basic training, troop morale was destined to plummet in war zones, where soldiers would live in foxholes, face rainstorms of bullets and shells, and witness war's greed for death and destruction.

In the summer of 1942, Trautman flew to Havana. While the mainland was not a hotbed of war activity, the waters surrounding it were.[55] German U-boats were an active menace, hunting the Atlantic for Allied supply ships and inflicting substantial casualties. Sinkings were frequent. In a single week in March 1942, the Navy recorded three separate torpedo attacks that claimed three American vessels off the coast of Cuba.[56]

While in Havana, Trautman paid a visit to "Sloppy Joe's," the bar on Agramonte and Animas Streets, where Ernest Hemingway was reputedly a regular.[57] In his youth, Trautman had read *The Sun Also Rises* and *A Farewell to Arms*, which was the beginning of a lifelong admiration of Hemingway. "Lean, hard, athletic narrative prose that puts more literary English to shame," was how the *New York Times* described Hemingway's writing; it was these qualities that Trautman revered.[58] More recently, Trautman had read *For Whom the Bell Tolls*, which only further sealed his esteem for Hemingway's manner of storytelling. Beyond his books, there was also the mystique that wreathed Hemingway as a death-defying, adventure-seeking, bull-fighting devotee who befriended literary celebrities like Gertrude Stein, James Joyce, Ezra Pound, and F. Scott and Zelda Fitzgerald.[59] An energy seemed to pulsate from Hemingway and his determination to wring every stimulating drop out of life.

Trautman took a seat at the bar and got his photograph taken—why not play the tourist, he thought—before settling into his drink. As he was nursing it, Hemingway appeared. Trautman's uniform attracted the writer. Hemingway had worn one himself, as a volunteer ambulance driver during World War I; he also covered the Spanish Civil War as a journalist.[60] Just recently, he had transformed the *Pilar*, his beloved forty-foot, black-and-green cabin cruiser, into an intelligence-gathering "Q-boat" for the US Navy. Camouflaged as a commercial fishing boat, the *Pilar* was equipped with state-of-the-art radio technology and, as a friend of his put it, "had machine guns, bazookas and high explosives, all disguised as something else."[61] If a German U-boat surfaced nearby, the *Pilar* would attack. Though he frequently expressed his hatred of war, Hemingway was drawn to it like a moth to a flame. He felt an affinity with those engaged in the fight.

Hemingway struck up a conversation with Trautman and learned that his drinking companion was the Army's chief librarian. The two bonded over their love of the written word and adventuring. Trautman's tales of his cross-country trip to the wilds of British Columbia to mine gold that ended in near-death disaster, and his CCC days spent navigating the backcountry of Kentucky, appealed to Hemingway's love of the outdoors and action.

Trautman made such a positive impression on Hemingway that the writer asked the librarian for help with a problem. For some time, Hemingway had been compiling an anthology, *Men at War*, consisting of the best war stories ever written, ranging from Bible excerpts to a recent piece on the Battle of Midway Island.[62] Hemingway's publisher, Crown, had mailed the galley proofs to Cuba before government censorship had taken effect, and now Hemingway needed to get them back to Crown with his revisions without censors butchering any offensive portions with their scissors or blue pencils. War-themed writings were stymied by censorship regulations. In 1942, the US Office of Censorship published a "Code of Wartime Practices" that prohibited the American press from publishing any information that might be helpful to the Axis.[63] *Silentium victoriam accelerat* (silence speeds victory) was the office's motto.[64] In addition, the US Navy produced a hefty list of topics that needed to be excised from writings before letters were mailed. And the US Army had its own litany of subjects that were off limits.[65]

Given that military censorship featured extremely wide safety nets—such as the elimination of any "information determined by the area commander to be of aid or comfort to the enemy"—Hemingway was concerned that his biting twenty-page introduction might ruffle feathers.[66] "This book will not tell you how to die," it opened. "Some cheer-leaders of war can always get out a pamphlet telling the best way to go through that small but necessary business at the end," he said. Though he hated war and "all the politicians whose mismanagement, gullibility, cupidity, selfishness, and ambition brought on this present war and made it inevitable," now that the world was engulfed in fighting, Hemingway believed that the only thing to do was win. And victory would come more swiftly were honest facts presented to the American people, and censorship wasn't used to cover the errors of those in power—whether military or political leaders. "Censorship can conceal mistakes, blunders and acts of almost criminal misjudgment and negligence," Hemingway wrote, but a "government which wants to keep the confidence of its people... should take the people into its confidence and tell them everything that they can know, bad as well as good." Yet with multiple tiers of government-created censorship watering down the news each day, people were being kept in the dark. To hide the truth was something the totalitarians did, and "rather than copy the methods of the losers," Hemingway hoped the US government would "realize the necessity of telling the people the truth... in everything that does not aid the enemy, because times are coming in this war when the government will need the complete and absolute confidence of all citizens if this country is to endure."[67]

Hemingway harbored no illusions that his caustic assessment of the government's chokehold on truth would survive the censors and arrive in New York untouched. Once a document was handed over to the scissor wielders, there was no knowing its condition once they were through with it—assuming anything was left. Celebrity was no shield. "The censor has written me a very stern letter about my remarks on the weather," Eleanor Roosevelt divulged in one of her "My Day" columns, which were carried in newspapers across the country.[68] Because eastward-moving weather patterns were deemed sensitive due to the vulnerability of possible aerial attacks along the coast, restrictions were placed on reporting weather conditions.[69] "From now on," Roosevelt wrote in her column, "I shall not tell you whether it rains or whether the sun shines where I happen to be."[70] Even war correspondent Ernie Pyle said of his overseas dispatches, "I wrote my stuff and sent it away [to the censors] with about the same assurance" that it would arrive in one, uncensored, piece "as if I had put it in a bottle and tossed it into the Mediterranean."[71]

Thanks to his chance encounter with Trautman, Hemingway believed he found his solution to getting the galley to New York. He asked Trautman to take the proof pages and personally deliver them to Crown when back in the United States. As an officer, Trautman experienced more relaxed oversight by censors, and if Trautman carried the galley, the pages would make it through unscathed. Trautman warned Hemingway that their delivery to Crown would not be immediate; the War Department had planned a tour that required Trautman to circumnavigate the globe. Delay seemed to trouble Hemingway less than censorship.

Trautman left Cuba with a new acquaintance, an edited galley, and a plan to visit New York when he arrived home.

* * *

Trautman's world tour swept him eastward from Havana to Australia, where he arrived in September 1942.[72] His next mission was twofold: take the temperature of the reading needs in this corner of the war, and meet with General Douglas MacArthur, the supreme commander of the Southwest Pacific Theater.

The Pacific had already seen several battles—from Wake Island and Midway to the Philippines and the ongoing campaign for Guadalcanal. There was little doubt that the Pacific Theater would see many more. The gradual advance toward the Japanese mainland would involve amphibious landings of "one damned island after another," as one GI described it.[73] It was turning out to be a brutal and prolonged campaign. Some islands had exactly one possible landing point, which the Japanese had spent years preparing to defend. For the invaders, it was like running into a firing squad, surrounded by bloodstained sand, burning landing craft, and cries for medics.[74] As E. B. Sledge, a Marine, described it, "To witness such a scene was worse than personal danger. It was absolute agony."[75] It is no wonder that from the beginning of the war, the morale situation in the Southwest Pacific was, as one biographer of Douglas MacArthur put it, "bleak."[76]

Trautman felt that if books were needed anywhere, it was in the Pacific Theater. To give troops what they wanted and needed most, Trautman endeavored to understand some basic questions about them, including: "Who is the soldier? What is his previous experience with books? What does he read?"[77] Officers tended to circulate only among other officers, but Trautman was determined to spend as much time as he could with the men he was serving—the GIs out in the field. He wanted to go where the enlisted men were baking in the heat, getting soaked in the rain, and eating their rations with a heavy peppering of sand no matter how hard they tried to keep the grit out.[78] These were the men who needed a morale boost.

When word spread that the chief librarian of the Army was paying a visit, soldiers rushed to request their favorite periodicals and book genres. "I was treated like royalty," Trautman said.[79] He was humbled by their hunger for print of any kind. Most said they would be grateful for anything to read, but, if they had a choice, bestselling novels, hometown newspapers, pin-up magazines, westerns, sports stories, comics, and even Sears Roebuck catalogs (Trautman referred to these as "wishing books") topped their list.[80] As one soldier stated, "You would have to [experience] the lethargy and isolation of the Southwest Pacific to realize the value of a book."[81] Because there were often long periods of waiting, it was handy to have reading material that was small enough to tuck into a pocket. Trautman observed that softcovers were extremely popular because of their compact size.[82] Unfortunately, this format was disfavored by mainstream publishers.

At the time, the paperback was in its infancy. In 1939, the first American paperback firms had been launched: Pocket Books—a venture headed by Robert de Graff with 49 percent funding coming from three individuals including Richard Simon (publisher at Simon & Schuster, but who funded Pocket Books personally)—and Ian Ballantine's New York outpost for Penguin Books, a paperback firm initially founded in 1935 in England.[83] Publishing powerhouses—like Random House, Simon & Schuster, Scribner's, and Doubleday—avoided anything in paper covers, finding them lurid, cheap, and reputationally harmful. Plus, at a quarter (as compared to $2 to $4 for hardcovers), the profit margin was a slim one; to make money, the print run typically had to exceed 100,000 or 150,000 copies and sales had to be robust. Between aesthetic objections and concern for their bottom line, traditional publishing houses refused to have their titles printed in anything other than hardcovers. Pocket Books and Penguin Books therefore specialized in classics that were in the public domain and in reprinting commercial and genre fiction, primarily mysteries, science fiction, and westerns. Contemporary titles and bestsellers were not to be found in soft covers. Moreover, because bookstores refused to carry them, paperback books were treated like magazines and sold only at newsstands, drugstores, tobacco shops, and railroad stations.[84] None of the publishers' qualms bothered GIs. The size suited their peripatetic reality, the genres were among their favorites, and they treasured every lightweight paperback that made the long journey to their theater.

Not only did overseas troops view the format of books differently than those on the home front, but they looked at the act of reading in an entirely different light. As Trautman observed, many troops were stationed in remote outposts where the only attractions were those provided by the military. Primitive living conditions were the norm. Under these circumstances, books were a rare luxury and even men who had never cracked a spine at home were willing to "read for lack of anything else to do," as one GI said.[85] One encounter made a deep impression on Trautman. Some of the Victory Books that the men had carried onto transports were still circulating, and he approached a young soldier to see what he was reading. The book was *Plato's Republic* "done in basic English." When the soldier learned Trautman was a librarian, he exclaimed, "Say this guy Plato is good! What else did he write lately?"[86]

Whether it was Plato or Tarzan, the men read and swapped books tirelessly, always handling them with special care to ensure they would last as long as possible despite being subjected to humidity, rain, and battle.

Trautman wanted to give the men what they desperately wanted, but there were obstacles. One of the biggest was the lack of a system for the storage of any supplies in the Southwest Pacific. This resulted in the destruction of brand-new weaponry and gear, and a crushing cycle of equipment shortages. During Trautman's visit in the fall of 1942, when matériel was unloaded off the coast of Australia, it was stacked on the beaches, fully exposed to the elements. Humidity and saltwater corroded the bottom tiers of containers as they sank into the wet sand and rotted.[87] A high percentage of supplies faced casualties without ever being removed from their crates. The urgent cries for more matériel carried on: More ships of equipment would arrive, a decent portion of the replenishments would succumb to nature, and the wasteful sequence would begin again.

Not only did the storage snafu frustrate the prosecution of the war, but it also eroded morale. While recreation items from the Special Services Division (the new name for the Morale Branch as of early 1942)[88] could bring some cheer, it became almost impossible to ship these items. Because war matériel was always in short supply, and cargo space on ships was finite, the Army created a priority system to ensure weapons and other "essential" equipment were loaded first. Entertainment was ranked low on the list. In the words of Major Ruel D. Harmon, an officer in the Special Services Division, one of the greatest challenges presented by the Southwest Pacific was "it was very difficult to get shipping space."[89]

One person who could make a huge impact on how books and other recreation equipment were treated was the theater's commander, General Douglas MacArthur.[90] Biographer William Manchester described the general as "a great thundering paradox of a man, noble and ignoble, inspiring and outrageous, arrogant and shy, the best of men and the worst of men."[91] This tangle of contradictions had served in the Army for over four decades, spending several years as Army chief of staff. MacArthur was used to commanding and having things his way, and he planned to keep a tight grip on his own theater. If Trautman was going to do his job, he needed to win the general's approval for prioritizing shipments of books.

MacArthur was rumored to be an avid book reader. His father, Arthur MacArthur, Jr., kept a library of 4,000 books that the general ultimately inherited.[92] Many nights, MacArthur turned to these books, often choosing challenging texts to sharpen his mind; light-hearted fiction was conspicuously absent.[93] Trautman hoped that if MacArthur was a bookworm, perhaps he would be amenable to his pitch. Yet, there was another side to MacArthur. Graduating from West Point as first captain and first in class, he was hardwired to operate under rigorous self-discipline, sacrifice, and sheer determination.[94] When he later returned to West Point to serve as its superintendent, MacArthur had mixed feelings about the school's recreational offerings. On the one hand, he discontinued the student newspaper because it was too independent and critical of him, and on the other, he enthusiastically supported athletics.[95] MacArthur, as biographer Geoffrey Perret wrote, "became convinced that the men who had taken part in organized sports made the best soldiers," because those who "contended physically against other human beings under rules of a game were the readiest to accept and enforce discipline."[96] Bodily strength, operating as a team rather than as individuals, and instinctively following instructions from a coach or the calls of an umpire—these characteristics reinforced qualities MacArthur wanted in his men. Independent reading did not.

When Trautman met with MacArthur, it quickly became clear to him that the general had no desire for his soldiers to be supplied with books and magazines. To MacArthur, solitary reading was antagonistic to the Army's aims. In fact, he was resistant to practically all entertainment and recreation offered by the Special Services Division because he wanted his men focused on soldiering.[97] Conveniently, MacArthur pointed a finger at the supply shortages and insisted that he needed every inch of cargo space for equipment that could arm, clothe, or feed his men.[98] On this point, MacArthur would not budge.

It was Trautman's job to get books into the hands of soldiers, and his initial refusal to give ground nearly cost him his military career. When Trautman attempted to explain the value of reading materials, how MacArthur's men hungered for them, and that books provided mental "armor," MacArthur fumed. Even though Trautman was a humble, soft-spoken, and unassuming young man, his gentle attempt to change the general's mind was interpreted as an act of dereliction. To subsist in MacArthur's good graces, one had to be "blindly subservient, even obsequious," as biographer William Manchester said. This was confirmed by Clare Boothe Luce, an acquaintance of MacArthur's, who stated that "MacArthur's temperament was flawed by an egotism that demanded obedience not only to his orders, but to his ideas and his person as well. He plainly relished idolatry."[99] Questioning MacArthur on the wisdom of depriving his troops of reading material was the opposite of hero worship. In no uncertain terms, MacArthur informed Trautman that a low-ranking librarian would not interfere with his operations in the Southwest Pacific. The general was so incensed that he even threatened to charge Trautman with insubordination.[100] Trautman backed down.

He left Australia feeling drained and carrying the weight of a lost opportunity. However, disappointment was soon replaced with determination. It would have been easier to have MacArthur's approval, but Trautman would find a way without it.

* * *

When Trautman arrived back in Washington, MacArthur's shortsightedness continued to vex him. MacArthur could pull rank as a four-star general and supreme commander of the Southwest Pacific, but Trautman was chief librarian of the US Army and was charged with the task of fortifying troops as they faced their darkest moments. The Southwest Pacific had the worst morale, and Trautman was convinced that books would improve the welfare of the troops stationed there. There had to be a way to get books into the Southwest Pacific without MacArthur's permission.

As Trautman sat at his desk, combing through a backlog of letters that had accumulated while he was away, he realized the answer to his problem was right in front of him. The mail. While theater commanders controlled the flow of practically everything entering their jurisdiction via normal supply channels, they had no authority over the Army Postal Service's delivery of letters and boxes.[101] All Trautman had to do was package books and magazines in packages small enough to be handled by the Army mail system. There was no need for approval from any high-ranking officials—MacArthur included. So long as the Army Library Service had an up-to-date address, they could provide reading materials to "all units, whether they requested it or not."[102]

* * *

Shortly after returning home, Trautman left Washington by train for New York, toting the unwieldy unbound galley (each page was two feet long) that he had been carrying around for two months. However, when he attempted to deliver it to Crown Publishing, Trautman was told he had arrived too late. Crown had already sent Hemingway a second set of galley proofs with strict instructions that the author return an edited version immediately. By the time Trautman showed up, *Men at War* was already being printed. Crown told Trautman to keep the galley he had faithfully carried around the world. Though the galley had been creased, stamped by the Commonwealth of Australia, and folded during its journey around the world, Trautman carefully transported it home, made plastic protective covers for each page, and treasured it for the rest of his life.

# 5

# Pass the Paper

We are crying for reading material.
—US soldier[1]

There was no question that foot soldiers needed lightweight books, yet Trautman had soon exhausted his softcover options. By 1941, Pocket Books and Penguin Books were joined by a third paperback publisher, Avon.[2] Costing twenty-five cents per volume, eight of these editions cost the equivalent of the least-expensive hardcover. However, the title selection was limited. "The same mysteries and bestsellers of the last decade kept turning up again and again," one post librarian complained. Overseas troops clamored for paperbacks of bestsellers and newly published books, but librarians were forced to explain that these were available only in hardbound editions.[3] As one soldier retorted, "books have weight—and the G.I. does not carry an unnecessary ounce." He added that when an infantryman only had a hardcover, "he gives it away or throws it away as soon as possible"—not because he doesn't want to read it, but because of its size.[4] As chief librarian, it tormented Trautman to fail at providing troops the books they really wanted.

The other type of reading material that soldiers pleaded for were periodicals. On the eve of World War II, the magazine industry was rapidly expanding, with dozens of titles selling multiple millions of copies per issue.[5] *The Saturday Evening Post*, *Life*, *Collier's*, *Reader's Digest*, and *National Geographic* were among the titles that were regularly devoured by a wide swath of the American public.[6] The popularity of periodicals only seemed to grow when a person was in uniform. "The soldier is first and foremost a reader of magazines," observed Elinor Kendall Evans, an Army librarian at Camp Blanding in Florida.[7] As a practical matter, articles took less time to read than a book, and tired eyes preferred to glance at pictures than tussle with tiny text. As one soldier explained, "Because the Army hates to see a man enjoy himself for more than ten minutes at a time, reading was often done in short spurts. Hence, comic books and magazines were more convenient because it didn't take so long to discover how the hero made out."[8]

To meet the diverse tastes of the growing Army, Trautman wanted to purchase a variety of magazines. Just as he was making plans to do so, the War Production Board (WPB), which was tasked with mobilizing American industry to further the war effort, announced that paper would likely face rationing.[9] Beginning with these rumors over the summer of 1942, the publishing industry—newspapers, magazines, and possibly books—feared losing one of the most precious resources in producing their wares.[10] Nothing sold newspapers and magazines like the war. Since Pearl Harbor, the public had a gluttonous appetite for every new detail. In the words of Brendan Gill, a journalist for the *New Yorker*, Americans "sat by their radios and listened with satisfaction to news bulletins, infinitesimally rewritten as they were repeated, about victories and defeats throughout the world, and then went out and bought newspapers and magazines and gorged themselves on the same information for a tenth or twelfth time."[11] At a time when the demand for periodicals was extreme, and rumors were flying that their supply of paper would soon be slashed, Trautman was hoping to secure tens of thousands of new subscriptions and bulk discounts. The timing was not optimal.

In 1942, Trautman received news that he was being promoted from captain to major. He soon found out that this boost in military stature did nothing to improve his bargaining position for bulk rates with civilian publishers.[12] What he lacked in rank, he made up for in talent and gumption. Trautman grew resigned to the fact that his low standing in and outside of the Army would always create obstacles, whether he was competing for funding or trying to convince publishers to partner with the Army. However, he also recognized that he was the only person who could grant publishers access to the Army's captive audience of millions; if soldiers liked what they read, they would likely become future paying subscribers. That had to be worth something to businesspeople interested in profits.

To test the waters, Trautman first approached *Time* magazine in the summer of 1942 to inquire about subscription rates for the Army. *Time* was early to recognize the value of building an audience by offering overseas subscriptions to American troops in England in 1941.[13] Trautman could extend *Time*'s presence beyond England to every country in the world where Americans were stationed. In exchange for this valuable benefit, Trautman hoped to be able to negotiate a discounted price.

Before purchasing subscriptions in serious numbers, Trautman wanted to first give overseas service a trial run with 120 subscriptions. In July 1942, he spoke with Francis Pratt, the circulation director of *Time*, and was under the impression that each subscription would cost $3. But the next time they spoke, Pratt insisted on $5. Trautman balked. In the words of a *Time* staffer, "He felt that since we were not paying [overseas] transportation charges on the magazines we could very easily come down to $3 per subscription or at least $3.50." Trautman told Pratt that if *Time* insisted on $5, he would take his business elsewhere, such as *Newsweek* or *U.S. News.*[14] Pratt, a graduate of the Harvard Business School,[15] was gifted at marketing and sales, and under his leadership from 1939 to 1955 *Time*'s circulation rose precipitously. However, this was a negotiation that he bungled.[16] When Trautman told Pratt that there were dozens of suitable magazines to which the Army could subscribe, he was not bluffing. He was fixated on getting the best rate to maximize the number of magazines he could buy for troops. Pratt decided to give Trautman a day to "cool off," as he put it, though he planned to agree to $3.50 per subscription. Days passed as the two played phone tag, and by the time Pratt reached Trautman, he was too late. *Newsweek* had proved far more accommodating, and Trautman placed his initial order with it.[17] When the next opportunity arose for *Time* to join the Army, it did with a much greater degree of cooperation. It was episodes like this, still early in Trautman's Army library career, that molded his approach to being outranked or underestimated. According to Trautman's son, Eric, whenever his father faced resistance from powerful figures, he adopted the mentality, "I can't make them do anything, but I can make them wish they did."[18]

After the drawn-out negotiation process with *Time*, Trautman was not eager to haggle with dozens of other magazines. He turned to the Washington News Company for help, as it offered discounted subscription rates on periodicals it distributed regularly, including mainstays like *Esquire* and *Reader's Digest*.[19] The Army began by placing orders for fourteen magazine titles, to be shipped to units in England, Ireland, the Pacific, Alaska, Puerto Rico, and the South Atlantic. These bulk orders resulted in overseas postal distribution centers receiving fourteen 200-pound boxes of periodicals, each box containing hundreds of copies of a single magazine. These headquarters lacked the time, personnel, and space to open every box, remove one magazine from each to create "sets" of fourteen *different* titles, and then repackage and mail these sets on to US units. What usually happened is the dauntingly heavy boxes of magazines never budged, or a unit would receive one hulking box with hundreds of identical issues of one magazine.[20] Obviously, this system didn't work. There had to be a better way.

In October 1942, the WPB turned rumor into reality when it announced that magazines would, in fact, face paper rationing starting January 1943.[21] Trautman believed the mere threat of paper rationing over the summer impeded his ability to negotiate bulk discounts. With the definitive announcement that paper rationing would take effect, Trautman predicted it would become even more difficult for him to buy periodicals for soldiers at a reasonable price. Yet the whole point of the WPB was to ensure the efficient production of war supplies by overseeing the conversion of private industry to serve the military's growing needs for all manner of equipment.[22] Automobile factories had been turned into manufacturers of jeeps, tanks, and airplanes. Where Ford and Chrysler once forged crankshafts and axles, they now produced mountings for anti-aircraft weapons.[23] If the WPB could transform the automobile industry, would it be willing to do the same with publishing? It would mean recognizing it as a war industry and reading materials as essential mental armor for overseas troops.

In late 1942, Trautman met with WPB officials to present his case that magazines were essential equipment in the Army. He argued that magazines were vital sources of information, education, and entertainment for the war effort, and asked the WPB to grant the Army an extra paper allotment for use by publishers producing periodicals for the military.[24] This way, he would not have to compete with the civilian market for the finite number of magazines being produced with rationed paper. Trautman's request fell on sympathetic ears. The WPB agreed to grant the Army whatever tonnage of paper was needed for GI reading needs.[25] Trautman suddenly became the most powerful figure in the magazine industry. The only way for publishers to print more magazines than what rationing allowed was to go through the chief librarian of the Army.

The WPB attached a few strings to its agreement with the Army. Disliking the optics of magazine publishers getting extra paper from the government and then selling magazines to the Army for a profit, the WPB advised Trautman to require publishers to sell their magazines to the Army at unit cost. It also insisted that the magazines carry no advertisements, which saved paper and stymied another source of possible profits to publishers. Finally, Trautman was asked to adopt policies that would economize the amount of paper being used, such as requiring publishers to use lightweight paper or a smaller page size.[26]

The latter was a sticking point. Popular magazines of the early 1940s were behemoths. *The Saturday Evening Post*, one of the most popular magazines of the era, produced issues weighing around one pound, with each page measuring around eleven by fourteen inches. When open, a reader was treated to over two feet of sweeping artwork and photographs that made stories come to life. In an age before television was a household staple, magazines provided an immersive visual experience, a window into other parts of the globe. *Life*, *Fortune*, and many other top titles fell within this heavyweight division. Trautman needed them to become bantamweights for the Army.

When paper rationing officially took effect on January 1, 1943, magazines were forced to conserve paper. There were a variety of approaches. *Time* and *Life* announced a reduction in newsstand copies, advertisements, and pages per issue. *Fortune* reduced its page size. *Redbook* printed one less issue per year. *Vogue* and *House and Garden* took a different tack, stretching their tonnage of paper by using pages as thin as newsprint.[27] While these adaptations for the home-front moved recalcitrant publishers toward the production of smaller and lighter-weight magazines, Trautman needed them to go further.

He considered the formats used by the less glamorous cousins to the industry's glossy-paged superstars: pulp magazines. In 1943, *Reader's Digest* weighed under three ounces and measured approximately five by seven inches; it resembled a paperback book and often contained excerpts from new and popular titles. Based on his conversations with soldiers in the field, Trautman knew troops would choose a *Reader's Digest* over a *Saturday Evening Post* based on size alone. To appease the WPB and the armed forces, the oversized magazines needed to adopt condensed formats. He needed miniature magazines that did not exist, at least not yet.

The offices of the Special Services Division, in which Trautman worked, were nestled together in the Adjutant General's Office. Brimming with ingenuity and creativity, they were a hotbed of ideas. Trautman could get an infusion of inspiration just by walking down the hallway.

One of the officers whom Trautman befriended was Major Eric Knight, one of the more colorful members of the Special Services team and a specialist with the Information & Education section. Like Trautman, Knight had had to work his way up. Born in England in 1897, Knight's father had died in the Boer War when Knight was a toddler, leaving the family destitute.[28] His mother became a governess to the children of Princess Xenia of St. Petersburg, Russia, and then, in 1905, she moved to the United States, leaving her three children with relatives in Yorkshire until she saved enough money to pay for their passage and sent for them, which she did one by one. Knight's turn did not come until 1912. In the meantime, he worked. Starting at the age of twelve, he toiled in a steel mill, a cotton mill, a worsted mill, a sawmill, and a glass-blowing factory.

When Knight arrived in the United States, he landed a position as copy boy at a Philadelphia newspaper and attended school. Art was his passion, and he ultimately studied at the Boston Museum of Fine Arts School and then the Art Students League and the Beaux Arts Institute. When World War I erupted, Knight joined Princess Patricia's Canadian Light Infantry and saw "much hard fighting." Two of his brothers were killed in France.[29] When he returned home and attempted to resume his painting career, he was stunned to discover he had become "almost totally color-blind." He tinkered with newspaper cartooning but ultimately gave up art forever.

Knight replaced his brush with a pen. He wrote short stories, and with the mentorship of e. e. cummings, the poet and writer, Knight dashed off several novels in the 1930s and published his three most successful books beginning in 1940. First, there was *Lassie Come-Home*, a story of a young boy and his faithful collie (it was also made into a movie in 1943, in which Elizabeth Taylor made her film debut).[30] In 1941, *This Above All*, a love story featuring a British soldier, became a bestseller and was turned into a movie. And in 1942, Knight published *Sam Small Flies Again* (also titled *The Flying Yorkshireman*), a collection of humorous short stories. In the summer of 1942, he joined the American military and was commissioned a captain in the US Army.[31] Knight was assigned to the Special Services Division, to put his writing talents to use for the war effort. When asked why he would abandon his commercial writing as his popularity was skyrocketing, Knight responded, "This war is too big to make any one man or his life of the slightest importance."[32]

Trautman and Knight bonded over their passion for the written word.[33] While Trautman was the Army's purveyor of popular literature, Knight was assigned the task of churning out "country guides," booklets that provided troops a crash course on a particular nation's customs, food, etiquette, climate, religions, and a glossary of common phrases with phonetic pronunciations.[34] Often, troops didn't know where they were being sent until they received a country guide on a transport ship.

Trautman talked over with Knight his need to inspire traditional magazine publishers to scale down the weight and size of their issues.[35] Days later, Trautman found sitting on his desk "A Short Guide to Great Britain," with a note from Knight: "The attached is the first of a series of similar pamphlets for overseas troops."[36] At 4.25 by 5.25 inches, it could be tucked into a uniform pocket. The cover was printed in color, and the inside was a mixture of text, maps, and cartoons. It was hard to think of anything more ideally suited for overseas troops. This was the dose of inspiration Trautman needed. What if American magazines could be sized to fit these dimensions?

Trautman noticed that Knight's guidebook was almost the same size as a reconstituted V-Mail letter, which the Army was advertising as the fastest and most efficient way to transmit correspondence overseas. V-Mail reduced the burden of shipping millions of pen-and-ink letters in their original size by photographing letters onto reels of film. While the original letters might fill a crate, the same number of V-Mail letters fit on a roll of film smaller than a carton of cigarettes. Like ammunition, V-Mail was assigned A-1 Priority for shipping, and delivery took days rather than a traditional letter's months-long journey.[37] Overseas, the film negatives were processed and reproduced at about 25 percent of their original size, measuring about four by five inches. Trautman wondered whether V-Mailed magazines might solve many of his problems—pocket-sized periodicals could be printed overseas while news was still fresh, and the cost would be minimal.

In January 1943, Trautman purchased a handful of identical *Newsweek* magazines and painstakingly clipped every article (omitting advertisements) and pasted them onto V-Mail forms. A V-Mail technician photographed each page, reconstituted the magazine from the developed negatives, and handed Trautman a thirty-seven-page magazine that he could slip into his pocket.[38] The size was right, but the font was punishingly small and difficult to read.

Sharing his V-Mail prototype with the production staff at *Newsweek*, Trautman asked if they could combine his idea with their expertise to produce a readable magazine in miniature format. They ran with

Trautman's idea by photographing pages from a full-size *Newsweek* and then reducing the page size for a servicemen's edition. At six by eight inches, a miniature *Newsweek* had clear images and legible text. By printing on newsprint, they produced a prototype that weighed less than an ounce and, when folded, could comfortably fit in a pocket. Dubbing the magazine a "Battle Baby," *Newsweek* set the standard for printing miniature overseas editions of popular magazines.[39] *Time* soon followed suit with its "Pony" edition.

Another early convert to minimizing its size for troops was *Omnibook*. Its publisher, Max Geffen, had worked as a correspondent and publisher before founding *Omnibook* in 1938.[40] The logic behind *Omnibook* was that books were being published faster than most people could read them—on average, Americans read ten books per year and thousands were published.[41] Every issue of the monthly *Omnibook* selected five of what it deemed the best books recently published and "abridged and excerpted" them without syphoning off the "spirit and flavor of the original." All this at the bargain price of fifty cents an issue.[42] The public devoured them. Even critics of abridgements praised *Omnibook* for—as one reviewer put it—"cutting, but not changing the author's word,"[43] and elevating "literary condensations" to an art form.[44]

Over the course of the magazine's first five years, *Omnibook* underwent several makeovers as Geffen tweaked the dimensions to make it more book-like. The early issues were oversized, measuring nearly eleven by fourteen inches.[45] Each page was so large that it had to be divided into quadrants, so that an open magazine displayed eight pages of a book at a time. With few, if any, illustrations, the large pages plastered in text were overwhelming. In 1942, *Omnibook* embraced a smaller format, 8.5 by 11 inches; each page had two columns of text and appeared more like a magazine.[46] When paper rationing took effect in 1943, *Omnibook* was forced to use 10 percent less paper than it had used in 1942—when it had already reduced its paper usage by adopting smaller-sized issues.

When Trautman approached Geffen in late 1942 to produce a miniaturized version for the armed forces, *Omnibook* was already planning to reduce its size because of paper rationing. In January 1943, *Omnibook* began printing an "overseas edition" for the military in a format that measured 5.25 by 7.75 inches—half the size of its 1938 iteration.[47] Within a few months, the domestic edition adopted the same small dimensions and was reduced in price to thirty-five cents per issue. Subscription rates soared.[48]

Not all magazines were as amenable as *Newsweek* and *Omnibook* when it came to the Army's list of demands. Even though the WPB's paper rationing caught *The New Yorker* "at its low point" after several "bad profit years," as Jane Grant, partner of the magazine's founder, Harold Ross, put it, Ross had little interest in taking his beloved magazine, distorting its dimensions, and sending the dehydrated monstrosity to troops.[49] Grant believed the magazine could not survive unless it produced an overseas edition and was determined to get Ross to come around.

She knew how Ross got his start in publishing by printing periodicals for troops during the Great War, and he would want his latest literary brainchild to entertain troops in this war.

Attracted to promises of being "first in France," Ross had signed up with the Eighteenth Engineers in 1917 with romantic visions of toting a gun while reporting the war from the front lines. Instead, he found himself digging ditches hundreds of miles from any shooting.[50] Bored stiff, Ross decided to amuse himself by creating a monthly regimental newspaper, which he called *The Spiker*.[51] Witty and sarcastic, featuring cartoons, gossip, and humor, the *Spiker* was a hit with Ross's fellow spade workers. The paper brazenly attacked everything that frustrated the men, even taking stabs at the Army's censorship regulations. "The boys on this side would like to experience the thrill of getting letters without knowing just what [city] they come from," one article jested. It urged the government to require all letters from home to bear mysterious return addresses, like "somewhere in California" or "somewhere in New York."[52] When Ross created *The New Yorker* in 1925, he replicated and tweaked many of the *Spiker*'s features.

Ross broadened his knowledge of wartime periodicals when he went AWOL from the Engineers and trekked 150 miles to Paris, toting a typewriter under his arm, to join the staff of *The Stars and Stripes*, an

Army-wide newspaper that was being formed. Ross barged into the paper's headquarters, claimed a desk, and promptly got down to work. Retroactive transfer papers were cobbled together so that Ross avoided being court-martialed.[53] He spent the rest of the war digging for scoops and learning what news soldiers hungered for.

Given this background, Grant knew that Ross had a soft spot for wartime journalism and would regret if *The New Yorker* did not make its way overseas. There was no arguing the business sense of the matter. As she told Ross, an overseas edition would help "keep up with our regular readers among our farflung fighting men and, even more important, to get some new ones in the youthful army."[54]

Grant reached out to Trautman, and the two worked together to land upon an advertisement-free six-by-nine-inch overseas edition. When Ross saw the first issue, he lodged any number of objections, growling that the "halftones took an awful licking in the miniature edition" and describing the cover art as "mutilated."[55] Seesawing between irascibility and perfectionism, Ross's performance may have been part spectacle and part genuine.[56] In any event, Grant persevered, and the miniature magazine began monthly overseas distribution in the fall of 1943, soon graduating to a weekly edition. Its popularity grew to the point that Trautman could justify increasing print runs and publishing two special editions devoted exclusively to *New Yorker* cartoons.[57]

By this point, some magazines were jumping onto the military bandwagon, willingly reducing their dimensions to make the overseas run; others insisted on maintaining their large pages, conceding only the elimination of advertisements and the use of thinner paper.[58] For example, *The Saturday Evening Post* produced an overseas edition with pages still measuring eleven by fourteen inches, but, by being ad-free and using newsprint pages, its weight was reduced from one pound to 4.5 ounces.[59] Still, the large pages were a turnoff for troops trudging through jungles or swashbuckling across the rugged terrain of the Mediterranean Theater. *The Post* decided to provide the best of both worlds. For those who were more stationary, the large overseas edition beckoned. For those on the move, *The Post* printed the most miniature magazine of the war,

*Post Yarns*. Only 3 by 4.5 inches, they could be slipped into a helmet liner. Ten million copies of thirty-six different issues were printed and distributed for free. Next to a letter from home, few things raised the spirits of combat troops like receiving copies of their favorite magazines in miniature formats.[60]

With these advances, magazine distribution within the Army rose astronomically, as did the periodical-reading audience. It took time to work out all of the kinks, but by the end of 1943, the Army was distributing one sorted package of seventeen different magazine titles to every 150 soldiers per month (with multiple copies of the most popular periodicals). The number rose to twenty-five titles by mid-1944, and thirty-five diverse offerings when the program reached its pinnacle in 1945.[61] These included: *Air Force*, *Coronet*, *Cosmopolitan*, *Country Gentleman*, *Detective Story*, *Esquire*, *Flying*, *Hit Kit*, *Infantry Journal*, *Inside Detective*, *Intelligence Bulletin*, *Life*, *McGraw-Hill Overseas Digest*, *Modern Screen*, *Newsweek*, *The New Yorker*, *Omnibook*, *Outdoor Life*, *Overseas Comics*, *Pic*, *Popular Photography*, *Popular Science*, *Reader's Digest*, *The Saturday Evening Post*, *Science News Letter*, *Sporting News*, *Time*, and *Western Story*.[62]

Other titles came and went over the course of the war. When magazine service first started in 1943, eight million issues were distributed—about one magazine per year for each man in the Army. A year later, having streamlined the entire process, Trautman was able to purchase sixty-three million magazines at a cost of less than four cents per issue. By 1945, 143 million magazines were being distributed. Occupation troops continued to be served with hundreds of millions of magazines through much of 1947.[63]

As troops' favorite magazines flooded overseas posts, letters of appreciation cascaded into the offices of magazine publishers and the Army Library Service. One unit stationed on a remote island in the South Pacific could hardly believe its luck when a "bundle of magazines [was] dropped off by a plane of the Air Transport Command." Apparently not knowing that General MacArthur would disapprove, the commanding officer for the area immediately contacted the Army Library Service to "request twenty tons of magazines...each month." He explained that the "very few magazines" his men had received had an "inestimable value," and as "dog-eared, torn and tattered as they are, they nevertheless are priceless and kept in constant circulation until they become practically unrecognizable."[64] Another batch of magazines that reached the Pacific generated the thanks of an entire squadron: "As you well know in this area, time has the habit of dragging; and in these lapses of time it is best [to]...have something to amuse. This situation your magazines aptly do take care of." Reading material was the only thing these soldiers looked forward to, and they hoped Trautman would "not forget us in the future."[65]

Praise for the variety of titles was commonplace among GIs. "My mouth has been watering for the 'Pony Edition' of *Time*, and lo and behold, here it came!" one man wrote. Having received a few issues of the magazine, he wanted the Army to know how they "lift me out of my little corner and put me on the roof where I can get that bird's eye view of the situation all over the world."[66] Seconding this sentiment, a letter from the *USS Iowa* described *Time* as "a godsend," noting "one copy will be read by 70 or 80 [men]."[67]

An unexpected favorite was *Omnibook*, with its monthly abridgements of bestselling books. From the Pacific, to the European and Mediterranean Theaters, troops wrote how special this little magazine had become to them. One man wrote about one issue that traveled through "the jungles of New Guinea," where it was passed from one soldier to the next; it was "like a letter from home and is a link...between the normal and the awesome desolation and turmoil" of war, he said.[68] From the Army Air Corps, an officer wrote that *Omnibook* was read "until the pages literally fall apart." "*Omnibook* fulfills the need in reading material better than any other publication," the airman added.[69] "I have enjoyed each issue of *Omnibook* for the past two years and hope to be able to enjoy your magazine for many more years to come," one soldier in the European Theater wrote. The "issues are eagerly read by all the fellows in my outfit, and *Omnibook* has gone with them through the campaigns in Algeria, Tunisia, [and] Sicily." *Omnibook* was the only way he could get his hands on the latest bestsellers from home, and that was what everyone wanted to read most.[70]

* * *

Trautman's miniature magazines proved to be a winning format for overseas troops. Yet while he found them uplifting, letters from soldiers about *Omnibook* were a bitter reminder of his inability to find a way to give troops the full range of book titles they wanted in the paperback design they needed. This shortcoming in Army Library Service haunted him.

Back at the Special Services Division in Washington, Trautman expressed his frustration to Eric Knight. The largest publishing companies claimed the bulk of bestselling titles and refused to print paperback editions. Troops wanted bestsellers, yet not hardcovers. Both sides were uncompromising. Trautman believed that the publishers were missing out on an opportunity to attract new readers, and that soldiers were losing a chance to develop a love of books.

As Trautman detailed his dilemma, Knight recalled an event he had attended at New York's Times Hall in May 1942, when he had been asked to speak before a large gathering of authors, publishers, journalists, and others interested in the role of the written word during wartime. The assembly was organized by a group called the Council on Books in Wartime, which was composed of nearly seventy publishers who adopted the motto "books are weapons in the war of ideas."[71] During the discussion, one panelist said that some books were so important in building understanding that they should be given away free. Knight noted that, in England, "sixpence [10-cent] editions are now hungrily absorbed by the public—books that are exceedingly good and books that just kill time," and that both types of books served an essential purpose in wartime. "America must come to cheap books," he declared.[72] Knight's idea was shot down by publishers. As the *New York Times* reported the next day, everyone agreed books needed to reach more people, but publishers had little "enthusiasm . . . for the suggestion that they be made cheaper."[73]

Inexpensive, popular paperbacks still eluded Trautman and his colleagues. But his experience with miniaturizing magazines had given him hope. He had been able to conjure up a paper deal with the WPB to coerce the cooperation of magazine publishers. And now American positions were flush with periodicals. Perhaps if he could understand the mindset that kept book publishers from producing paperbacks for the Army, he could suggest a way around it. After all, if publishers really believed that "books are weapons in the war of ideas," why were they hoarding the ammunition?

# 6

# Go Small or Stay Home

> A war of ideas can no more be won without books than a naval war can be won without ships. Books, like ships, have the toughest armor, the longest cruising range, and mount the most powerful guns.
>
> —Franklin Delano Roosevelt[1]

Trautman had not solved his paperback plight by the fall of 1942 and therefore had little choice but to support the renewal of the Victory Book Campaign for 1943. The Army had swelled to 5.4 million troops by the end of 1942, and this number was on pace to rise to over 7 million by the end of 1943.[2] New Army facilities were being built across the country so quickly to train and house these new recruits that there was a lag between securing supplemental appropriations from Congress for post libraries and getting books onto shelves. According to Trautman, it could take as long as four or five months after a camp had opened for books to be delivered.[3] During these first few months, many new recruits curdled with resentment at the loss of their civilian freedoms and the inanity of Army discipline, rules, and control over their every movement. As one private said about his new home in the Army, "I want to get the hell out of this hole." When others were asked if they agreed, only one of thirty did not.[4] Trautman was convinced—based on personal experience and the anecdotes troops shared with him—that books could help ease the hardship of adjusting to the military. Given that Victory Books could be sent to a camp at the very moment it opened, a book drive was his best bet to swiftly fill the stacks.[5]

When the 1943 campaign opened, the pace of donations was disappointingly slow. Pleas for books regularly appeared in newspapers, and yet the public response was underwhelming.[6] And the quality was wanting. As a librarian from the Enoch Pratt Free Library, Trautman's former employer, relayed to him, "I think I shall never recapture my... attitude toward the materials of librarianship." He had received 140,000 donated books, and in sorting them, discovered at least 50,000 books were "utterly useless" and "now on their way to the digester at the waste-paper plant." Another 10,000 were eliminated because they concerned "female" themes like housekeeping, sewing, cooking, childrearing, and the like; and there were thousands of children's books that could not be sent to the Army. Thus, of the original 140,000 books, only around half would be headed to troops—and many of these were older fiction and nonfiction, not modern titles or recent bestsellers.[7]

Five months into the campaign, only 4.2 million books had been donated—less than half the number from the year before.[8] Trautman felt it was time to make his move. While he deeply appreciated the help of his fellow librarians in gathering books for new Army libraries at domestic training facilities, he remained keen—even desperate—to open a new literary front: paperbacks specifically designed for GIs. The book he needed—lightweight and stowable—did not exist, so Trautman took a page out of the Information & Education Branch's playbook and invented one.

* * *

The first place he looked was *Omnibook*, which had already reduced its size twice in five years. Trautman thought its staff might provide helpful advice on what magic tricks would shrink a book. Additionally, Trautman was hoping its publisher, Max Geffen, might be receptive to producing an even smaller troop edition than the 5.25 by 7.5 inches they had launched. He and Geffen discussed page margins, font type and size, paper weight, and typical word counts for full-length books. Geffen provided Trautman with blank pre-constructed magazines to tinker with.

Back at his desk at the Special Services Division, Trautman tried to figure out how small he could make an *Omnibook* without ruining legibility. He wondered whether, if he included only one or two stories per issue, he could reduce the size without compromising readability. Guiding the question of scale were the dimensions of the pockets of a standard-issue US Army uniform. The ideal were the little guidebooks Eric Knight was making down the hall that could fit snugly in a pocket. A good book would always be within arm's reach.

Trautman sliced a blank *Omnibook* in half. Measuring just over three by five inches, it was smaller than Knight's guide to Great Britain and slimmer than a wallet. Testing the prototype on his own uniform pockets, Trautman found that it smoothly slid into his breast pocket and swam in the back pocket of his trousers. Believing only one condensed book would fit, Trautman made a mock label for the inside front cover that read "Omnibook Abridged Editions: This book, originally published in abridged form in *Omnibook*, the book-magazine, is reprinted in this special edition for the Armed Forces. . . ."[9] Trautman did not finish writing the sentence. Midway, he seemed to have an epiphany. If five condensed books could fit in a full-size *Omnibook*, then two and one-half abridged books could, theoretically at least, fit in the halved version. Trautman wondered whether there might not be enough space to print one entire, unabridged, book.

There was only one way to find out. Trautman didn't want to repeat the failure of his V-mailed *Newsweek* with its microscopic print. He tracked down the individual in the Special Services Division who helped with the format and layout of the country guides that Eric Knight produced. He was H. Stahley Thompson, a gifted graphic arts specialist for the Information & Education Branch, who developed a reputation as a maverick when it came to inventing new layouts and printing techniques.[10] During the war, he figured out how to print books, booklets, and Army reading materials in shapes and sizes that fit unique military needs; after the war, he helped develop plastic plates for book printing, which became the industry norm, and became vice president in charge of production at the American Heritage Publishing Company, where he designed hardcover magazines.[11] Thompson proved so helpful that Trautman secured permission for him to take temporary leave from his job producing country guides to assist the Army Library Service with its book project.[12]

Trautman and Thompson studied their options for printing equipment, paper, and how to format the interior pages. Improving on the size, weight, and shape of the halved *Omnibook* prototype that Trautman had made seemed impossible. The main difficulty was there was no book press capable of mass-producing such tiny paperbacks. Plus, only certain types of printing equipment, like magazine presses, could process the newsprint-thin paper for the interior pages. Since no printing press was designed to print such small-sized books, it was resolved that they would have to be paired and printed "two-up," one on top of the other on a single page.[13] After printing, the conjoined books would be sliced into two. Wider than they were tall, these squat volumes were unlike anything that the publishing industry—even those companies involved in producing paperbacks—had ever made.

Before going any further, Trautman and Thompson needed to calculate the cost. Trade paperbacks were twenty-five cents each, and to make this project attractive to the higher-ups in the Army, the cheaper these books were, the better. After researching the issue, Thompson discovered that because of wartime rationing, the production and sale of consumer goods had taken a substantial drop, which caused the printing of commercial catalogues to plummet. This meant that companies operating rotary magazine presses—the type of machine needed to print these books—not only had the capacity for an extra project but were eager for business.[14] Thompson located over a dozen companies that could help with the job. Their estimates provided that a print run of 50,000 would result in a unit cost of ten cents; the cost would be reduced to five cents per book in a print run of 100,000 or more.[15] The price was right.

Still, if the books were unreadable, none of it would matter. For the books to be pocket-sized, they had to remain small *and* thin. Testing showed that a book measuring 5.5 by 3.8 inches (the size of a halved *Omnibook*) would fit in the breast pocket of a uniform so long as it was under 384 pages, and the hip pocket could accommodate a book measuring 6.5 by 4.5 inches so long as it was no thicker than 512 pages. Playing with font sizes, Thompson discovered that if he copied the interior format of *Omnibook* by printing two columns of text on each page and reducing the margins, they could use a highly legible ten- or eleven-point font.[16] Printing two columns per page improved readability because it was easier on the eyes to read shorter rows of text.[17] This was especially important because troops would likely read in poor lighting. After Thompson had crunched all of this data, he concluded that complete shorter works could be squeezed into these miniature books without any editing or omissions. Lengthier tomes would need to be abridged.

Having settled on a design and a format, Trautman now needed to broach the idea to book publishers who wanted nothing to do with paperbacks. Once again, he turned to Eric Knight for advice. Knight encouraged Trautman to try the Council on Books in Wartime. This was the group of publishers that had invited Knight, in May 1942, to speak on the role of books in the war. It was possible that Knight had planted a seed in their minds when he urged them to print cheap paperbacks to increase reading as Britain had. Maybe, by now, the idea had germinated.[18]

Knight's assistance to Trautman was cut short when Knight was assigned an overseas mission by the War Department. On January 15, 1943, a transport plane carrying Knight and dozens of others crashed in a remote jungle along the Guiana coast.[19] There were no survivors. The loss was devastating to Trautman; Knight had become a close friend and a strong supporter of the work he was doing.[20] Without Knight, there would have been no paperback prototype to show publishers. To honor his friend and the ideas they shared, Trautman steeled his nerve and prepared to persuade publishers to print modern titles in soldier-friendly paperbacks.

* * *

The Council on Books in Wartime was founded in early 1942 by a formidable group of bookmen welded by a single belief: books had a key role in fighting World War II. Among its members were W. W. Norton, of W. W. Norton & Co.; John Farrar, of Farrar & Rinehart; Richard L. Simon, of Simon & Schuster; as well as representatives from Doubleday, Doran & Co.; Charles Scribner's Sons; G. P. Putnam's Sons; McGraw-Hill Book Co.; Little, Brown & Co.; Grosset & Dunlap; Harcourt, Brace & Co.; and Columbia University Press. A smattering of other like-minded institutions was represented, from the New York Public Library to the Book of the Month Club.[21] For all the experience in the room, no one had a clear idea of how to use books to fight a war. During the organization's first year, it dabbled with a variety of activities, all of which were geared toward the home front and book promotion. The council hosted radio broadcasts about war-related books, crafted dozens of "must read" book lists for everyone from children to sophisticates, and produced movie "shorts" about significant war books, including John Hersey's *Into the Valley* and Konrad Heiden's *Der Fuehrer*.[22] All of these activities promoted their lists and therefore increased sales of their titles, yet none was geared toward the military. Publishers likened books to weapons, but they were not sending their weaponry to war zones.

These publishers nonetheless knew that American troops were embarking for places where expression was distorted by propaganda, silenced by censorship, and controlled by laws. GIs would not only face attack by the enemy's guns, mortars, mines, and bombs, but leaflets, posters, and radio messages specifically targeted to demoralize them and weaken their resolve. By weaponizing words, the Axis believed it could soften the enemy and persuade Allied troops to surrender without a fight.[23] If anyone needed mental and spiritual armor, it was those facing this psychological warfare.

In late January 1943, Trautman and Thompson approached Malcolm Johnson, the publisher at Doubleday, Doran & Co. and an executive committee member at the council.[24] Why they singled out Johnson is unclear. Given that none of the paperback houses were represented on the council's executive committee (nor do records suggest that they were even invited to become members),[25] Trautman and Thompson had no choice but to approach a paperback skeptic.

Recognizing that business leaders communicated in the language of profits and losses, Trautman tailored his pitch along sales lines. The home-front market for books was already saturated, and the public had less free time to read than ever before. According to *U.S. News*, one in every three men between the ages of eighteen and forty-four would don a military uniform.[26] As these men left the workforce for the armed services, women were leaving the home and venturing into factories to take their place and perform essential war work. Nights and weekends were filled with volunteer work. With the nation at war, the public had less free time for reading, not more. What the book industry needed was a new reading market.

Trautman happened to know of one. He told Johnson how, in the oppressive heat and humidity of the South Pacific, he had witnessed troops passing along soiled, grimy books because it was all they had to read. Though damp, dog-eared, and dilapidated, they handled them as delicately as ancient artifacts, for there was no knowing if more would arrive. Trautman cited a poll asking troops what they wanted most, and they ranked books above athletics in popularity and use.[27]

While headlines suggested the war consisted of action-packed days and a rapid succession of battles, the reality was that most troops experienced snippets of intense activity followed by long stretches of idleness. "Hurry up and wait," they called it. During these seemingly interminable periods, homesickness had a chance to take root, discomforts and irritations won the mind's attention, and boredom made time stand still. In most theaters, there was no relief—no escaping to town for an evening out, no meals outside of rations or the KP's latest concoction spooned into their mess kit, and not even a chance to take a bath or launder their uniform. War was a monotonous routine of foxholes, tin-can dining, and poor hygiene. Trautman asked Johnson to consider what it was like to wear a soldier's boots, and how much an entertaining book might mean to a GI.[28]

Few books were truly portable for an infantryman in a warzone, who had to carry every single necessity on his back, a load that easily weighed fifty pounds or more.[29] Lugging a two-pound hardcover was out of the question. Foot soldiers were known to carry only two types of books. One was a Penguin paperback, usually jammed into a rear pants pocket.[30] The other was a small Bible sized to fit into a breast pocket. It served more than one purpose. The so-called "heart shield" Bible was designed to fit in a breast pocket and its covers were clad in gold-plated twenty-gauge steel that could supposedly "deflect supercharged 38-caliber service bullets at five paces... and may as miraculously deflect either bayonet or shrapnel."[31] Steel-clad or not, these books had one thing in common: They fit inside a GI's pocket.

Trautman presented his paperback prototype to Johnson. He explained all of the considerations he and Thompson had put into its design: its pocket-sized dimensions, lightweight paper, and dual columns of text to ensure a legible font size even in dim lighting. Because only mainstream publishers had the rights to bestsellers, works by modern popular authors, and timely nonfiction, they offered the only hope that the Army could supply soldiers the books they wanted in the pocket-sized format they needed. By producing them, Trautman argued, publishers would gain an entirely new audience of readers who would become lifelong customers. The war wouldn't last forever. If book publishers could follow the example of the magazine industry and produce GI reading material to sell to the government at cost, they would stand to profit for decades to come when troops returned home with a habit of reading books.[32]

Intrigued, Johnson offered to present Trautman's miniature paperback to the council at its next executive committee meeting in February 1943.[33] Johnson knew that council members felt that they had not maximized the potential role of books in the war, and, indeed, as a history of the council put it, were "in search of a project."[34] Printing books for those battling both the Nazis and the Nazis' chokehold on free thought was a fitting way for publishers to fight the war.

At the February meeting, Johnson urged his fellow bookmen to consider providing the government with "brand new little books printed from special plates and unlike any books heretofore issued in this country." He explained they would be paperbacks for servicemen only, sold directly to the government and not available for resale.[35] In response to Johnson, a few publishers offered to research the idea and report back on its feasibility, cost, profitability, and desirability.[36]

Meanwhile, Trautman was kept busy with constant travel. From February to March 1943, he attended a slew of successive conferences at Army Air Force bases that required him to travel cross-country twice, often by train as most servicemen on Army business did. Beginning at Mitchel Field in Long Island, New York, Trautman's next destination was the familiar Randolph Field, Texas. Though he did not have the eyesight to be a pilot, he maintained a lifelong love of aviation and never turned down a flight when one was offered. He then went to a conference in San Francisco before proceeding north to Fort George Wright, in Spokane, Washington, where there was a convalescent hospital for injured airmen. From there, he traveled to the Southeast Air Corps Training Command in Montgomery, Alabama, and then back home.[37]

Like most soldiers, whenever Trautman faced empty stretches of time he tended to think of home and grow lonely. If he had a book—and he usually did—he read. When he had writing paper handy, he wrote to Jane. "Came up from Los Angeles last night on the sleeper and stayed awake…watching the breakers dashing against the rocky shore in the moonlight. How I yearned for you to enjoy it with me—then it would have been perfect," he wrote Jane in mid-February. "I can't enjoy anything fully unless you are there to share it with me. . . . I'm just so much in love with you that my part of the world just rotates around you." Yet even when Trautman was working near their home in Arlington, Virginia, he never saw Jane for long. A typical day at the office might end at 1 a.m. and the next would start a few hours later.[38] With the war nowhere near an end, Trautman knew Jane faced years of him being absent. And he wished he could ameliorate the emptiness that caused. "Why don't you buy a cat or dog while I'm gone to help break the loneliness," he suggested in his letter. "You might phone the Humane Society," he added.[39] Soon after, a dog named Count joined the Trautman family, though he did not seem to take to Jane all that quickly. As Trautman wrote a few weeks later, "I am looking forward to getting back home and if our dog has decided to like you, I'll have a job building a fence for him."[40]

When Trautman returned to Washington in mid-March, updates from the council were waiting for him. It seemed that Johnson never mentioned to council members that the miniature paperback prototype originated with Trautman and Thompson. It must have shocked and amused Trautman to learn that the council had determined that officers in the Special Services Division (most likely meaning Trautman and Thompson) were "excited at the prospect" of troop-friendly paperbacks.[41] Trautman never corrected this lack of direct credit; if he could supply troops with the books they wanted, that was reward enough. As expected, not everyone on the council was supportive. Richard Simon, publisher at Simon & Schuster who had personally helped bankroll the launch of Pocket Books in the United States,[42] floated the idea that Pocket Books might consider printing paperbound books for the Army on a nonprofit basis. Immediately, other publishers expressed enthusiasm at the idea, eager to maintain no association with paperbacks.[43]

But by March this suggestion was abandoned, and the original idea of the council's members banding together to offer their own titles to be reprinted in a paperback designed for troops was back on the table.[44] However, there was a long list of conditions. Publishers wanted to select the titles. A royalty of one cent would be worked into the price, with one-half cent going to a book's author and the other half cent to the original publisher.[45] The government would pay for composition, printing plates, binding, overhead, and shipping. Plus, as it did with magazines, the government would need to provide paper since the WPB required, as of January 1943, book publishers to reduce their paper consumption to 37.5 percent of the paper tonnage they used in 1939.[46]

Even with all of these provisos and precautions, several publishers remained apprehensive. Would a legion of paperbacks for the military flood the domestic book market and depress sales? The print runs being floated were enormous—50,000, 100,000, 150,000. If the public learned that the government was purchasing books for troops for five or ten cents each, why would it shell out $2 to $4 for a hardcover? These and other night terrors encouraged a contingent of wary publishers to vehemently oppose printing cheap paperbacks for anyone.

The insider who soothed these worried minds was William Warder Norton, chairman of the council. He had established W. W. Norton in 1924 with the philosophy that "serious modern subjects should be presented in well-written, well-designed and good-looking books written especially for the average person who wished to acquire exact knowledge."[47] Books, he believed, were for everyone, not just the wealthy and privileged. Having built an admired and successful publishing house from the ground up, Norton commanded the respect of his fellow bookmen. He seemed to intuitively understand the book-reading and -buying habits of the public and knew what was good for business. His confidence that publishers would be fools to let this opportunity pass them by helped create consensus behind the project.

At council meetings, Norton tirelessly addressed questions and quelled concerns. To those who fretted that cheap paperbacks (and their thin profit margins) would destroy the market for hardcovers (and their hefty profit margins), Norton argued that the home front would still prefer attractive hardcovers and pay the price for them; the pocket-sized readers for troops were expendable. In response to worries that the domestic market would be flooded by free books, Norton pointed out that the flimsy paperback editions—with interior pages akin to newsprint—would not last long. His main argument remained that this was an opportunity to expand the book-reading and -buying audience. Paperbacks would reach millions of men who had never purchased hardcovers as civilians; an entirely new market would be stoked. Soldiers would become lifelong customers. Norton's incessant cheerleading for, and wholehearted endorsement of, Trautman's paperbacks was instrumental in persuading publishers to sign on. In the words of John Jamieson, a librarian who worked in the offices of the Army Library Service and wrote the definitive history of its work, "Norton's personal standing in the industry was the chief factor in creating unanimity," and for many publishers, decisive. By May 1943, the project got the green light from all the major publishing houses.[48]

Now Trautman's challenge was gaining the government's approval. As Norton was preaching the gospel of paperbacks to his publishing brethren, Trautman was opening a second front by lining up support within the Army, which would be footing the bill for these books. Not everyone in the War Department felt that books had a role to play in this war. That Johnson and the publishers were taking credit for the paperback plan proved handy. Johnson, Norton, Simon—these were the starred generals of the publishing world, and they commanded respect from even those outside their profession. Johnson proposed coming to Washington to meet with Trautman and other government officials to discuss the paperback proposal, financing, and the publishers' conditions on the partnership. Trautman was overjoyed.[49] Someone with clout had joined the fray. With surprising ease—given the reluctance of some, like General Douglas MacArthur, to supplying overseas positions with books—Johnson secured official authorization from the Army.[50]

Now it was up to Trautman to dot each bureaucratic *i* and cross every *t* so that the plan would gain administrative approval. Cooperation across different sections of the Army was essential—including the Quartermaster, the Procurement Division of the Army Service Forces, and the Assembly Branch.[51] For example, the staff in the Quartermaster General's Office needed to make adjustments to the contract so the council was set up as a publishing business that could satisfy the Army's requirements on pecuniary responsibility; the Procurement Division had to assist with contractual language that would keep books from being "dumped" into the domestic book market at war's end; and the Assembly Branch would need to bundle and ship the packages of books.[52] Trautman was creating more work for multiple Army offices, and some objections and complaints were made. When he encountered resistance, according to Jamieson, Trautman "always took the line that the person he was dealing with was the only man in or out of the Army who boggled at the idea. If those who hesitated or raised objections had known how much company they had, the project would never have been approved."[53]

Finally, in early summer 1943, after months of planning and preparations by both the publishers and the Army, a contract was signed to make the partnership official. To placate publishers worried about the GI paperbacks inundating the domestic market, the contract specified they would be distributed overseas only. (This provision was slightly altered in August 1944, when publishers also permitted limited distribution of the paperbacks to military hospitals within the United States.)[54] Although the Army Library Service had performed the bulk of the work in negotiating, organizing, and launching this paperback program, the Navy shared in its benefits. When the first order of 50,000 paperbacks was made, 40,000 were allocated for the Army and the remaining 10,000 for the Navy; this was roughly in proportion to the respective size of each military service.[55]

By July 1943, thirty titles were selected by council members and military library staff to compose the first month's batch of books. The first group, called the "A series," included *Oliver Twist*, by Charles Dickens; *Tortilla Flat*, by John Steinbeck; *Storm Over the Land*, by Carl Sandburg; *My World and Welcome to It*, by James Thurber; *The Fireside Book of Dog Stories*, by Jack Goodman; *World Series*, by John Tunis; and a smattering of other titles.[56] Trautman's miniature paperbacks were called the Armed Services Editions.[57] To facilitate future ASE selections, a three-part book selection process was adopted to give both publishers and the military a role in choosing what titles would be printed. First, each publisher scrutinized their own lists to identify all titles that might be appealing to young servicemen. Next, these lists were culled by the council's Advisory Committee—a rotating group of men and women with book expertise—to ensure a good variety of titles for each month's batch of ASEs. Lastly, the Advisory Committee's recommendations—which could number well beyond sixty titles per month—were reviewed by Trautman and the Navy's head librarian, Isabel DuBois, since ASEs were distributed across both services.[58]

Trautman appreciated the opportunity to work with DuBois, an experienced librarian who understood the Navy's reading needs and preferences. She began her career as a librarian at the Drexel Institute in Philadelphia in 1910 and joined the ALA's war service work during World War I before being named assistant director of libraries in the Navy's Bureau of Navigation. She remained with the Navy through World War II.[59]

As one newspaper commented in a 1935 article about DuBois, "The Navy is a strictly masculine domain, but a woman picks the books read by its personnel, from bluejacket to admiral."[60]

When Trautman and DuBois made the final cut for each month's batch of ASEs, some titles were rejected because the Army and Navy had already purchased hardcover versions for training camps and new titles were preferred. Later in the program, troops wrote the Army and Navy librarians about what titles they wanted, and so Trautman and DuBois would ask that the most requested books be added.[61] They typically aimed to include titles scattered across twelve main subject areas: contemporary fiction, historical fiction, autobiographies and biographies, westerns, adventure novels, mysteries, classics, short story collections, travel, history, science, and poetry.[62]

According to Trautman's son, Eric, his father felt DuBois never got the credit she deserved for running an exceptional library service for the Navy.[63] In the 1940s, it was rare for a female librarian to serve in a leadership role (the VBC's Althea Warren was another exception), even though 90 percent of librarians at the time were women.[64] In the Navy, DuBois was the only woman on the staff of the Bureau of Navigation and likely became accustomed to working in a male-dominated workplace due to her long tenure.[65] The membership of the council, which was almost entirely male, likely had little experience receiving orders from a woman on what to print.[66] Council records show that the publishers grew irritated by DuBois's ASE suggestions, with private memoranda between members complaining how she made "a huge issue of a triviality."[67] It is likely an understatement that it must have been difficult, and even lonely, for DuBois. Perhaps because Trautman often felt like an underdog, he made sure to include DuBois when others tried to leave her out, even inviting her to council meetings when the publishers did not. At the end of their time working together, Trautman sent DuBois a telegram to express his appreciation. "A well done to you for your achievements in planning and directing a great library service," it said.[68]

* * *

In late September 1943, the first ASEs rolled off the presses. They were transported to sorting centers so that book bundles containing thirty different titles could be prepared for shipment overseas. Wrapped in waterproof brown paper and bound by white twine, each bundle measured nine by six by seven inches and weighed only seven pounds.

To celebrate the achievement, the council ordered Moroccan leather slipcases sized to fit a single ASE, and presentation copies were given to President Roosevelt, General George Marshall, Admiral Ernest King, and many of the publishers.[69] Trautman received one as well and kept it as a precious memento of this chapter of his library work. Around the same time, the Army also recognized Trautman's work by promoting him to lieutenant colonel.[70]

Beginning in December 1943, the ASEs made their way overseas, delivered by jeep, parachute, plane, or the mail. No one had seen a book like this before. Given the timing, some thought the Army had sent them a holiday present. Those who read the Army's most popular periodical, *Yank the Army Weekly*, knew that these packages comprised their new monthly reading ration. *Yank* had claimed that these paperbacks would be "easy to read, about one-fifth the size of a normal book," and sized to "fit into any uniform pocket." To many, it had sounded too good to be true. Yet here they were.[71]

Trautman, Thompson, and the publishers waited to hear what troops thought of the ASEs. Did they like the selection? Were they readable in foxholes? Did the paper covers and thin pages disintegrate under combat conditions? Most importantly, were the soldiers reading them?

# 7

# Roads Paved in Books

From that time on, the world was hers for the reading. She would never be lonely again, never miss the lack of intimate friends. Books became her friends and there was one for every mood. There was poetry for quiet companionship. There was adventure when she tired of quiet hours. There would be love stories when she came into adolescence and when she wanted to feel a closeness to someone she could read a biography.

—*A Tree Grows in Brooklyn*, Betty Smith[1]

Trautman well knew that the average American soldier did not consider his hometown library to be "an important cultural center" worth visiting. A GI's "previous use of books was largely confined to necessary school work," he said. Although most soldiers did not go into the Army as book readers, they did have a civilian habit of reading magazines and comics.[2] Publishers skeptical of the ASE project wondered whether they were gambling with their business model to produce books for people who did not even want them.

These concerns were exacerbated by a fall 1943 article in the *New York Times Book Review* by Ralph Thompson, a critic and future editor at the Book of the Month Club, who was serving as a sergeant in the US Army. Thompson argued that American soldiers in England, where he was stationed, read little more than their mail, with the occasional newspaper or magazine—usually *The Stars and Stripes* or *Yank*.[3] "As for books, practically no one pays much attention to them," Thompson wrote. His fellow soldiers had not been "in the habit of reading books before," and it was Thompson's opinion that "the Army in wartime is no place to learn how to cultivate" this custom. Although there were not many books available, Thompson believed that there was no point in sending more. "You soon enough learn in the infantry not to accumulate a single ounce or square inch of personal baggage (books or otherwise) for sooner or later every ounce and every square inch takes its toll." There was no way that troops who shirked books as civilians would voluntarily carry a book. "If you could see what an infantryman's normal impedimenta consist of, you'd understand why he doesn't run out and buy a couple of 1,000-page historical novels to top off the load."[4] The council's membership undoubtedly read the *New York Times Book Review*. Those who had been reticent about participating in the ASE undertaking likely felt a sense of vindication.

However, one month after Thompson's account, *Publishers' Weekly* printed a counteroffensive, written by another man in the Army, Paul McPharlin. While it was true that most soldiers and sailors had not turned to books to fill their spare hours as civilians, McPharlin nonetheless insisted that "many who are stationed at quiet posts will become readers in spite of themselves."[5] For those overseas, "comparatively few are engaged on actual battle fronts," and "thousands find themselves on tropical isles—without Dotty Lamour" movies. "Under the circumstances," McPharlin said, "men become voracious readers."[6] Isolated, homesick, and bored, troops in "their enforced solitude,... become not only bookworms but bibliophiles."[7]

With these mixed verdicts, publishers were eager to hear directly from troops. But the later months of 1943 slipped by with no word whether they had received ASEs, let alone welcomed them.[8] The publishers had not anticipated the lag, as they were unversed in military supply lines, red tape, and the Army's prioritization system. For soldiers on the move, mail could arrive months late. For the vast majority, no ASEs reached them until late December 1943 or early January 1944. The publishers grew so impatient to receive testimonials that they even placed an advertisement in *The Stars and Stripes* that asked troops to write publishers to share their opinions about the ASEs. After their first foray with these paperbacks, many earnestly shared their two cents.[9]

One early letter came from a private whose transport received a bundle of ASEs before heading to India. He described:

> Now after a seemingly interminable voyage made bearable only through the ministrations of these books, I can pay personal tribute to their effect on the morale of the transient soldier.
>
> On this ship, everywhere one looked, one saw soldiers eagerly devouring these books, oblivious of overcrowded decks, a blazing sun, and a heaving ocean. Even lipreaders stubbornly plodded their laborious way through them. Whenever a spare moment or an empty space permitted, the books emerged from hip pockets....
>
> Every soldier is indebted to the Council for the free Armed Services Editions.[10]

Another soldier wrote that he and his fellow soldiers had quickly "become book readers, traders, hoarders."[11] A sailor marveled, "[I'd] bet dollars to G.I. Spam that half the men... never cracked a book before," and yet now they couldn't last a day without reading one.[12] The ASEs were praised from all fronts for their portability, popular titles, and wide selection of genres. The main refrain was "keep 'em comin'."[13]

Trautman, however, did not need testimonial letters to prove what books meant to soldiers in the field. He had toured training facilities, spoken with despondent men burrowed in holes wondering if they would survive another day, and witnessed the boredom and brooding of troops isolated on Pacific islands. They were elated to receive a book, *any* book, to distract them from homesickness, morbid thoughts, and oftentimes both.[14] Because so many GIs were stationed in remote areas where a USO celebrity show couldn't reach them and setting up a movie screen wasn't possible, the ASEs—as Paul McPharlin had said—converted even the most reluctant readers into patrons of paperbacks.[15]

It was not just soldiers who were elated by the ASEs. To have your book made into an ASE was perhaps the highest compliment an author could receive. Some of the most moving letters sent to Trautman were from writers. Using his pseudonym of Stefan Heym, Helmut Flieg, a Jewish author who had been uprooted from his home in Germany by the Nazis in 1933,[16] wrote Trautman in November 1943 after he received word that his second book, *Hostages*, was being produced as an ASE. At the time of his letter, Heym had enlisted in the US Army and was a private stationed at Camp Ritchie, Maryland. He was overjoyed that his book would be among the paperback volumes being shipped overseas. "Since I am in the Army myself, I don't think I need to mention how delighted I am with the job."[17]

Trautman's friend Jesse Stuart told him how much it meant when his books were purchased by the Army. Before the ASEs, 2,000 hardcovers of Stuart's books had been obtained for Army hospitals and training camps.[18] After Stuart's *Taps for Private Tussie* was crowned the December 1943 selection for the Book of the Month Club,[19] it was made into an ASE and distributed to troops in March 1944.[20] (Another Stuart title, *Head O'W-Hollow*, also became an ASE and was distributed shortly after V-J Day.)[21] Despite the fact that he was an award-winning, bestselling author, Stuart believed that it was his induction onto the shelves of Army libraries and into uniform pockets that had capped his writing career. "Ray, you don't know how much I thank you for this," Stuart wrote Trautman in May 1943. "If you hadn't been in the position you are in, my books wouldn't have made the Army Libraries," Stuart said. "I am grateful that you did this Ray."[22]

Trautman could not take credit for Stuart's being an ASE author—or anyone else's. He was the last to have a say in what titles made the cut. Stuart's publisher would have had to nominate his books first, then the council's Advisory Committee would have had to select them as good additions to a particular month's reading fare, and then Trautman for the Army and Isabel DuBois for the Navy would make the final determination.[23]

However, this did not mean that Trautman didn't feel some gratification when he saw the works of his friends made into ASEs. Two of Eric Knight's bestselling books were chosen, and one of his short stories was included in *The Fireside Book of Dog Stories*, which was one of the first

In November 1940, Trautman was selected as chief librarian of the Army, a position he held until late 1945. In this role, he worked with magazines to make troop-sized editions, developed the prototype for the pocket-sized Armed Services Editions, and helped create the format for *Overseas Comics*. Distributing over 140 million books and hundreds of millions of magazines and comics, Trautman built the largest library system in the world.
*Credit*: Courtesy of Eric Trautman

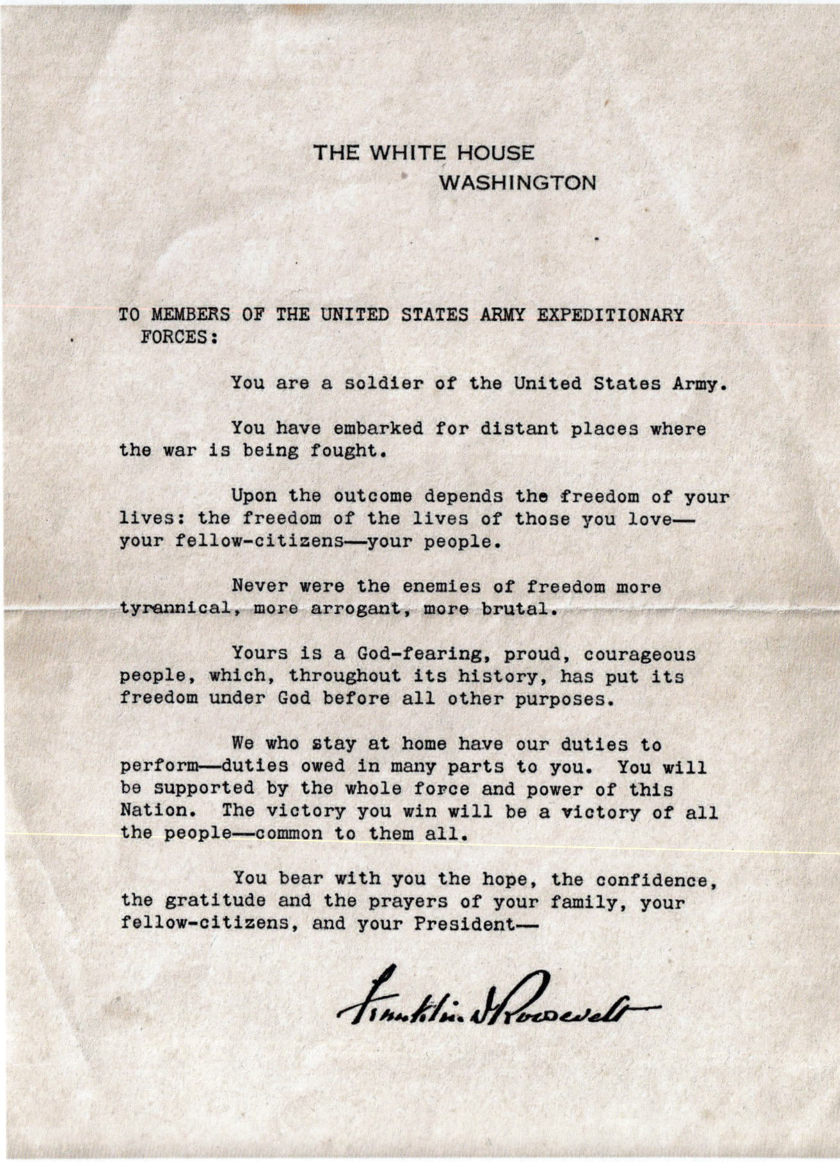

THE WHITE HOUSE
WASHINGTON

TO MEMBERS OF THE UNITED STATES ARMY EXPEDITIONARY FORCES:

You are a soldier of the United States Army.

You have embarked for distant places where the war is being fought.

Upon the outcome depends the freedom of your lives: the freedom of the lives of those you love—your fellow-citizens—your people.

Never were the enemies of freedom more tyrannical, more arrogant, more brutal.

Yours is a God-fearing, proud, courageous people, which, throughout its history, has put its freedom under God before all other purposes.

We who stay at home have our duties to perform—duties owed in many parts to you. You will be supported by the whole force and power of this Nation. The victory you win will be a victory of all the people—common to them all.

You bear with you the hope, the confidence, the gratitude and the prayers of your family, your fellow-citizens, and your President—

Franklin D Roosevelt

In early 1942, the White House asked Trautman to research famous speeches given to embarking troops. Trautman prepared this letter, which was lightly revised by White House staff and signed by President Franklin Roosevelt; a copy was given to every soldier as they left the United States for battle.

In mid-1942, Trautman traveled around the world to observe the book needs of troops, and his first stop was Havana, Cuba, where he visited Ernest Hemingway's favorite watering hole, Sloppy Joe's Bar. Before Trautman left, Hemingway arrived and the two discussed the war, books, and a revised galley Hemingway needed to send to New York.
*Photo*: Courtesy of Eric Trautman

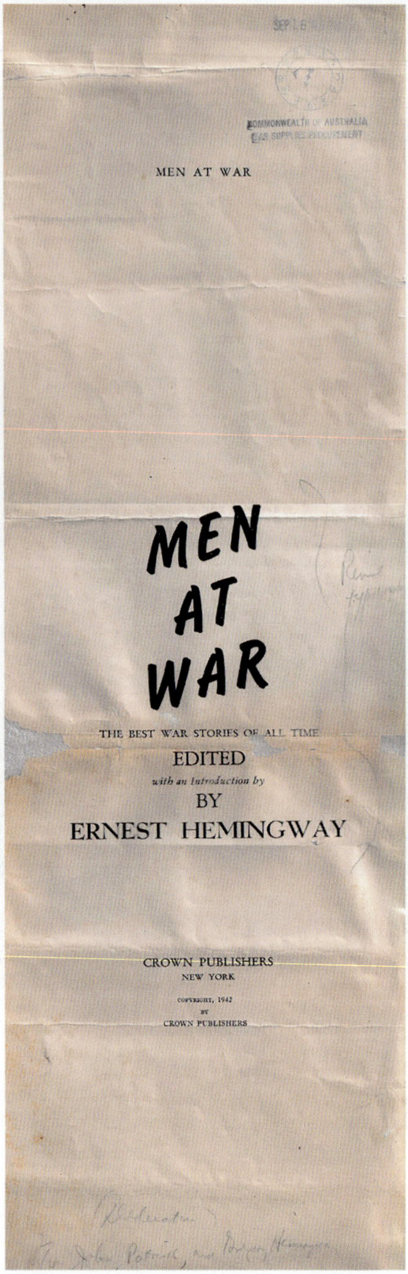


Concerned about censorship, Ernest Hemingway asked Trautman to hand deliver this revised galley of *Men at War* to Crown Publishers in New York. Trautman agreed, carrying it around the world while he was on Army business. The top-right corner is stamped by the Commonwealth of Australia, marking Trautman's stop-over to meet with General Douglas MacArthur. Handwritten notations to the first page of the galley indicate that Hemingway disliked the typography and wanted to add a dedication to his sons, John, Patrick, and Gregory Hemingway.
*Credit*: Courtesy of Eric Trautman

Trautman traveled extensively as chief librarian. Here, he is attending an April 1943 Army Librarian Conference in Atlanta, Georgia. As this image shows, most of the Army's librarians serving in training facilities in the United States were women. Trautman is sitting in the front row, to the right of the podium.
*Credit*: Army Signal Corps

In 1942 and 1943, the Victory Book Campaign was hosted by the American Library Association, American Red Cross, and the USO. Posters like this one encouraged the public to donate good books for distribution to servicemen. Approximately eighteen million volumes were collected by librarians for military training facilities. Most books were hardcover and were suitable for stationary troops, while foot soldiers overseas clamored for lightweight paperbacks.

Trautman helped create the Armed Services Editions, pocket-sized paperbacks specially printed for troops in World War II. Each month, a new selection of titles was wrapped in waterproof packaging and heavy-duty twine. This image of the "B-series," the second monthly installment of ASEs, consists of thirty books and measures nine by six by seven inches and weighs seven pounds. These bundles were mailed to troops around the world beginning in late 1943. When the ASEs were discontinued in 1947, over 123 million had been distributed to American troops.

While serving as chief librarian, Trautman became a father. Pictured are Trautman and his wife, Jane, with their first son, Eric. The inspiration for their son's name was Eric Knight, the author of *Lassie Come-Home*. Knight worked in the same Army offices as Trautman and helped inspire the Armed Services Editions. He was killed in an Army plane crash. Throughout the war, Trautman carried this photo of his family in his wallet.
*Credit*: Courtesy of Eric Trautman

Trautman's fact-finding mission for General Eisenhower brought him directly into the Battle of the Bulge. On a road like the one seen here (the 82nd Airborne Division is pictured heading to the front), soldiers poured out of the woods and flagged down Trautman's car. They formed a makeshift unit and, after being stranded for nearly a week, the group fought their way to safety. Like most veterans, Trautman maintained a lifelong reluctance to talk about battle. However, it crystallized his mission to do anything to get books to combat troops. Reading was their only escape.
*Credit*: Army Signal Corps

After the Battle of the Bulge, Trautman followed orders to return to Paris, but he could not stop thinking of the soldiers still fighting. This silhouette of Trautman, made days after he led troops into battle, suggests the toll of combat—his eyes are cast downward, his chin is lowered. Knowing the only comfort he could provide to those still fighting was to give them books, Trautman purchased 17,000 editions from Paris bookstores and personally supervised getting them to the front lines. *Credit*: Courtesy of Eric Trautman

Books were one of the most popular forms of recreation during World War II, and the Army Library Service successfully shipped Armed Services Editions to even the most remote outposts. When the Sixth Army was stationed in northern New Guinea in July 1944, torrential rain flooded the area. By propping a stretcher on stilts and using a wooden box for a pillow, this private created a respite from the water so he could relax and read a book.
*Credit*: Department of Information

Some of the only books that made it to the Pacific Theater were Armed Services Editions. Pictured here is the Third Marine Division's library on Iwo Jima. It is housed in a large tent, with a wall of sandbags around its perimeter. On top of the sandbags are several crates of paperbacks and ASEs.
Credit: Cpl. R. Impenachio, Headquarters, Third Marine Division

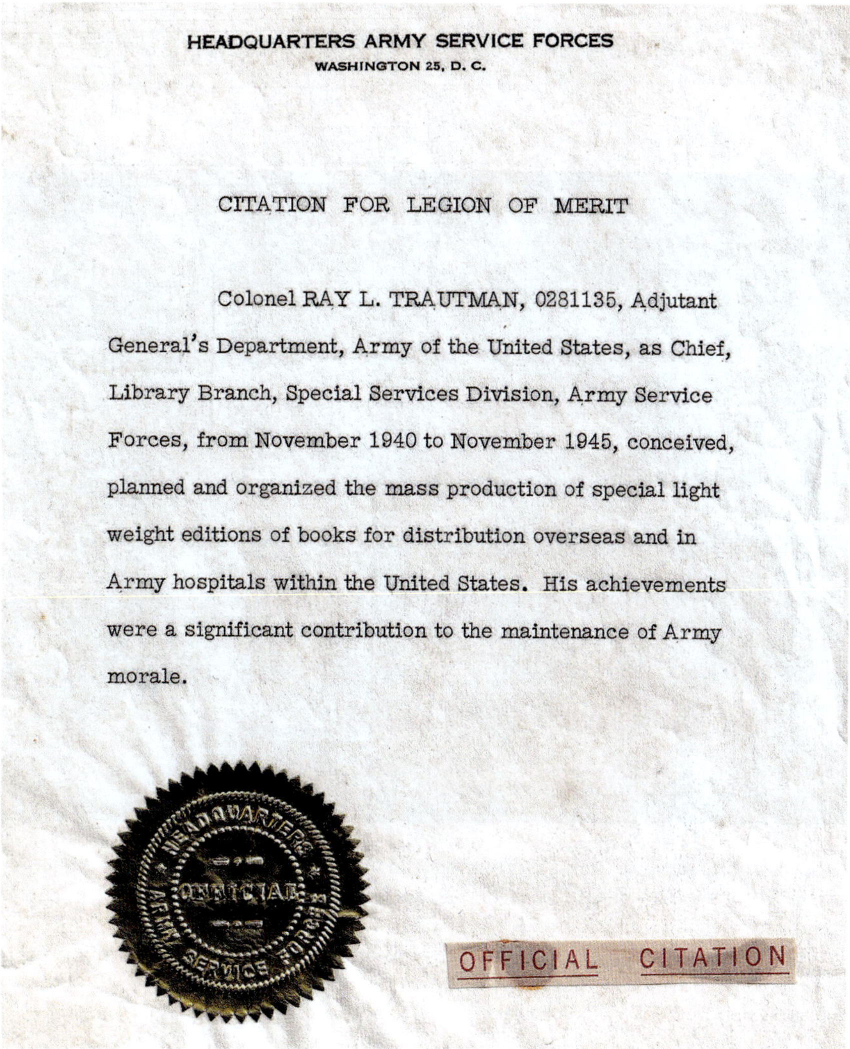
HEADQUARTERS ARMY SERVICE FORCES
WASHINGTON 25, D. C.

CITATION FOR LEGION OF MERIT

Colonel RAY L. TRAUTMAN, 0281135, Adjutant General's Department, Army of the United States, as Chief, Library Branch, Special Services Division, Army Service Forces, from November 1940 to November 1945, conceived, planned and organized the mass production of special light weight editions of books for distribution overseas and in Army hospitals within the United States. His achievements were a significant contribution to the maintenance of Army morale.

HEADQUARTERS OFFICIAL ARMY SERVICE FORCES

OFFICIAL CITATION

Trautman is likely the only person awarded the Legion of Merit for distributing books to the armed forces during wartime. This citation credits Trautman with conceiving, orchestrating, and distributing the Armed Services Editions and for making a "significant contribution" to maintaining morale in the Army.

Trautman had become such a luminary in the world of books that Frederic Melcher, on behalf of the American Booksellers Association, invited him to partake in a 1945 ceremony providing President Harry Truman with hundreds of books for the White House Library. The president is in the middle of the photo, and Trautman is the rightmost figure, wearing his Army uniform.
*Credit*: American Booksellers Association

In 1948, Mildred Young became the first female chief librarian of the Army. Here, she appears with publisher Stanley Rinehart, Jr., to present a copy of *The Best Army Short Stories 1950* to Major General Edward F. Witsell, the adjutant general of the Army. While Trautman favored a writing competition for troops during World War II, it was Young who gained the necessary approval postwar, launched the contest, and had the best pieces published. On the shoulder of Young's uniform, the Army Library Service patch is slightly visible; she fought to secure this insignia to honor the unique education and specialization of Army librarians.
*Credit*: US Army photo

In 1948, Trautman became a professor of library science at Columbia University. For decades, Trautman taught while continuing to serve in the Army Reserve and working on projects that would increase literacy and the availability of books and libraries for all. One of his last contributions to teaching was developing a course, Institutional Libraries, which highlighted the need for more libraries serving all communities.
*Credit*: Courtesy of Eric Trautman

thirty titles printed.[24] This was only appropriate, given that it was Knight who had inspired the ASE format, encouraged Trautman to pursue it, and had recommended the Council on Books in Wartime as the agency best suited to take on the project. In February 1944, an ASE of Knight's *Lassie Come-Home* was distributed to troops overseas, and the following month Knight's bestselling *Sam Small Flies Again* made its way into soldiers' pockets around the world.[25]

Around the same time that Trautman approved 50,000 ASEs of each of Knight's books, Trautman honored his friend's memory in a more personal way. On December 13, 1943, Jane and Ray welcomed a baby boy, Eric Ray Trautman. This deeply touched Knight's widow, Jere, who would send birthday and holiday gifts to her husband's namesake for years to come.[26] But it was perhaps Max Geffen of *Omnibook* who sent the most fitting words of congratulation to Jane: "My best wishes on your abridged edition of Colonel Ray."[27]

* * *

Early in 1944, while the initial reports from overseas showed the ASEs were a success, Trautman faced his first showdown with the publishers. They felt they should have exclusive control over choosing titles; they knew the reading habits of Americans—whether serving or not—better than the military and did not want their judgment second-guessed. However, Trautman and Isabel DuBois had reams of data on troop reading preferences; they both knew there was a chasm between what publishers thought servicemen should read and what they wanted to read.

One sticking point was Trautman's determination to include an array of books across different reading levels, while publishers grumbled about including titles for "illiterates." Army classification paperwork showed that over 30 percent of draftees—nearly one in three—had attained no more than an eighth-grade reading level.[28] Additionally, the Army required that all inductees have a minimum of a fourth-grade-level education so that they could "comprehend written instructions, orders, signboards, and regulations." By December 1941, over 200,000 men had received deferments because they were illiterate. This was too large a number for the Army to ignore, and so these men were inducted and shepherded into special training units where they were taught to read.[29] Instructors employed cartoon strips and heavily illustrated materials; not only were these visually appealing, but the images also helped reinforce and confirm comprehension. By the end of the war, over 300,000 troops had cycled through the Army's literacy program and gained the ability to read.[30] Publishers, in making their ASE nominee lists, had a tendency to ignore the needs of the Army's novice readers.

A related issue was that publishers exhibited a strong preference for nonfiction, classics, and what might be called "highbrow" works, while soldiers' preferences hewed to westerns, mysteries, stories of adventure, and page-turning fiction. When Trautman picked titles, he always tried to give troops the books they wanted most, based on the conversations he had had with soldiers in training facilities and overseas; on reading preferences documented in military hospitals; and on letters from soldiers about books they enjoyed or had found transformative. Based on these experiences, it was obvious to Trautman that the war was taking a psychological toll on servicemen, and books seemed to provide relief. This was hard to explain to publishers, especially since there was a dearth of medical or scientific research to back up Trautman's observations.

The Royal Army Medical Corps had coined the term "shell shocked" in 1915 to describe soldiers with no external wounds but who seemed stricken by "a severe psychical shock" that made them emotionally and mentally "unsteady."[31] Though medics believed the condition was caused by exploding shells jostling the brain, this hypothesis was weakened when troops had symptoms of shell shock despite being far from any explosions. "Neurasthenia," was the label placed on these men, whose symptoms of physical and mental exhaustion were believed to be caused by the stress of war.[32]

In World War II, troops who exhibited the telltale signs—slurred speech, bewilderment, depression, nightmares, tremors, a mental haze—were diagnosed with "psychiatric collapse," "battle fatigue," or "war neurosis."[33] They were typically treated by being given a rest period, then sent back into combat. Needless to say, this was entirely ineffective. Not until 1980 was posttraumatic stress disorder recognized by the American Psychiatric Association.[34] This late bloom of knowledge did little for the 1.4 million Americans who were diagnosed with battle fatigue in World War II.[35] And this number represented only the documented cases. Social stigmas tethered to stereotypes of masculinity caused some troops to hide their suffering.[36] This was only reinforced after the highly publicized 1943 incident in which General George Patton slapped a hospitalized private diagnosed as "battle-shocked" because, in Patton's words, the private was using "'battle fatigue' as an excuse for cowardice" and he needed to "get up, join his unit, and make a man of himself."[37] Patton was later forced to apologize.

Trautman was convinced books could offset the emotional wounds of war. Drawing from the principles of "bibliotherapy," he believed reading had a therapeutic quality that could help soldiers process the trauma they endured. Practiced in United States hospitals since the early 1800s—the physician Benjamin Rush was one of its first proponents—bibliotherapy typically involved a trained librarian selecting titles that might help a patient "solve a personal problem, develop skills needed for living, and/or bolster self-image."[38] In stories, readers might observe traits they admire and wish to develop, or gain ideas to help them through their own difficulties. A character—David Copperfield, the Lone Ranger, Superman—might impart upon a reader a dose of strength, courage, validation, acceptance, or hope.[39] Trautman sometimes referred to the ASEs as tools in his "first aid" kit for troops.[40] Others recognized the therapeutic value that books provided. One soldier who spent time in a hospital referred to them as "life savers."[41] And an Army medic ranked ASEs, alongside penicillin, as "the greatest improvement in Army technique."[42]

As Trautman continued to ask for page-turning fiction, popular short stories, and books that would be accessible to soldiers building literacy skills, publishers grew increasingly frustrated with Trautman's suggestions. At one point, council members asked Trautman to justify why the Army and Navy should be able to request titles for ASE production in the first place, or indeed have any control over what titles were printed.

Trautman's response was sent to Philip Van Doren Stern, the council's manager of the ASE project.[43] Practicing the art of diplomacy, he began by praising the publishers' work with the ASEs, and then suggested that it would be "unlikely that the Advisory Committee would disregard the first-hand information available" to the military on the "reading tastes and demands of servicemen." After all, "the Armed Services Editions were intended primarily to supply soldiers and sailors with the books they desire rather than to reflect a selection of books of which the publishing industry is most proud." Given the wide swath of reading abilities and tastes across the Army, a good selection of books was the only way to serve everyone. The ASEs could be a failure if they consisted only of titles "selected by highbrows for the minority highbrow group in the Army."[44]

To prove his point, Trautman provided feedback from troops. "Ease up on the historical novels," one soldier had advised. And "it might not hurt to try a single classic a month."[45] "There is one bit of criticism I have to offer," wrote another GI. "I believe that the majority of the fellows prefer fiction, especially of the modern type."[46] A private in a field hospital commented, "I believe you have struck the proper balance in providing books that appeal to every literary (and non-literary) taste."[47] When it came to requests for specific titles, soldiers seemed to overwhelmingly seek books that reminded them of home and family. Two popular titles, Rosemary Taylor's *Chicken Every Sunday* and Betty Smith's *A Tree Grows in Brooklyn*, featured fictional stories of intimate family life. These books reminded GIs of their mothers, siblings, and hometowns, and they soaked up every nostalgia-inducing page.[48] To Trautman's point about bibliotherapy, one hospitalized Marine said that two years of combat had numbed him; he carried a "dead heart" and "dulled mind" and had no hope for the future. To pass the time, a nurse happened to give him the ASE of *A Tree Grows in Brooklyn*. "I can't explain the emotional reaction that took place," the Marine said, but "this heart of mine turned over and became alive again," and he dared to believe that "maybe a fellow has a fighting chance in this world after all."[49] There was no medicine that could bring such a result. But a book could. These testimonials were not isolated; during the war, Trautman heard the stories of thousands of troops eager to share anecdotes of what these and other titles meant to them.

The publishers couldn't argue with these letters or Trautman's first-hand observations. After all, the military consisted of a group of readers they had not confronted before. Reviewing Trautman's data on troop reading preferences, they came to appreciate that Trautman and DuBois knew this cohort better than the council did. For the duration of the program, the publishers stopped questioning Trautman's judgment when he made suggestions on what titles publishers should nominate for consideration as ASEs. While the first step of the ASE-selection process still required publishers to identify all titles on their backlists and front-lists that would appeal to young men, when Trautman made recommendations on specific titles to include, they listened.

* * *

By the early months of 1944, it was obvious to all that the ASEs were a hit. The publishers had found a way to do their part for the war effort by spreading the gift of reading to millions of fighters. Authors were thrilled that their books had been selected. Servicemen were devouring them. Books were being read in places they had never gone before. According to a report by Elinor Kendall Evans, an Army librarian, ASEs were consumed in "the cockpits of combat planes" as "the pilot and his crew kill time by reading."[50] On a transport making its way to the Caribbean, "out of twenty-one passengers, perched on odd-shaped bundles of freight, sixteen were reading these handy little paper-covered volumes," one member of the crew reported.[51] A month later, when poor weather delayed the invasion of Normandy, leaving thousands of American troops stranded on lurching landing craft with little to keep them company, men turned to the ASEs they had stashed in their pockets. "These little books are a great thing," one soldier said to A. J. Liebling of the *New Yorker*. "They take you away."[52] And one didn't have to be a low-ranking private, an infantryman storming a beach, or a foot soldier hunkering down in a foxhole to appreciate the ASEs. After publishers sent a copy of one of their first ASEs to General George C. Marshall, Army chief of staff, Marshall became, according to the *New York Times*, "a regular reader of these books." In fact, "a complete set of the latest issue [was] always kept in his private plane, and when one issue failed to reach him on time…an aide promptly demanded the reason for the delay."[53]

The main complaint was that there were never enough books. When the first monthly batches of ASEs were printed, 50,000 copies of each of thirty titles were published—this equaled 2.5 million books per month. However, by the time these books were distributed overseas, in December 1943 and January 1944, the Army's ranks had swelled to over seven million troops.[54] Not only was one title for every three men inadequate, but the paperback books quickly deteriorated when subjected to war conditions. Foot soldiers read ASEs in the rain and snow until they turned to mush. Some accompanied readers to hospital beds or makeshift morgues.[55] As one combat officer told Trautman, "from Naples to Rome, the road was paved with bodies and council books."[56] Some were destroyed—by losses in transit or enemy attacks—before delivery to American fighters.[57] Demand for them was insatiable, and each month's supply rapidly vanished.

Trautman pleaded for more funding and urged the council to adopt every economy to maximize print runs from their finite funds. Even before the first ASEs reached troops, in October 1943, Trautman urged publishers to increase output to 60,000 ASEs per month. He explained that the YMCA's War Prisoners Aid would be syphoning 2,000 ASEs per month from the Army's supply to send to prisoner of war (POW) camps for captured American troops in Europe and Asia.[58] And this number was expected to climb. Used books could not be sent to POWs,[59] and some POW camps placed size and weight restrictions on incoming packages; ASEs were ideal because they were new, lightweight, and small.[60] POWs, of course, craved an escape from their surroundings and begged for books. "When you send a package…please put in candy, warm underwear and clothes, [and] books (novels)," one man wrote from a German POW camp.[61] Seconding this sentiment was a POW in Japan, who said his "existence here is rather monotonous" and his only respite was reading. "I have read about 90 books," he said, and begged for more.[62] There was no debating the issue: ASEs were needed for soldiers facing every guise of war.[63]

Despite Trautman's pleas for higher print runs, the council delayed, wanting to ensure that they had the printing infrastructure to increase their production. Perhaps encouraged by the accolades of servicemen who received their first ASEs, in January 1944, the council agreed to increase the number of books from 18,000,000 to 30,000,000 each year. This would be achieved by increasing the print run for each title from 50,000 copies to 77,000 copies, with an increase of an extra 3,000 copies of each title per month thereafter.[64] Additional boosts in print runs occurred. By January 1945, as the war in Europe was in its last phase, 125,000 sets were printed for the Army, and this number increased to 155,000 starting July 1945. Additionally, the number of monthly titles gradually increased from thirty to forty titles.[65] At the height of the ASE project, 6.2 million books were distributed to troops overseas each month—just shy of one book per soldier.

* * *

Even with hundreds of millions of ASEs and miniature magazines, most military personnel wished for one more category of reading materials above all others: comics. Practically every recruit in the armed forces had a habit of reading the funnies. One poll showed that seven out of ten Americans who read newspapers perused the cartoons.[66] While the New York publishers—particularly the higher-end houses—had no interest in reprinting cartoons, soldier requests for them eventually became impossible for the Army Library Service to ignore. As Elsa Maxwell of the *St. Louis Star-Times* noted in her column in January 1943, an officer insisted that what his men wanted most was Superman and Dick Tracy. He said that, on a recent troop transport, there were only four comic books on board and that "they must have gone completely around the [ship] six times."[67] This sentiment was echoed by Basil L. Waters, the executive editor of the *Minneapolis Star-Journal and Tribune.* He relayed how during an overseas tour of an American bomber base, he happened to have been carrying a Sunday newspaper and a crewman who just finished a flight mission begged for the cartoon supplement. "It's little things like this they are missing," Waters said.[68]

Trautman's philosophy was that soldiers should be given whatever material interested them—including cartoons. Yet in the 1940s, there were outspoken critics who believed that comic strips had little value and indeed contributed to societal ills like delinquency and the corruption of young minds.[69] Some military leaders saw comics as undermining the chain of command. *The Stars and Stripes* and *Yank the Army Weekly* published military cartoons, with GI favorites including Dave Breger's *Private Breger*, Milton Caniff's *Male Call*, and Bill Mauldin's *Up Front*.[70] George Patton, for one, loathed them, even writing letters of complaint to *The Stars and Stripes* for printing material that was "subversive of discipline,"[71] and threatening to throw Bill Mauldin in jail for producing cartoons of disheveled soldiers who griped and stewed about the hardships they faced.[72] Trautman had spent enough time touring Army installations to know that, "in a foxhole, one was more apt to welcome a magazine containing the misadventures of the 'Gumps' and 'Snuffy Smith' than a weighty tome concerning the New England Transcendentalists." "I think the comics come near to having a universal appeal," he continued, "just as Walt Disney's motion pictures strike a responsive chord in the hearts of people in every land." It irked him when people "patronizingly" putdown comics. "I know quite a few deep thinkers who follow 'Terry and the Pirates' as faithfully as any young G.I. or sailor."[73]

Trautman believed that comics brought laughs to weary troops who desperately needed them. He decided to find a way to deliver a weekly dose of the Sunday funnies soldiers most wanted—Popeye, Li'l Abner, Blondie, Terry and the Pirates, Dick Tracy, Buz Sawyer, Joe Palooka, and Superman. As no compact periodical containing these popular strips yet existed, Trautman decided to make his own.

In January 1944, after visiting a newspaper stand and buying all the Sunday papers, he crafted a booklet the size of a small magazine. He drew a layout for each strip, clipped all of the panels out of newspapers, and pasted them onto his mock-up.[74] In the space of one winter afternoon,

Trautman had created the template for what became the Special Services Division's most popular periodical, *Overseas Comics*. It would take months to gain permissions and Army approval, but by mid-1944, 700,000 copies were distributed to GIs.[75] They were such a sensation that, in under two months, an order for 16,750,000 issues of *Overseas Comics* was made for the Army, which would consist of reprints of the previous year's strips to help troops get up to date on their favorite pen-and-ink characters.[76] Of all Army publications, none was printed in greater quantities than *Overseas Comics*.[77] The insatiable appetite for cartoons warranted the addition of two more comic books in 1945—*G.I. Comics* and *Jeep Comics*.[78]

* * *

In late 1943, Trautman learned that the Information & Education Section would be separating from the Special Services Division, and, in March 1944, the Special Services Division's branches for athletics, entertainment, music, libraries, and arts and crafts would be relocating to New York City.[79] Given that practically all of the major book and magazine publishers were located in Manhattan, this move would make it much easier for Trautman to build an even stronger connection between the Army and literary worlds.

In March, Ray and Jane returned to the metropolis where they had many fond memories. They purchased a single-family home in the "suburban village" of Bronxville, in Westchester County, just north of New York City and conveniently situated on the Harlem Rail Line, which went directly into Grand Central Station. Their new home had big bedrooms, a large lot with a garden, and a wood-paneled living room that gave it a homey feeling.[80] The move went smoothly except for a small hiccup when the movers discovered that the "personal effects" of a small family included over 1,500 pounds of books. The moving company insisted on charging an "excess" fee for surplus weight.[81] Trautman paid the ransom. He knew a thing or two about the difficulties of shipping books; he was, after all, the man who created, as Elsa Maxwell put it, the "readingist army in the world."[82]

# 8

# Tell Them to Stuff It

A book is no good unless it is read.
—Ray Love Trautman[1]

Beginning in late 1943, Trautman and his squad of Army librarians found themselves under assault in a multi-front battle over censorship and book bans. A handful of critics—from civilians to Army officials and legislators—challenged the availability of certain titles in military libraries, citing morality, politics, and offensiveness. They demanded the removal of hundreds of volumes—ranging from Hemingway to history books. Trautman was obliged to follow military orders on what books he could distribute, yet was also bound by his library training and belief that every book had a place on the shelves. A democracy did not tell its citizens what they could and could not read. Rather, it insisted upon the freedom to choose any book, on any subject.

To Trautman, it was baffling that any restrictions could even be suggested in America. Book burnings and bans were the tools used by fascism—whose ideology the United States was supposedly fighting against. He—along with American politicians, librarians, and the public—remembered the 1933 book burnings across Germany and how tens of thousands of volumes were destroyed because of their ideas. The significance of those bonfires had only become more apparent over the decade that had passed. On May 10, 1943—ten years after the Berlin book burning—flags were flown at half-mast at libraries across the United

States, and President Roosevelt spoke of the power of books in fighting against totalitarianism and oppression:

> We all know that books burn—yet we have the greater knowledge that books cannot be killed by fire. People die but books never die. No man and no force can abolish memory. No man and no force can take from the world the books that embody man's fight against tyranny. In this war we know, books are weapons.[2]

Books were considered so crucial to preserving and spreading freedom that the US Office of War Information designed posters saying as much. One depicts a bonfire licking the base of a skyscraper-sized book, with small figures wearing Nazi armbands throwing books into the flames. The giant book appears unscathed by the fire. On its cover, an excerpt of President Roosevelt's speech is provided.[3] A second poster by the Office of War Information shows an image of the 1933 Berlin book burning and states: "Ten years ago: The Nazis burned these books...but free Americans CAN STILL READ THEM."[4] Distributed for free, these posters were hung in storefront windows and libraries, often accompanied by a display of books banned by the Nazis and recommendations that Americans enjoy these forbidden books.[5] Banned authors included Helen Keller, Ernest Hemingway, John Steinbeck, Langston Hughes, Dorothy Thompson, Edna Ferber, Eric Knight, Carl Sandburg, Jack London, and Kay Boyle.[6]

Yet even as they were commemorating the burnings and the United States' commitment to the freedom to read, Trautman and the Army Library Service began to face serious challenges to printing certain titles as ASEs. Brigadier General Ernest J. Dawley, who was serving in Europe, lodged a complaint against the distribution of the ASE of Ernest Hemingway's *Selected Short Stories*, finding Hemingway's "frank" descriptions of the "nature of sexual relations" to be highly offensive and "unfit to be issued to decent-minded soldiers."[7] Though Dawley did not specify which of the twelve stories caused him to bristle, it was likely "The Short Happy Life of Francis Macomber." Margot Macomber, deeming her husband a coward for fleeing from a wounded lion while on safari, has an affair with the heroic guide. Perhaps the general was offended by the guide's policy of bringing a "double size cot on safari" because "women did not feel they were getting their money's worth unless they shared that cot" with him.[8] The general may also have found "The Snows of Kilimanjaro" offensive for its references to taking lovers, going "whoring" to "kill loneliness," and the narrator's admission of loving a woman other than his wife.[9] Whatever the source, Dawley passed the volume along to Colonel L. Curtis Tiernan, a chaplain at the theater headquarters, who agreed with him.[10] Dawley also wrote to the Army Library Service threatening to "have all copies of the book within his command area destroyed."[11]

Dawley and others did not seem to grasp that others might view the book differently. One hospitalized soldier credited Hemingway's short stories with rescuing him from depression upon learning that he required a partial leg amputation. "I read the story about the nurse, the gambler, and the radio, in which the hero discovered that crying relieved the pain in his broken leg," the soldier recounted in a book he published after the war. Until he read this story, "I never dared cry." However, given the protagonist's example, "I put my head under the blankets and cried a little, softly, and that helped ease things and I [felt] better."[12] One man's indecency could be another's saving grace.

Army librarians knew this wisdom well. As a matter of principle, they worked to ensure that no books would be banned or destroyed. In preparing a response to Dawley, an assistant in the Library Branch began with the "customary reply"—librarians were growing accustomed to this form of attack—that "men old enough to be drafted into their country's service and to die for it were also old enough to be aware of the facts of life." The assistant added, "nothing in Hemingway's book went beyond the accepted literary limits of decency," nor were any sexual innuendos all that different from Shakespeare's comedies and tragedies, which "alluded openly to the facts of sex." Given that a response from a low-ranking librarian would hardly appease a general, the draft letter was funneled up the chain of command to General Oscar Solbert, chief of the Special Services in the European Theater of Operations (ETO).

Not only did General Solbert approve of the assistant's letter, he felt the need to add one final sentence: "Council Books are expendable but not destructible." No copies of Hemingway's *Selected Short Stories* were to be harmed on indecency grounds.[13]

Despite bawdy nose art on airplanes, cartoons featuring women in various attitudes of undress, full-page pinups in *Yank the Army Weekly*, and the ubiquitous wake-up call of "off your cocks and grab your socks,"[14] books somehow bore the brunt of having a "corrupting" influence. No two books came under greater heat for containing prurient stories than Lillian Smith's *Strange Fruit* and Kathleen Winsor's *Forever Amber*. Of the two, however, *Strange Fruit* seemed to attract the greatest number of objections. The book tells the story of forbidden love: a white man and Black woman are attracted to one another and ultimately share a romantic relationship. When pregnancy results, the couple considers marriage, which would make the child's birth more respectable. However, many states in the 1940s criminalized interracial marriage, and so arrangements were made for the pregnant woman to marry someone of the same race.[15] When the woman's brother learns of his sister's pregnancy, he kills his sister's lover. This murder results in the lynching of an innocent man.[16] With a page-turning narrative, *Strange Fruit* illuminated the corrosive effects of racism, earning it both praise and controversy.[17]

Among the book's outspoken critics was Senator Theodore Bilbo of Mississippi, an unabashed white supremacist who denounced *Strange Fruit* from the floor of the Senate: "It is regrettable that . . . perhaps millions of the pure-minded white people of America . . . have already been polluted and corrupted by the reading of this dirty and obscene book, which is an indictment against the South, a gross misrepresentation of the facts, and a puny attempt to integrate the American Negro into the social life of the white people."[18] Though he described the book as "obscene," Bilbo did not list sexual intimacy in his objections.

The book also had its proponents. Soon after its publication in February 1944, the book was banned in Boston on "obscenity" grounds.[19] To test the legality of the ban, a squad of police officers were called to the University Law Book Exchange in Cambridge to witness its owner,

Abraham Isenstadt, sell a copy of *Strange Fruit* to the well-known author, journalist, and critic Bernard DeVoto[20] (DeVoto won the Pulitzer Prize in History in 1948).[21] DeVoto told the *Boston Globe* that he considered *Strange Fruit* "a decent book" that "will be universally praised" and he resented that it had been banned.[22] A summons was issued for Isenstadt, and counsel for the Boston Civil Liberties Union represented him.[23] He was ultimately convicted and fined.[24]

Kathleen Winsor's *Forever Amber* was also banned by some locales, including Boston, for "obscenity."[25] This book provided a titillating journey through the life of a young woman who used her sexual appeal to attract rich suitors and gain social standing. It earned popularity and a reputation for its steaminess.

Ranked among the top ten bestselling books of 1944,[26] both titles were prime contenders to become ASEs. The sexual references proved a selling point for troops. As one soldier wrote to the Council on Books in Wartime, "We're all looking forward to... *Forever Amber*" because "We get curious about all books that are banned in Boston—and who wouldn't?"[27] However, there was concern about these two books making their way into Army libraries. After both were printed as ASEs, the Army Library Branch received a letter from New Hampshire Congressman Sherman Adams, who had himself received a complaint from a constituent that the Army was providing obscene books to troops in the Pacific Theater, namely *Strange Fruit* and *Forever Amber*.[28] Out came the "customary reply." Representative Adams was informed that the Army Library Service "regards soldiers as adults and it is consequently the policy to provide them with popular and readable books that are generally available to adult civilians in the United States." Polls administered to troops established that "there is a great demand for both of these books among overseas soldiers,"[29] with *Forever Amber* and *Strange Fruit* ranking as the most-requested and second-most-requested titles, respectively.[30] It was the Army Library Service's position that "the specific books in question are not obscene and that in light of their popularity it would be an injustice to deprive soldiers of the opportunity to read them."[31] This response apparently satisfied Representative Adams, who did not pursue the complaint further. The Army Library Service thus maintained its policy of providing popular books to troops. Other titles facing bans in the United States on indecency or obscenity grounds—including Joseph Pennell's *The History of Rome Hanks* and Erskine Caldwell's *Tragic Ground*—were also printed as ASEs due to demand.[32]

Validating the importance of sending every kind of book—including those featuring lusty romance—were yet more testimonies that came to Trautman about how these stories served a unique role in helping troops through difficult times. One nurse who worked in a military hospital shared in a letter her experience caring for three men whose hands were so badly burned that they couldn't even hold an ASE (which only weighed a few ounces). The three men begged the nurse for *Forever Amber.* Ordinarily, she would never harm a book, but she had no choice but to tear pages out of the ASE, giving the men a few at a time, as that was all they could bear to hold. As one man finished his pages, he passed them down the line to the next. "The exploits of Amber took their minds off their pain as a more innocent story might not have done," the nurse remarked.[33]

* * *

For every fire the Library Service extinguished, another managed to flare. The National Organization for Decent Literature (NODL), a Roman Catholic pressure group that aimed to restrict access to reading materials that were offensive to its code, took an interest in what Army libraries stocked on their shelves.[34] Its "Code for Clean Reading" warned against literature that glorified crime, was "predominantly sexy," featured "illicit love," contained illustrations considered "indecent or suggestive," or included "disreputable advertising."[35] Because all of these categories are loose and subjective—whether a drawing is "suggestive" or an advertisement is "disreputable" is a matter of opinion and disposition—a dangerously large amount of reading material easily fell within these parameters. During World War II, the NODL targeted ninety-five magazines in general circulation as offending the code, and flagged thirty-one titles that were distributed outside mainstream channels.[36] Local volunteers of the

NODL formed vigilance committees that scoured newsstands, drug stores, and other establishments that sold magazines, comic books, or paperbacks. If what they deemed an offensive publication was discovered, NODL volunteers demanded its removal, threatened boycotts, and promised regular follow-up visits.[37] When it came to books, some of the era's most prominent authors were targeted, including Ernest Hemingway, D. H. Lawrence, Henry Miller, John Steinbeck, and William Faulkner.[38]

The Army Library Service featured books by all of these authors, magazines with excerpts of their work, and was responsible for the mass distribution of periodicals and comic books. In addition, as a surprise holiday "gift" to troops from the Army Library Service and *Esquire* magazine, miniature pinup calendars with twelve illustrations of semi-nude women were distributed in 1944 and 1945.[39] On a daily basis, the Army Library Service ran afoul of the NODL's standards, and records show the NODL was monitoring the Army's literary offerings. Knowing his libraries were under watch, Trautman wasn't going to change a thing. Those eager to ban books over concern that they caused harm ignored how harmful censorship was.

Having spent time with servicemembers across all theaters—in training facilities, combat zones, hospitals, and everywhere in between—Trautman understood that while some men wanted challenging books, most simply wanted an entertaining and escapist read. It was not his job to pass judgment but to give troops what they wanted. They were counting on him. "Pay no attention, absolutely no attention, to whatever organization tries to influence your selection of books," read one soldier's letter to the Library Service. "If the legion of decency approaches you, please leer at them in your most offensive manner and tell them to stuff it." The closing line of this letter read, "Yours in deepest belligerency toward all moral societies."[40]

In the period when the NODL was interested in surveying Army reading, Trautman received a letter addressed to John Steinbeck, an author whose works the NODL wanted to ban. The soldier wrote:

> I have been overseas nearly 23 months, from Casablanca up through Northern Africa to Tunis, Panterleria Island, all of Italy, both the

> Mediterranean and Adriatic coast, as well as inland, over to the island of Corsica, for the invasion of Southern France, up to Dol[e] in France, then back to Rimini in Italy, Ravenna, etc., until [V-E Day].... [N]ow I am back to Naples.... Naturally there wasn't many times for roaring laughter, I mean real, downright old fashioned laughter that's from way down deep. Once back to Naples we felt that our job was done and we would soon sail for home, but we were told a few days ago that there was one more job for us to do—getting gear in condition for the Pacific. Naturally I felt pretty down-hearted for it meant no boat for home. . . .
>
> So tonight found me... pretty restless, chain smoking, trying to read a few old newspapers, and I happened to pick up... [*Cannery Row*] and started to read it. Felt I would no doubt never finish it, but a way to pass a few hours anyway, but in short order I was beginning to grin, chuckle, laugh a little, then really laughing like I haven't laughed in years.... So, sir,... I thank you for finding a laughter that I thought I had lost for good.... I have found that which I thought was a lost art—to really, truefully laugh again. I shall surely read it again and shall tell my buddies, for I am sure they will enjoy it as much as I.[41]

If he took Steinbeck out of circulation, all Trautman would do is deprive some men of laughter. He was not going to add to the hardships of foot soldiers by withdrawing books that made them smile.

In the end, the NODL kept watch over the Army Library Service but never targeted a specific military library or demanded the ban of certain books, comics, or magazines. If it had tried to do so, Trautman could point to the ALA's "Library Bill of Rights," first adopted in June 1939, which called for the "unbiased selection of materials, balanced collections, and open meeting rooms."[42] Amended in 1948, the ALA expanded its Bill of Rights to specifically address groups operating like the NODL, stating that libraries were not spaces to be policed by "volunteer arbiters of morals or public opinion" so as to "establish a coercive concept of Americanism."[43] Americanism required choice, freedom, and providing people access to all viewpoints, perspectives, subject matters, and ideas. Nazi Germany had already demonstrated to the world how democracy withered as books were sorted into subjective categories like "acceptable" and "unacceptable" and taken off of library shelves.

* * *

Having survived charges of promoting indecency and obscenity, Trautman's most formidable foe in curbing what books the Army Library Service could provide turned out to be the United States Congress.

In 1943, Public Affairs Committee, Inc.—a nonprofit educational organization—published a booklet, *The Races of Mankind*, written by two Columbia University anthropologists, Ruth Benedict and Gene Weltfish.[44] The thirty-one-page pamphlet, one of a hundred or so that addressed issues affecting the American public—including health, education, democracy, and the wartime workplace—[45] featured cartoon-like illustrations and data that debunked connections between race and aptitude.[46] To establish this point, *The Races of Mankind* cited statistics from World War I intelligence tests administered by the Army that showed that Black and white troops from the North scored higher than Black and white southerners, and that Black troops from the North scored higher than white troops from the South.[47] Benedict and Weltfish explained, "The differences did not arise because people were from the North or South, or because they were black or white, but because of differences in income, education, and cultural advantages."[48] They also noted that the intelligence test scores were in direct correlation to the amount spent by states on schools, and there was also a connection between higher scores and better housing and diet, and higher income.[49] The pamphlet essentially dismantled the idea of any race being superior. The Information & Education Branch of the US Army ordered fifty-five thousand copies of the booklet for use in orientation courses and to sell to troops.[50] The Army Library Service planned to obtain copies from the Information & Education Branch to include in stationary libraries across the world.[51]

In January 1944, before the Army began distribution, newspapers reported that the president of the USO, Chester I. Barnard, had banned the booklet from USO centers because it was too "controversial."[52] The USO was a popular nonprofit organization that catered to the recreational needs of American GIs—ranging from hosting celebrity shows for troops to providing recreation centers with a variety of amusements—and its public position of banning *The Races of Mankind* attracted attention. The Alfred P. Sloan Foundation, a sponsor of the Public Affairs Committee, publicly chastised the USO. "Of course, if you happen to believe that the earth is flat, you will find every book on geography 'controversial,'" Harold Sloan, the foundation's executive director, said in a statement to the press. "I fear that epithet is used by people who don't like to have facts presented. It is a paradox that the USO should withhold from our service men a statement of the facts on which our democracy is based, and for which they are fighting."[53]

Irving Abramson, the chairman of the Congress of Industrial Organizations (CIO) War Relief Committee, announced in February 1944 that the CIO would mail free copies of the pamphlet to every serviceman on its mailing list. Abramson told the press that the pamphlet "is one of the best weapons in the hands of our soldiers. It certainly is one of the best answers to Hitler's Aryan creed."[54]

The media attention surrounding these warring organizations drew the attention of the House Military Affairs Committee.[55] The committee had ten representatives from the South, and they were determined to quash the Army's circulation of the pamphlet.[56] According to the committee, *The Races of Mankind* came to its attention while investigating the "infiltration" of ideas that were, as it put it, "inimical to the interests of the people and the government." Its first objection was that one of the illustrations depicted Adam and Eve with navels,[57] thus suggesting that they were "born in the normal manner."[58] The second objection was that the pamphlet aimed "to teach racial equality, especially the equality of white men and Negroes."[59] Senator Theodore Bilbo, who had earlier attacked *Strange Fruit* from the floor of the Senate, publicly accused Benedict and Weltfish of being Communist conspirators who performed "some mysterious undercover manipulation" to get the Army to purchase fifty-five thousand copies. It was, Bilbo announced, a plot to "repeal . . . all laws forbidding the intermarriage of the races."[60]

The Information & Education Division pushed back, countering that the booklet was "good ammunition against the ignorant racial prejudices fostered by Nazi propaganda."[61] Representative Andrew J. May of Kentucky threatened that there would be "a fight against the War Department," if it persisted in its plans for distribution.[62] In the end, the

Army's copies of *The Races of Mankind* were placed "in cold storage in the War Department," never to be distributed.[63] The claims made by the House Military Affairs Committee provided fodder for pundits and columnists. A book titled *The Natural History of Nonsense* noted that the committee was "uncertain of... the scope of their duties and in consequence assumed that Navel Affairs came under their jurisdiction; but the chances are that they were just laying down a smoke screen.... and struck a mighty blow for white supremacy—right on the button!"[64]

In the end, Trautman never received the copies of *The Races of Mankind* that he intended to distribute throughout Army libraries. There was little he could do on his own, and the high-ranking officers of the Information & Education Division were not poised to fight Congress over the pamphlet. Defiance by a single librarian would likely result in his removal, not a reversal of the ban. As one newspaper summarized the episode, "Prejudice Wins a Round."[65]

The story of *The Races of Mankind* still spread across the US military thanks to Trautman's magazine distribution. When *Time* magazine ran a piece on the Military Affairs Committee's ban, troops read the story in their "pony edition." Many were outraged that Congress did not trust them to read information and draw their own conclusions.[66] One soldier wrote to *Time*, "As one of the servicemen affected, I was appalled at the shortsighted and presumptuous action... in halting further distribution of the pamphlet *The Races of Mankind*.... I shall do my damndest to obtain a copy."[67] Many back home felt the same way. By 1946, *The Races of Mankind* had gone through eleven reprintings.[68] It served as the basis for the 1945 film *We Are All Brothers*,[69] and it inspired countless exhibits in schools, libraries, and YMCAs.[70]

* * *

The backlash did not deter Congress from continuing to meddle in what reading materials were being distributed to soldiers. As the 1944 presidential election neared, Congress faced public pressure to ensure that troops stationed around the world would have the opportunity to cast votes and have them counted.[71] With the exception of New York, all states lacked absentee voting laws that were conducive to wartime voting.[72] On average, most state legislation included a one-month deadline for a person to request an absentee ballot and return it completed. For troops overseas, this timeline was impossible. On average, a letter from the United States took approximately twenty-two days to arrive in North Africa, thirty-seven days to reach Europe, forty-three days to travel to the Pacific, and fifty-two days to enter the China-Burma-India Theater.[73] Given that a serviceperson would have to make a written request for an absentee ballot, wait for that ballot to be mailed to their military address, and then return the completed ballot to the secretary of state in their state of official residence, these time frames would need to be tripled to reflect the amount of time a soldier actually needed to vote. Rather than gamble on having each state pass individual legislation to extend the time period for absentee voting, Congress considered creating a streamlined federal ballot that states could opt to use. It could be printed well in advance of the 1944 election and improve the chances that completed ballots would return in time to be counted.

While all politicians generally agreed with the notion that soldiers should be able to vote in a presidential election, they disagreed about the details. Republicans and Democrats fought over the format of the federal ballot and whether certain features might favor one party over the other.[74] Ohio's Republican Senator Robert Taft grew preoccupied with the idea that President Roosevelt's Democratic government might inundate American troops abroad with campaign tracts.[75] Taft drafted a provision to add to the federal voting legislation that would prevent the Democratic-led government from distributing political reading materials to influence the soldier vote.[76] Around the same time as Taft slipped this censorship provision into the bill, he stoked racial prejudices by pointing to the possible expansion of voting rights for Black troops. Just as the suggestion of racial equality had doomed *The Races of Mankind*, this monopolized the attention of many legislators.

First, Taft questioned whether a federal absentee voting law could steamroll states' rights by abolishing the poll tax.[77] Second, he opposed the circumvention of in-person voter registration for servicemembers who turned twenty-one while in uniform.[78] Both the poll tax and in-person voter registration requirements were tools used in several states—mainly in the South—to disenfranchise Black voters through rigorous enforcement (white voters faced relaxed standards) and intimidation tactics.[79] As Taft likely anticipated, despite arguments that it would be fitting to eliminate race-based voting practices at a time when the United States was fighting against the idea of an Aryan race, southern politicians were unmoved. Many agreed with Louisiana Senator John Overton, who argued that the poll tax and in-person voter registration had to remain intact "to maintain white supremacy" in "the Solid South."[80]

While Taft's colleagues were distracted by impassioned debates over states' rights, ballot formats, and whether Congress was overreaching its constitutional authority, Taft's provision censoring soldier reading material received scant congressional attention or debate. When the Soldier Voting Act was passed (without abolishing the poll tax or in-person voter registration requirements for troops),[81] it contained Taft's Title V provision to prevent "pernicious political activities." "It shall be unlawful for any officer of... the Army" to distribute material "containing political argument or political propaganda of any kind designed or calculated to affect the result of any election."[82] Books, magazines, and newspapers were all specifically targeted.[83] Anyone who violated Title V could be fined and imprisoned.[84] Overnight, Trautman's procurement of ASEs and miniature magazines for the Army made him feel like the kingpin of what could be an international criminal enterprise.

How, he wondered, could one run a library program and stay out of prison? As Trautman and his colleagues brainstormed, the War Department devised a policy to deal with Title V. It was not just the ASEs and magazines that drew concern—the War Department had a robust educational program, and even textbooks were vulnerable to violating the new law. "Leave it out when in doubt" became the military's mantra for its bookshelves.[85] The Army Library Service thus had to review every book before purchase to ensure it did not contain political ideas. Trautman had no choice but to follow the War Department's orders, which meant resolving any ambiguity regarding the political nature of a book in favor of prohibition.[86] Civilian librarians were hired to carefully read every page of books the Army Library Service wished to purchase, flagging even a passing reference to a political issue.[87] Within weeks, nearly one hundred titles were determined to run afoul of the law, ranging from westerns to history books; librarians across the Army Library Service were told not to purchase them.[88] Trautman grew disheartened. A library was supposed to be a clearinghouse for all ideas and viewpoints; now it was being stifled by imaginary dangers. According to Army librarian John Jamieson, adding to Trautman's sense of despondency was the fact that "nobody outside the army grasped what was going on," as the "full extent of the book banning had not been brought to public notice."[89] Congress did not make the public aware of Title V; it advertised the creation of an absentee ballot for troops.

The ASEs, of course, were made in cooperation with civilian publishers, and when Trautman informed them that previously approved ASE titles had to be revoked because of Title V, they exploded. As Jamieson explained, publishers "felt that their function was to select books *for* soldiers, not to keep books *from* them." If they were to comply with Title V, publishers would find themselves "obliged not only to ban books, but to ban books precisely, it seemed, because they did deal with the underlying issues of the war." Publishers believed the American public should be informed that Congress was foisting a ban on books for soldiers. Trautman did what he could to help by pointing out the absurdities and inconsistencies of the law whenever he could.[90]

There was no shortage of absurdities for Trautman to share. When a congressperson suggested that the *Congressional Record* be included in army libraries, Trautman replied that the publication contained "political argument" that might influence votes, and it would be criminal of him to do so. When Trautman was asked why the *AAF: The Official Guide to the Army Air Forces* was banned, he replied that it contained a full-page image of President Roosevelt in the front matter and was "just the sort of thing Senator Taft had protested against."[91] Trautman's cautious approach was justified. In the summer of 1944, Colonel Egbert

White, a recipient of the Legion of Merit and supervisor of the Mediterranean Theater's *The Stars and Stripes* newspaper, was removed from command and ordered home for trying to include a two-thousand-word daily digest of Associated Press news.[92] Meanwhile, all editions of *The Stars and Stripes* were ordered to discontinue reprinting content from such magazines as *Collier's*, *The Saturday Evening Post*, and *Reader's Digest* because of Title V.[93] The Army could not afford to take the law lightly.

Trautman was already on the congressional radar. In 1943, a number of officers in the Special Services Division, including Trautman, were brought before Congress to justify the funding they had requested as part of the 1944 National Defense Appropriation Bill.[94] Presided over by Senator Gerald Nye, a Republican from North Dakota, and assisted by Senator Rufus C. Holman, a Republican from Oregon, Trautman was asked to defend the $6.5 million being requested for the Army Library Service for the upcoming year. This was no easy task. Rather than listen to Trautman, Senator Holman seemed to advance his own ideas. As Senator Holman admitted at the start of the hearing, the point of the interrogation was political. "Frankly, and I might just as well be frank about it, some of this stuff I am convinced is political propaganda for the fourth-term election of Roosevelt, under the guise of keeping up the morale of the soldiers."[95] Trautman responded by explaining that the Army Library Service aimed to give troops the books they requested. "They are entitled, we think, to read what they want to read, in the same manner as the civilians or people back home," he said. Holman asked about the composition of the selection committees for the Council on Books in Wartime and the Army and Navy. Trautman began to describe how the council's representatives selected titles for consideration based on their judgment as to what books would be suitable for an Army of young men. Holman immediately interrupted, "Representative in their judgment? They may not be representative in my judgment. They are representative in somebody's judgment. Whose judgment?" Trautman then explained how the council consisted of more than one hundred publishers and representatives in the book industry, and it was this diverse body whose "judgment" was relied on in making the first-round lists of titles that might be appealing to millions of young men starved for reading material.[96] Holman temporarily stood down.

But not for long. He asked Trautman about publishers' royalties, whether they were pressuring the military to make new titles into ASEs so that they might become bestsellers, and whether the Army independently evaluated all books. There was questioning about whether the Army "circulated any books by a Mr. Roosevelt, either No. 1 or No. 2, First or Second"—the answer was no. Then, another senator read from page 207 of Henry C. Cassady's *Moscow Date Line*—an ASE selection—which mentioned that presidential candidate Wendell Willkie had attended a cocktail party.[97] Immediately, Senator Holman jumped in: "Do you see the danger of transmitting the political expressions of avowed candidates for the Presidency? I think it is all wrong," he declared.[98] Finally, other senators on the committee had enough of Holman. "The boys don't have to read that," Senator Elbert Thomas, a Democrat representing Utah, snapped. "They're all of age, and they certainly know what kind of material they want to read. If they want to read the Bible—and no doubt many of them do—nobody would criticize them for calling for the Bible and carrying it around with them." Holman had to have the last word: "There is a difference between a request coming to the library and shoving the stuff out."[99]

Perhaps to temper Holman's innuendos, Senator Nye offered a few kind words to Trautman: "I want to compliment you on doing a grand job. I was about to remark that if there was any pressure on you from outside to depart from the path that you have reported here to be your purpose, you have succeeded very well in resisting that outside influence."[100]

Trautman left Washington knowing he was walking a tightrope. Any misstep in approving titles, and there were senators all too eager to make an example of it. This made Trautman's handling of Title V even more challenging. As a librarian, he felt he could not purge bookshelves of every title that contained a political idea. As a law-abiding Army officer, he was required to.

* * *

For the ASEs, things quickly escalated from bad to worse. As books were reviewed for political argument or propaganda, the council determined that fifteen titles that were on the verge of approval as ASEs had to be rejected because of Title V. These titles were:

*Watching the World*, by Raymond Clapper
*Lend Lease*, by Undersecretary of State Edward Stettinius
*Time for Decision*, by Sumner Welles
*America Unlimited*, by Eric Johnston
*Tell the Folks Back Home*, by Senator James M. Mead
*My Ten Years in Japan*, by Joseph C. Grew (former ambassador)
*Yankee from Olympus*, by Catherine Drinker Bowen
*One Man's Meat*, by E. B. White
*Basic History of the United States*, by Charles and Mary Beard
*The Republic*, by Charles Beard
*Chiang Kai-Shek*, by H. H. Chang
*State of the Nation*, by John Dos Passos
*Rich Land, Poor Land*, by Stuart Chase
*Under Cover*, by John Carlson
*Slogum House*, by Mari Sandoz[101]

The council, Army, and Navy would now need to scramble to swap these titles out for others that did not offend Title V. As the *Saturday Review of Literature*'s Norman Cousins commented, ASE nominees were bouncing back "like a batch of bad checks."[102]

Publishers had had enough. In June 1944, they issued a press release to every major media outlet, and sent copies to President Roosevelt, the Senate, and the House of Representatives. "Recognizing the special importance of a free literature in wartime, the Council on Books in Wartime believes it to be its duty to take note of an increasing tendency on the part of some branches of the government to encroach on that freedom," the press release read. "We believe that censorship of matters other than those affecting security in wartime cannot be left to the arbitrary will of individuals, even if legally authorized, without grave jeopardy to democratic freedom." The press release explained how a host of bestselling titles could no longer be distributed to troops because Congress had banned them.[103]

As the publishers predicted, people of all political persuasions expressed their disapproval of limiting what a soldier could read. Editorial pages in newspapers across the country were filled with letters disapproving of the ban. The *Miami News* opined that Washington seemed "afraid that the American soldier might read something significant, something important, something that would make him think and perhaps raise a question or two about the war and the world and the great nation he was defending with the only life and body and mind he has."[104] An opinion piece by William L. Shirer, the journalist and historian whose works on the Third Reich would become classics, was printed in the *Washington Post*. "Cannot this great democratic Nation of ours treat its fighting citizens as adults? Wouldn't it be wise—especially if they are to vote intelligently this year—to let them hear about our controversial issues at home, to let them read the outstanding books of the year and actually encourage them to argue and debate the state of the world and the way they would like to have things after the guns have died down for good?"[105]

An editorial in the Kentucky *Courier-Journal* argued that while no one believed campaign tracts should be sent to troops, "the severity of Title V denies our soldiers and sailors one of the great democratic privileges for which we are fighting—the right of free access to information, the right to select and judge for oneself what to read and what to believe and what to think."[106] Dorothy Thompson, in an article published in the *Cleveland Plain Dealer*, said that under Title V, "the servicemen's libraries and reading rooms are now going through a regular Goebbels' purge." She suggested that since Senator Taft could not bar books that might "influence soldiers to become New Dealers, he has cut the Gordian knot by barring books that might influence them to become anything."[107] An editorial in the *Detroit Free Press* described Title V as a "dangerous" law that could justify banning "everything from the Bible to comic books."[108] And a concerned reader of California's *Fresno Bee* believed that Title V violated "the freedom of thought and expression" guaranteed by the Constitution, and stated Americans at home needed to fight for the right of troops "to read and... think for themselves."[109]

As news spread overseas, a number of servicemen railed against the hypocrisy of fighting for freedom while theirs was being taken away. One soldier on the island of Tulagi in the Solomons—a site of fierce fighting against the Japanese in August 1942—accused legislators of wanting to "keep the GI mind pure and vacant."[110] Another wrote, "It will be recalled that Mr. Hitler got his start by banning and burning books with which he, in his wisdom, did not agree."[111] Troops stationed in Europe had a firsthand glimpse of what a society subjected to book bans looked like, and it was not the type of society they were fighting for.

Some Republican senators even launched an attack against the continued distribution of the letter Trautman had ghostwritten for President Roosevelt, and had been distributed to all troops leaving the United States for overseas service since February 1942. They believed that troops might form a positive opinion of Roosevelt by receiving his personal well wishes, affecting how they might vote.[112] Citing the tradition of presidents providing troops with a motivational send-off, and recalling how President Woodrow Wilson had written a similar letter to troops in 1917, President Roosevelt remarked that many things can be seen to have a "political intent between now and the election." However, the letter had been created before he had given any thought to the 1944 presidential race.[113] The GOP decided to drop this issue.

In the end, the publishers' public opinion campaign achieved results. In August 1944, the law was amended and loosened so that the Army could distribute whatever books soldiers had clearly indicated that they wanted to read. The bookmen and Army officials who were privy to the behind-the-scenes work by Trautman knew the ban would have remained in effect had it not been for his efforts. As Richard Simon, of Simon & Schuster, said in a letter to Trautman, "you have a miraculous way of cutting through red tape. I want to applaud you on your stand about the Army censorship rules. You have handled this in a most statesmanlike manner [to ensure] the servicemen [are] getting all the books which we all know they should read."[114]

Trautman received a glowing commendation from Brigadier General Robert Cutler for battling Congress's censorship so capably. Cutler, who was the War Department's coordinator for soldier voting, watched as Trautman endeavored to follow and fight the law simultaneously. It was an unenviable task, and yet Trautman had managed it, and well. The commendation praised "the greatest assistance" Trautman provided in following the Army's Title V policies while overseeing the continued "distribution to soldiers of books, magazines, and newspapers." Cutler valued Trautman's "technical knowledge, his good sense, and his steady temperament during the very difficult period of public controversy concerning the Army's course of action." The commendation stated: "I placed great reliance in Lt. Col. Trautman's judgment and capacity, and was never disappointed in his performance."[115]

Years later, after Cutler retired, he reminisced with Trautman about their Army days. "We sure had fun over" Title V, Cutler remarked. "I guess it was because we believed in our course and knew it was right."[116]

# 9

# Temporary Widow

Midway in the journey of our life
I came to myself in a dark wood,
for the straight way was lost.
—Dante Alighieri, *Inferno*[1]

In October 1944, Trautman received travel orders to go overseas. This was hardly unique; he had traveled extensively throughout the war. But these orders were the first labeled "secret." Trautman was given a few days to secure winter clothing from the quartermaster, get a typhus inoculation, pack a limited number of personal items, and prepare to be away from home for at least ninety days. All Trautman knew was that his first destination was Paris.[2]

Only months earlier, Paris was liberated from over four years of Nazi occupation. France's swift capitulation to Germany in 1940 had preserved the city's buildings, gardens, and monuments from destruction, but the spiritual cost had been devastating. With their city "infested by Nazi soldiers and Nazi spies," as an op-ed in the *New York Times* put it, Parisians had had to tolerate the tricolor's replacement by swastika flags, onerous restrictions placed on practically everything, and curtailments on the city's cultural offerings.[3] Paris's celebrated libraries and bookstores lost their independence. Initially, almost all libraries were closed.[4] The Nazis pilfered anything deemed of especial value and sent it to Berlin. In September 1940, the Nazis distributed the *Liste Otto*—named for Otto Abetz, the German ambassador to France during the

Occupation—which identified approximately 1,400 titles that were subject to immediate removal from libraries and bookstores.[5] Libraries typically reopened after being "reorganized" by the Nazis, meaning books containing a hefty dose of Nazi indoctrination were on prominent display while prohibited titles were removed from circulation.[6] The Nazis warned that non-complying libraries and bookstores would be permanently closed or confiscated.[7]

Despite its liberation, little news trickled out of Paris on what post-Occupation life was like. Trautman had no idea what to expect. With few days to prepare, he was too busy to investigate. He and Jane agreed that it made sense for her and ten-month-old Eric to visit her parents in Cincinnati for at least the first six weeks of Trautman's absence.[8] In mid-October, they parted, not knowing when they would see each other next, and yet aware Trautman's top-secret mission could take him into an active war zone. In an attempt to lighten the mood, Trautman referred to his absence as Jane's "temporary widowhood."[9]

When Trautman's plane arrived in Paris, he was surprised to learn that General Dwight Eisenhower had sent a car and chauffeur to bring him to ETO headquarters. Waiting at the airport was a Bentley.[10] Trautman was not accustomed to such red-carpet treatment. He was aware that Eisenhower had strong views about maintaining soldier morale. As he wrote in his memoir after the war, Ike believed that "morale, given rough equality to other things, is supreme on the battlefield."[11] Eisenhower subscribed to everything the Special Services Division offered (and personally turned to golf and western novels to relieve stress and clear his mind).[12] For Trautman—after his ordeal with MacArthur—reporting to a general who wanted books was a boon.

Eisenhower wanted Trautman to help with the reorganization of the Special Services Division in the ETO. Specifically, he wanted the Library Branch to be put on an equal footing with the other recreational offerings, which included athletics, movies, theater, and information and education.[13] This would enable Trautman and his team to dedicate their attention to maximizing the production and distribution of reading materials. When Trautman shared this update in a November letter to his New York staff, he predicted "things will begin to *hum* soon."[14] For the first several weeks of Trautman's time in Europe, he split his time between London and Paris to meet with various Special Services Division personnel and expand the Library Branch in the ETO.

As he toured areas surrounding London and Paris, Trautman detailed his observations for his New York office. For starters, troops in transit did not seem to have any ASEs at their disposal. "There ought to be a table full of [ASEs] at Aerial Ports, also at stopover points, but I never saw a Council Book...except the few I took along," Trautman said. When he encountered troops in rear areas who had ASEs, Trautman was astonished to learn that they had "been circulated more than 20 times." Trautman spoke with support troops who recently received packages of ASEs that included Betty Smith's *A Tree Grows in Brooklyn*. The book was such a sensation that servicemen made waiting lists to read it; when Trautman saw the lists, he could hardly believe that four copies had already been read "a total of 67 times, 18, 16, 19, 14 respectively." Soldiers eagerly gave Trautman recommendations for future ASEs. "Thorne Smith is <u>very</u> hot," Trautman told his New York office, referring to the author of several humorous fantasy fiction novels. There were many requests for westerns by Zane Grey, new releases, and bestsellers. In addition, troops devoured their copies of *Overseas Comics*.[15]

But access to books and reading materials was inconsistent. While sending much higher quantities of books and magazines would obviously help, the upcoming winter holidays promised to slow mail delivery, as millions of care packages and holiday presents would be on their way to troops. Under the circumstances, "it is doubtful whether ASE books and unit sets of magazines can be received in satisfactory quantities," Trautman wrote.[16]

There were also challenges on the home front. The Council on Books in Wartime was having a hard time finding new titles to print as ASEs; the publishers felt they had exhausted the latest bestsellers, popular classics, and the most coveted titles in all genres that would appeal to young men. At a time when more books were needed, the council wanted to reduce the number of monthly titles from thirty-two to twenty-six.

"The [council] is scraping the bottom of the barrel to secure new titles," the Library Branch was informed.[17] Knowing Trautman needed even more books, his battalion of librarians in New York came up with a possible solution to share with their boss thanks to a letter from a private in Europe.

The letter is memorable. "Kindly excuse [the] stationery for my writing pad is soaking wet, and I had to substitute this paper bag, picked up during my travels through France," the private's letter began. Over the past few weeks, his home, as he put it, was a "wet and muddy slit-trench," and his companions were "rain, bugs, flies, mosquitoes," along with a unit of German soldiers who liked to bombard his position. Each time he emerged from his "bachelor apartment" to stretch his legs, he knew it was only a matter of time before the Germans would try to kill him. When the "music" began, this private said that he retired to his "fortress," and after praying fervently, started to read. The ASEs distracted him from the very real possibility that he would be "eliminated, or in plain army slang, knocked-off." He included these details to show he knew all about the "horrors of war" that most books "completely by-passed." Yet he thought that he could write truthfully about his Army experiences. "I believe I can dish out a complete story on the feelings, the intimate everyday feelings, of our men abroad which are usually tucked away in memories and only for the consumption of a few, later on in years, over a bar-rail or at conventions." This private wanted to write his story and submit it to publishers so it could become a book, but first he needed advice about how to proceed.[18]

This letter, along with those from other aspiring authors, inspired Trautman's team to float the idea of hosting a writing contest—soldiers could submit novels or short stories they had written and the best ones would be printed as ASEs.[19] The Special Services Division had just sponsored an Army-wide art contest, asking troops to submit illustrations, paintings, and drawings of their military experiences with the finest pieces eligible for prizes and display at the National Gallery of Art in Washington, DC.[20] If the Army could approve an art contest, why not a writing competition?

"The idea of a clearinghouse for getting G.I. writing is excellent," Trautman replied. Publishing ASEs of "cartoons, short stories, articles, novels"—by and for soldiers—could fix the publishers' dearth of new material while encouraging troops to practice their freedom of expression.[21] They would need War Department approval, he warned them, which would require reams of paperwork and time. Meanwhile, an immediate solution to the publishers' plight in running out of new ASE titles was not to reduce the number of books printed, but to reprint some of the most popular ASEs from the early months of the program, such as *A Tree Grows in Brooklyn* and H. Allen Smith's *Low Man on a Totem Pole*.[22]

As he gathered information on the state of soldier reading in Europe, Trautman grew increasingly alarmed at how much work needed to be done. He attended a large gathering of Special Services and Information Officers from across Europe, at which it was "emphatically voted that there should be many more books. At least a book per man per month under combat and field conditions." While the ASEs in rear areas and hospitals typically withstood over a dozen readings, those carried by troops into combat zones could only survive a maximum of three readings, Trautman learned. As he relayed to his office staff, "The book casualty rate is pretty high."[23] A dramatic rise in book production and distribution was absolutely necessary. For the rear areas, where books were not being carried in pockets, Trautman wanted to build fifty new libraries, each with 5,000 volumes.[24] Shipments of hardcovers could be sent to stock the shelves for these stationary troops, and the ASEs could exclusively go to foot soldiers most in need of portable entertainment. Trautman asked his office to prepare a list of qualified librarians to run these libraries; they would need to be self-starters and unafraid of challenges.[25] Trautman duly received a three-page list of librarians. Not one was a woman.[26] It was clear that volunteers in the Women's Army Corps (WACs) with library credentials had not been given any consideration, as 90 percent of all librarians in the United States, and most of the Army's librarians serving across the United States, were women.[27] This irked Trautman. He knew that many in the military harbored chauvinistic views on the abilities of women to serve, and although over 100,000 women became WACs, it was the Army's position that their delicate constitutions prevented them from serving in combat, and that they should generally be kept from zones of danger.[28] As one military historian wrote, "The Army had its share of a conservative element that had scarcely recovered from the shock of the mechanized horse when confronted with the militarized woman."[29]

Having supervised the Army Library Service for several years, Trautman had witnessed the work of female librarians in Army libraries at home; he needed their experience and know-how in Europe. Trautman replied to his office that he wanted a list of qualified women.[30] If there were any problems in bringing female librarians to Europe, Trautman knew that Eisenhower would readily throw his support behind the move. Eisenhower had recently announced that he wanted WACs for various jobs in the ETO and if none arrived, he was going to hire local women in England to fill the positions. The reason why he wanted WACs? "They are good soldiers," Eisenhower said.[31] It was rare for a commander to openly express such favorable opinions about women serving in or near combat zones. In the Pacific, Trautman not only faced MacArthur's disapproval of running libraries but also knew that Chester Nimitz, who commanded millions of troops across the Pacific, openly "disliked seeing women in uniform," as one of his biographers put it, and opposed women serving "anywhere near the war zone."[32] Trautman knew the WACs were not only capable soldiers but outstanding librarians. For Europe's Army libraries to be managed by them would prove their abilities to the world, and especially to those in the Pacific. The next letter from New York included the names of female troops with library experience. "Thanks for the dope on WACs," Trautman responded. He had performed his own search in the meantime and had identified many others.[33]

* * *

Nearly every letter Trautman sent to his New York office was strictly business, though he would occasionally add observations about the conditions in Paris and how palpable the deprivations from years of Nazi occupation still were. As he confided in a November 1944 note:

> There is no heat in any homes, hotels, or office buildings. Temperatures hover at slightly above freezing and will be much colder. There is warm (tepid) water one day a week in most places troops or officers are quartered. It rains almost every day. There are no street lights although electricity is available most of the time. Walking up and down 7 flights of stairs is not unusual. One doesn't ride an elevator (even where they are in operation) for less than 4 or 5 floors. I am sitting in a fancy office with WOOLS—heavy uniform, sweater and overcoat on. This is not, is not, a complaint. It is heaven here to what our men have in combat.[34]

The late fall gloom and wet chill seemed to exacerbate homesickness; Trautman began to feel the weight of missing the holidays and Eric's first birthday. On Thanksgiving Day, Trautman tried to keep thoughts of home at bay by busying himself with Army work and a little book shopping in the afternoon. However, when he spied a window display showcasing an illustrated alphabet book featuring the elephant Babar, Trautman ached to see his son. He purchased the book, returned to his frigid office, and wrote a note to Eric inside *ABC de Babar*: "Thanksgiving, 1944, in Paris. Eric—Here is a little picture book for you to play with and tear. All little boys need things to tear and break. I will hurry home so we can go hiking before you grow too big for those things. Your daddy, Ray."[35]

In the days and weeks following Thanksgiving, Trautman's homesickness seemed to subside. Some of his letters revealed his enchantment with Paris. Walking the cobblestoned streets of the Left Bank, admiring the historic buildings, and seeing the statues and monuments that reflected pride for a glorious past, moved him. In the pocket-sized diary he carried everywhere, he began to jot down ideas for possible ASEs by French authors—Victor Hugo's *The Hunchback of Notre Dame*, or Molière's *The Misanthrope*; and any of the novels by Alexandre Dumas, Gustave Flaubert, and Guy de Maupassant—among others.[36] "Paris is a wonderful city and some day you all should see it," he wrote in a letter to his office. He ended it by circling back to work, "Hope you can keep all papers shoveled off my desk."[37]

* * *

In early December, Trautman felt like he had accomplished the bulk of the work Eisenhower had assigned him. There were plans for Army libraries to dot the landscape of liberated Europe, librarians were being scouted to run them, and book acquisitions were in the works. An Army *Guide for the Operation of Small Army Libraries* was being prepared to crystallize Trautman's plan for library service across the ETO.[38] As Trautman told his office, "My job is 2/3+ complete."[39]

Eisenhower had other ideas. On December 13, 1944, Trautman was surprised to receive restricted movement orders stating he was to proceed to Namur, Belgium, where he would join the US First Army until he had "carri[ed] out the instructions of the Theater Commander."[40] Eisenhower had tasked Trautman with observing the field conditions and book needs of American troops in France, Germany, Holland, Belgium, and Luxembourg. The Allies had liberated the areas Trautman was to tour, and Trautman was assured that the region was a quiet one.[41] In fact, throughout this sector, the battle-tested veterans whose divisions had fought across Europe were being relieved by replacements, recent recruits who were being given a soft introduction to warfare. Many high-ranking officers believed the battle for Europe would soon end. Eisenhower had an outstanding bet with Field Marshal Bernard Montgomery that the war in Europe would be over by Christmas.[42]

Trautman prepared for his journey. He would have at his disposal a chauffeur and command car, and so he packed a few ASE bundles, his typewriter, and a rucksack with clothing. Feeling slightly nervous, he was relieved when four unexpected boxes arrived for him. They were filled with Christmas presents, personal notes, and small tokens from his New York staff. Trautman was so touched by the gesture that he spent the evening before his trip preparing a box for New York. "Am enclosing little notes to those of you who helped give me the biggest bang (outside of a V-2) I've gotten in this war. Your letters were wonderful and while I must become tough and a crusty old man after I return, right now I can say you are a swell gang and I like every one of you a lot." Because of the secrecy enshrouding Eisenhower's travel orders, Trautman could not mention to his team where he was headed.[43] Not knowing how hectic the days ahead would be, Trautman also sent a card to Jane. "*Joyeux et Gai Noel Bonne Heureuse Annee*," the embossed message read; on the inside, Trautman added "To the girl of my dreams with the fond hope that I can tell her Merry Xmas in person."[44]

The next morning, Trautman purchased a map of France, replaced his worn-out shoes at the Paris Quartermaster Sales Store, and began his trip to connect with the First Army.[45] He, along with the entire US military, was unaware that Germany was poised to launch a massive surprise attack across a thinly guarded eighty-five-mile stretch across the Ardennes—precisely where Trautman was headed. For Germany's offensive to be a success, stealth was essential. The Wehrmacht had spent weeks transporting men and equipment under the cover of darkness; trains moved tens of thousands of troops and tons of matériel into the Ardennes overnight, returning to the Rhine before daylight.[46] Roads were blanketed in thick beds of straw so that when German machinery and cavalry approached American positions at night, the clatter of horses' hooves or clanking treads were largely inaudible.[47] By December 15, 250,000 German soldiers and thousands of artillery and tanks stood ready to attack Allied positions.[48] The Americans were outnumbered by at least three to one.[49] Although some US outposts reported "unusual noise" in the days leading up to December 16,[50] and recently captured German POWs had insisted that an "all-out attack" would occur within days, these murmurings were ignored as nothing more than paranoia or isolated rumors.[51]

At 5:30 a.m. on December 16, the Ardennes erupted in deafening sound, as the Germans' mortar shells, rockets, and 88s pummeled Allied positions.[52] It was chaos on the ground. As George W. Neill, a rifleman in the 99th Infantry Division, recalled, he and the rest of his platoon burrowed into their foxholes as the earth trembled under "the apocalyptic bombardment of screaming, whistling, whining and crashing."[53] "I attempted to crawl into my helmet," recalled John Schaffner, another soldier in the 99th Infantry Division, and when that failed, he tried "to get down as far as possible but I found my buttons to be in the way."[54] Many simply hugged the ground and prayed.

When this hellfire abruptly stopped, the silence was broken by muffled noises approaching the Americans' foxholes. Squinting through the fog, troops saw advancing German soldiers and heard the crescendo of approaching tanks.[55] The Germans began to open fire at the Americans and the tanks behind them came up to finish the job. Some men, paralyzed by fear, could not move. Their foxholes became their graves.[56] Others took turns shooting at anything moving ahead of them and then frantically retreating.[57] Those who reached the safety of the dense woods became separated from their units. As one man in the 106th Infantry Division futilely looked for others in his company, he concluded they were "scattered from hell to breakfast."[58] Rag-tag groups of soldiers from different divisions, platoons, companies, and units banded together. Some were badly wounded, but they did not dare to cry out for fear of being found. These men knew they were being hunted by the Germans.[59] As one soldier said, "Four-letter expletive[s]...seemed to best describe our situation."[60]

Because the Germans had knocked out telephone wires and jammed radio communications, Allied command posts struggled to communicate and confusion reigned. Many commanders initially believed the Germans were engaged in mere skirmishes in discrete sectors; it took over ten hours for the American leadership to learn that a massive attack had been underway since morning.[61]

All the while, Trautman was motoring toward his rendezvous with the US First Army. Making periodic stops to inspect Army depots, hospitals, and replacement centers, Trautman chatted with troops about their impressions of the Army's Library Service and whether the selections of books and magazines met with their approval. Trautman learned that the quality of titles was good, but the quantity wasn't. The Army Library Service needed to double, even triple, its production of reading materials—and even then, troops probably would not have enough. Trautman was also told how desperate soldiers were for writing paper. Although stationery fell outside the literary supplies he furnished, Trautman still wrote to his office, "V-mail forms should be included in [the] magazine kit if possible," or, "better yet, enclose them in all C and K rations," since "a guy eating these is usually beyond normal distribution channels."[62] Anything that boosted morale was worth doing.

He began to hear gossip that Germany had launched an offensive in the Ardennes. No official reports confirmed these rumors and Trautman had been assured by Eisenhower that he would be traveling through neutralized regions. As he clambered into his car to continue toward Namur, he was unaware that the 2nd Panzer Division was on its way to the same place.[63]

Hints of trouble began to appear in the form of missing road signs at intersections.[64] Trautman's driver was no longer sure where they were. Trautman also noticed that the telephone wires running along the road appeared to be torn and disconnected; under ordinary conditions, miles of these multicolored ribbons were deployed so that localized units could connect to higher headquarters by telephone. Severed wires signaled sabotage.[65] As dusk descended, Trautman peered into the woods and thought he saw silhouettes of human figures. Before he could alert his driver, a small group of soldiers emerged and blocked his car. The men wore frayed uniforms and weary expressions.[66] They were shivering, wet, and filthy. One had a bloody stump where his hand used to be.[67] All wore American insignia. Stories spilled out about huge forces of Germans overtaking US positions, firing as they ran, and tanks following from behind. These men had fled for the woods, where they had been hiding with no resources or commanding officer. As the highest-ranking officer, Trautman took command.

Trautman maintained a lifelong reluctance to discuss his experiences over the next several days, but one snowy night several decades later, he revealed them to his son, Eric.[68] As Eric recalled, his father described how he quickly took charge, remembering information he had learned while auditing medical courses at the University of Kentucky. Trautman examined wounds and ordered the able-bodied to help with supplies and treatment. Bandages and tourniquets were made from fabric scraps and belts. Trautman spotted a beehive and asked one of the soldiers to retrieve it. Honey could act as an antibacterial barrier and prevent infection. The hive was scraped and honey gently slathered on the mangled arm of the most injured soldier.[69] Meanwhile, Trautman ordered those who were physically able to build a sled from fallen trees and branches that could be pulled by his command car. Once completed, everyone piled into or onto Trautman's car and they made their way into an unnamed village, where they stopped for the night. The car was hidden in a back alleyway, and the group moved into the upper floors of an abandoned building and bedded down.[70]

When Trautman peered out the window the next morning, only the lightest etchings of the landscape were visible through the curtains of fog. Lacking food and any information on where they were, Trautman sent out a small reconnaissance team. They did not get far. German tanks had moved in overnight, blocking the road and any hope that Trautman and his men could leave.[71] Things were not looking good. The Allied command of the skies had been denied by the persistent fog, heavy clouds, and frequent bouts of precipitation.[72] To flip the scales, the Allies needed to reclaim air dominance. Trautman had spent enough time as a flying cadet to know that, under these conditions, no planes could go up, no reconnaissance could be gathered, and no bombers could hit a target. Everyone was socked in and had to wait it out.

But for how long? The group needed supplies, food, and weapons. If the fog and darkness had helped the Germans launch their surprise attack, then maybe the same conditions could help the Americans. Under moonless skies, Trautman dispatched small teams to search the town. One group found an impressive cache of wine in the basement of the village's church, along with some food; they filled their arms and returned to their hideout. The food resuscitated the men, and Trautman let them drink some wine.[73] There was little doubt that if the Germans found Trautman's squad, they would be killed. They had nothing to defend themselves with, and stories of atrocities against civilians and captured Allied troops were legion.[74] They might as well enjoy themselves while they could.

Later, as Trautman eyed the pile of wine bottles, he was struck with an idea. Although infantry manuals instructed that only bazookas, antitank guns, antitank mines, and self-propelled tank destroyers could knock out German Panther and Tiger tanks, Trautman was short on supplies and needed to find another way.[75] His car, which remained hidden, had gasoline in the tank. In the middle of the night, Trautman ordered his men to silently gather the empty bottles and siphon gasoline into them. Plugging each bottle with a wad of fabric, they made as many Molotov cocktails as they could.[76] They might not have guns, but they wouldn't be empty-handed.

On the morning of December 23, the fog grew translucent, and it seemed the sky was brighter than usual.[77] If the weather improved, Trautman planned to use an improvised radio one of his men had cobbled together to send a message asking for help. But first, he and his men readied themselves by writing letters home, knowing that these notes could be their last. Trautman wrote to Jane. "Tho I haven't written to you in almost one week, you are and always will be the number one interest of my life. I think of you many times every day and worry if all is well with you and Eric," Trautman said. He promised to write her again as soon as he could and signed the letter with "all my love."[78] Trautman's second letter was to his New York office. What he had witnessed and experienced had changed his tone. "Dear office: There are a few things that we will need to radically change if we are to survive as a supply agency for reading materials." The distribution of books and magazines "has been unsatisfactory almost to the point of failure to units on the continent of Europe." Books and magazines were second only to movies in popularity, yet "reading materials are extremely scarce." There needed to be more ASEs, but mail delivery was shoddy, and the books that did arrive quickly disintegrated as they warred against the weather and the Germans. Trautman did not care what it took. "I could write on for hours," though he only had minutes. "WE MUST GET *MORE* READING MATERIAL TO THE FIGHTING MEN."[79]

As Trautman wrote, the fog continued to lift and he saw snippets of blue sky for the first time since he left Paris. A hum began to crescendo. American planes were in the air. In the words of Roscoe C. Blunt, a private in the 84th Infantry who fought in the Bulge, "Combat continually offered isolated instances of unexplained fateful luck."[80] Trautman immediately messaged his position and situation. Whether kismet, or because his transmission had been received, one of the planes took out the first German tank in the column that blocked the main road of the village. Another disabled the last tank in the row. Bookended, all the tanks in between were trapped in the clutches of the narrow street. Trautman ordered his men to grab their homemade incendiaries and take the rest out.[81] Lighting their Molotov cocktails, the Americans dropped them into tank turrets and threw them against the tanks' lightly armored rears to knock out engines and set them aflame; if their crews were inside and tried to bail out, Trautman's men would have to fight as best they could.[82]

After it was over, Trautman spent the next two days evacuating his men, helping them reconnect with their units, and tending to those who were wounded. He spent Christmas Day in a hospital in Belgium with his injured men. He distributed some of the ASEs he had packed in his car. While he was leaving the hospital, he spotted an ASE on the floor of the operating room. Picking it up, Trautman reflexively fanned the pages only to discover that "on about page 35 there was a thumb smudge in blood which was repeated 2/3 through the book where it suddenly ended." Trautman never revealed whether the man reading this book had survived or not. When he shared this story, his point was to convey how troops relied on books wherever the war took them—even to death's door.[83]

The fighting in the Ardennes made it impossible for him to continue on his planned route into Germany and Luxembourg, and he had already been away far longer than his orders had directed. Trautman reluctantly returned to Paris. His heart remained with those fighting. He could not get the image of the ASE with the bloody thumbprint out of his mind. For many men, the ASEs were the only source of comfort during the darkest hours of their lives. The line from his December 23 letter to his office resonated. "WE MUST GET *MORE* READING MATERIAL TO THE FIGHTING MEN."[84] He had never before felt such a sense of urgency. As he walked the streets of Paris, his mind reeling, Trautman happened to pass a bookstore with English-language editions. Without a second thought, he went inside and purchased every book. Having familiarized himself with Paris's bookstores in the weeks preceding his trip to the Ardennes, he spent the next few hours going bookstore to bookstore and buying every English and American edition he could get his hands on. According to one newspaper account, it amounted to 17,000 volumes.[85] Trautman secured a truck and personally made sure they were sent to the front.[86] This one-man book crusade was a risky move. The Army had administrative channels that one had to work through, with matters of budget, requisition paperwork, approval for expenditures, and other protocols to follow. Trautman knew all this but no longer cared. He couldn't stop the fighting, but he could fight boredom and offer distraction from the horror of war. If his superiors decided to court-martial the chief librarian for providing books to troops without specific authorization for their immediate procurement, so be it.

Almost a week had passed since Trautman had written his office, and his last letter had been preemptory. His staff was working so hard on the ASEs, mini magazines, and streamlining library service to make it run efficiently. He felt a pang of guilt for suggesting they were not trying hard enough. "My letter to you dated 23 Dec. was written in the 'heat of battle' so to speak and may be a bit strong in spots." Nonetheless, he added, when it came to the urgency in ramping up book production and distribution, "I wouldn't tone it down much even now."[87] He told them that he would be submitting paperwork for overseas librarian positions, and would be working on securing the approval of General Eisenhower to improve book and magazine distribution across Europe.[88] When he returned to New York, he planned to work on publishers to maximize book and magazine output. "I am anxious to get back... to get re-acquainted with my family at home and my office."[89]

In early January 1945, Trautman returned to Eisenhower's ETO headquarters for a meeting to report on his trip to Belgium. Eisenhower apologized for sending him on a mission that had almost gotten him killed. Trautman replied that he was grateful. What he had witnessed only magnified the importance of books and only made him more determined to boost production.[90] Eisenhower signed a cable authorizing the "shipment of council books and unit magazines by the most expeditious surface means available."[91]

With fresh resolve, Trautman returned to the United States in mid-January.[92] Over the course of the next several months, he would squeeze every book he could out of publishers to serve the troops.

# 10

# Fighting *Your* War

We all spread out and began to dig in,
While the shells were exploding with a terrible din.
Each man was ready for his part in the show
For he knew it was rough in the E.T.O.

—Pfc. Dennis R. Gilliam[1]

Trautman felt an overwhelming sense of gratitude to be home and with his family. When he arrived back in New York in January 1945, he was deeply moved to learn that his friends had been looking out for Jane and Eric while he had been away. When Eric's first Christmas came around, Trautman was still emerging from the Battle of the Bulge and presents were the last thing on his mind. But Trautman's friend, publisher Max Geffen of *Omnibook*, marked Eric's first Christmas by sending him a war bond with a note: "For your sake and for your country's too, here's a good way to start saving. . . . Merry Christmas!"[2] Eric Knight's widow, Jere, sent her husband's namesake a book with a note wishing him a very Merry Christmas.[3] Paul Postell, one of Trautman's assistant librarians in New York, had sent notes to Jane throughout the months Trautman was abroad, offering encouragement and sharing updates.[4] These and dozens of other caring gestures lifted Trautman's spirits and invigorated him as he returned to work.

Trautman would need all the fortitude he could muster. While he was in Europe, he had asked friends and Special Services officers in other theaters to provide reports on the state of reading where they were stationed. When Trautman returned to his desk, their responses were waiting. Little of the news was positive. Unsurprisingly, the Southwest Pacific, MacArthur's territory, remained a difficult sector to crack. For neutralized areas, where there was no threat of bombardment, the Army Library Service had planned to send hardcover books so that ASEs could be reserved for front-line troops who required pocket-sized paperbacks. To this end, the Army Library Service developed a 2,000-volume book kit so stationary troops could have an instant library.[5] However, the crates of pre-made libraries were too large to go through the mail; they had to be shipped as Army cargo. Because MacArthur refused to allocate shipping space for books, libraries were extremely rare in the Southwest Pacific. As Major Everett T. Moore, an Army Information & Education specialist, observed during the fall of 1944, "Libraries and reading rooms for troops in Australia and New Guinea were virtually unknown." Unless "someone would have books sent to him from the States," the "Armed Services Editions and lightweight editions of magazines were depended upon almost entirely."[6] Sergeant Martin P. McDonough seconded these sentiments. McDonough, who was stationed in Australia, said that a Red Cross Library opened in 1943, but that the books "must have [been] picked up in a Brisbane second-hand juvenile book-shop." "What really saved the day," he added, "were the Armed Services Editions and the occasional book-gifts some of the fellows received."[7] This only confirmed that Trautman's plan to mail reading materials did result in books and magazines reaching the Southwest Pacific. Still, Trautman's inability to launch libraries across the region felt like a lost opportunity.

More favorable news came from the Persian Gulf. Susan Klein, a friend of Trautman's who was attached to the British Ministry of War Transport, wrote from Basra to report that US troops read incessantly. "Of course, the men down here aren't in the fighting lines—but they are bored to death with nothing (or almost nothing to do)," and "a great majority of the men here read." Stationed alongside British troops, many Americans gained an appreciation for how fortunate they were to have an Army that supplied free books to them. "The British are very jealous of our books," Klein said. "They'll beg and borrow them at any time," and US troops tended to share. "I find at least a couple [ASEs] in every house I visit here in Basra. Our soldiers are very generous and as soon as they finish with a book, they pass it on to friends. Often the friends are civilians, but it makes no difference." Klein believed that those in the Army Library Service would never know how profoundly they were influencing reading habits around the world. The ASEs were making readers out of soldiers and locals alike. Klein closed her letter encouraging "you and all the people who are still working to get the books out" to continue their outstanding work.[8]

Perhaps the most difficult theater to supply logistically was China-Burma-India (CBI), which was tasked with driving the Japanese from Burma, building a thousand-mile supply road from the jungles of Assam to Kunming, China, and then transporting supplies to the Chinese Army and American Air Forces in China. Chief of Staff George Marshall described the CBI as having "the thinnest supply line of all."[9] Because practically all ship cargo space was reserved for ammunition, food, and medical equipment, only a minimal supply of books arrived through early 1944. Establishing libraries was futile because the theater consisted of hundreds of thousands of troops scattered in small clusters across a huge territory. If these men received books, it was because they had carried them from the United States or received some in the mail. So desperate were these troops for entertainment that one wrote, "it was a real tragedy to finish one book and not have another to pick up."[10] When Trautman had hatched his plan to circumvent MacArthur by mailing the ASEs, he also stumbled upon the most effective solution to supply books to the CBI. Not only did mailbags bring precious letters from home, but they also brought the small paper-wrapped packages of ASEs.[11] "The best way to spell *morale*... was m-a-i-l," one soldier in the CBI theater said.[12] A private in India wrote that "we ravenously read all the books which the Council on Books in Wartime, Inc., have sent over," and it was not unusual to read the same book "three times" because it was all they had.[13]

William Sloane, publisher at Henry Holt and a council member, went to China on business and visited troops stationed in Chungking while he was there. Sloane wrote in a letter, "You simply cannot appreciate the vacuum in which the men...live out here." There was hardly anything to break the monotony of each long day, except for books. It was in this spirit that the soldiers looked forward to ASEs with "pathetic eagerness." They did not care what titles arrived, so long as they had something to read. "The book itself is all that matters," Sloane said.[14] A letter from a soldier who worked on the Ledo Road in India and Burma mirrored Sloane's observation. He stated that the ASEs were "my chief, and almost only source of recreation" for twenty-two months. "It was an event when a new series arrived and the selection...offered satisfaction to almost every reader's taste."[15]

* * *

Having secured General Eisenhower's order to prioritize distribution of reading materials in the ETO, and hearing the chorus of demands for more books around the world, Trautman was more determined than ever to increase the number of ASEs being printed. This would take the full cooperation of the publishers, who were reticent about embracing change, particularly if it affected profits. When Trautman was invited to give a talk about his recent trip to Europe at the February 1, 1945, annual luncheon of the Council on Books in Wartime, he would have a platform and a captive audience. He decided he would broach a topic that he knew would ruffle feathers and possibly even risk the entire ASE program. If his powers of persuasion prevailed, however, more ASEs would be printed than ever before. He had to try.

When the Army first came to an agreement with the Council on Books in Wartime to print ASEs, one of the publishers' conditions was a one-cent royalty for every ASE printed, to be divided evenly between the original publisher and the author of the work.[16] At the time, a number of publishers were resistant to the ASE idea, and Trautman's paperback program received the tepid approval of the Army. It had not been a time for hard bargaining; he simply needed to get the program up and running. If the publishers, who were doing much of the legwork in appeasing the brass hats in the Army, wanted a half-cent royalty, Trautman was willing to go along with it. However, once the initial contracts were signed, the ASEs were printed and distributed, and the popularity of the program was obvious, Trautman began to see the royalty in a new light. The magazine publishers printing "pony," "peewee," and "baby" editions for the Army received no such royalty; their payoff would come after the war, with skyrocketing subscriptions coming from veterans who returned home wanting to maintain their wartime reading habits. Why should book publishers receive any royalties for the ASEs when the same postwar bonus awaited them? If the publishers' royalties were instead reinvested into the ASEs, tens of thousands of additional ASEs could be printed each month.

In the summer of 1944, Trautman had urged the publishers to forego their royalty on all ASEs so that more ASEs could be printed on the Army's limited budget. He did not challenge the half-cent royalty for authors likely because it would be too time-consuming and complicated to negotiate with each of thirty to forty authors per month. The ASEs required a streamlined process for timely printing. In contrast, practically all publishers were council members; in theory, they could all agree to eliminate their half-cent royalty per ASE and future contracts would simply eliminate it. At the time, the average unit cost of an ASE was five and one-half cents, and about 10 percent of this cost consisted of their royalty.[17]

The publishers scoffed at Trautman's request. Pointing out that their half-cent royalty on each ASE was a fraction of their regular royalty on a hardcover book, the publishing companies felt they had already sacrificed a great deal for the Army.[18] S. Spencer Scott, treasurer of the Council on Books in Wartime and publisher at Harcourt Brace, met with Trautman for lunch in late August 1944. Going into the meeting, Scott told publishers that "so long as we continue to live in a capitalist society, I shall insist that publishers . . . should be rewarded the same as producers and inventors are rewarded in other fields." Scott and the publishers were not going to budge. The tense meeting culminated with a threat from Scott. "I warned Lt. Col. Trautman that I would use my best efforts to terminate the contract [for ASEs] with the Army and Navy January

1st if any further attempts were made either to reduce the royalty or to do the work on a royalty free basis," he wrote in a memo to the council.[19] Trautman kept his composure but privately fumed that the publishers would rather pull the plug on the entire ASE program than waive a half-cent royalty per book. After their lunch, Scott told the council at their next board meeting that they wouldn't be hearing anything more from Trautman about adjusting their royalties.[20] And for the time being, that was the case.

But in early 1945, Scott and the council were dealing with someone determined to win the next skirmish in the royalty battle. After the Bulge and witnessing the preciousness of books to troops facing death, Trautman felt he owed those men every ASE he could get. Sharing some of the things he saw and experienced—like the bloody thumbprint—would be the best ammunition. Trautman knew browbeating and confrontation would not work. Instead, Trautman merely laid down the facts—they were compelling enough. Although he never even used the word "royalty," the publishers knew exactly what he was alluding to.

On February 1, 1945, as the publishers enjoyed a gourmet lunch at the Hotel Ambassador in New York, Trautman was invited to the rostrum. Still reeling from his experiences in Europe, Trautman choked down his reticence in sharing some of the things he saw. Removing a few slips of paper from his pocket, Trautman scanned the audience of more than seventy publishing notables—including W. W. Norton, Richard Simon, Stanley Rinehart, Alfred Knopf, Joseph Lippincott—not to mention luminaries in the library world like Carl Milam of the ALA and Franklin Hopper of the New York Public Library. These were the biggest names in the universe of books; Trautman had little more than a uniform, library degree, and a sense of mission on his side:

> I should like to talk to you about some observations made on my recent trip to England, France, Belgium, Holland and Germany. First, I must admit that there were far too few books. There should have been 5 times as many to really go around. When a soldier with a monthly pay of $55 is willing to pay 500 francs or $10 American dollars for the privilege of being next in line to read a particular Council Book they are pretty scarce.

One thing which impressed me is the short life these books have under combat conditions. One or two readings is all that can be counted on. A man reads a book to death very quickly while standing in the rain or snow without any shelter to keep the pages dry.

It is not unusual for a man to tear off the portion of a book he has finished to give it to the next man who doesn't have a book to read saying—"I'll save my pages for you."

I saw books which had been read to a state of "combat exhaustion" but when I asked if I might have them to bring back as samples I was reproached with "You wouldn't take our books away would you? We can still read them some." So I haven't any examples of book casualties to show you—dirty books with covers gone, pages curled or missing at both ends and looking worse than an old magazine that's lived in a barber shop for a year. I picked up a Council Book in the operating room of a hospital in Belgium on Christmas day (I don't remember the title) but on about page 35 there was a thumb smudge in blood which was repeated 2/3 through the book where suddenly it ended.

As casualties are drained back from combat positions so too are Council Books carried to the rear. It takes thousands of extra books at the front each month to replace those carried out of action in this manner. . . .

Some of the uses of Council Books which may not be too well known are by our soldiers who have been captured by the enemy. From 60,000 to 200,000 books per month are made available to the International YMCA which is the only agency permitted to supply reading materials to Prisoners of War. The books are of utmost importance in making life bearable to Prisoners of War.

Hospitals both overseas and in this country wouldn't get along without Council Books. Before they were put in all hospitals here, sick and wounded men used to complain that regular books were too heavy and hard to hold up and that there were never enough good titles. Hospital use of Council Books is now fully accepted and even the dyed in the wool librarians who scoffed at them before are now their staunchest promoters. . . .

When troops were being sent to marshalling areas in England getting ready for D-Day . . . Council Books were distributed to all who desired to have them for the jump off. Here also men were told to examine and sort their belongings because "if you don't want to lug it with you, don't take it." All kinds of things were left behind such as extra clothing, toilet articles, souvenirs and even cameras, but there were no Council Books to be found after a group moved out. A man just couldn't take the chance on being without something to read until a new supply caught up with him somewhere in France.

Having established how cherished books were overseas, Trautman wanted the publishers to also understand the men who were reading them. Could these publishing executives imagine what it was like to be thousands of miles from home, with nothing to eat but two meals of K-rations per day? Or what it was like to live outdoors in the winter, periodically shoveling the hole they lived in to prevent the constant snow from turning into a bath of slush? Could they relate to stuffing their clothing with newspapers (if any arrived) for insulation because their winter uniform wasn't warm enough? Had they ever felt the hairs on the backs of their necks stand up straight as death skulked in the shadows around them? These were the conditions facing hundreds of thousands of lonesome, homesick, scared souls whose only respite could be found in the pages between two covers. As one soldier said about an ASE, it was his "ration on pleasure."[21]

Trautman knew he had the publishers' attention when many among them softly laid down their forks and knives and listened. An ASE was a soldier's emotional survival gear, the only thing that helped alleviate the stress, grief, anxiety, and misery they endured each day. Although the production of ASEs had increased from twenty to fifty million a year, Trautman was resolute: "There are still not enough books to go around."[22] Couldn't the publishers do whatever it might take and get the job done?

As straightforwardly as he could, Trautman stated his case:

> Those men overseas are giving so much to the common cause and we here are doing so little in comparison that it is nothing short of criminal to let any little want they may have go unfilled. They want many millions more books than they are now getting and when they are told that there isn't enough money... they can't understand why.
>
> The least we can do is to get soldiers all the books they want and stop worrying about cutting down or quitting until the need has been satisfied. As long as millions of American soldiers are overseas fighting *your* war the work of the Council in helping produce books cheaply must go on.[23]

Against a backdrop of polite applause, Trautman left the lunch and let his words percolate. Within weeks, publishers on the executive committee of the council moved to reconsider waiving publishers' royalties on the ASEs. With Scott as the council's treasurer, his vehement opposition was enough to temporarily quash further debate.[24] It seems that to Scott, it was a matter of principle that publishers deserved a nominal royalty—it was, after all, only one-half a cent per ASE—for the extensive amount of time and effort they devoted to the project. And many other publishers agreed with him. Much to their chagrin, the issue kept resurfacing.

On May 2, 1945, Trautman met with the council's executive committee and again addressed the continued need for ASEs—there was still a dearth of books in Europe, the Pacific, the CBI, and at outposts around the world. Trautman said that if "enough funds were available, the Army would increase their order for ASE books" to 175,000 copies of each title per month—totaling seven million ASEs per month, nearly one million more books per month than what was currently being produced.[25]

After Trautman's earnest plea, the publishers' unanimity on the royalty issue began to fissure. Some insisted on eliminating their royalty. Others fiercely opposed such action. Tempers flared, and Scott ended up recusing himself, for unrecorded reasons. W. W. Norton took the helm and presided over the discussion. Norton felt that Trautman's position was the better one, and with his assured guidance, the publishers ultimately resolved to give each publisher the option of waiving their royalty so that more ASEs could be made. According to the meeting minutes, "The Executive Committee requested Mr. Scott to draft a letter to be sent to all Council members (on Council stationery) advising them of this resolution."[26] Scott surely did not appreciate this assignment.

Though Trautman won the royalty battle, it was never about winning or losing for him. The quest to eliminate royalties was purely about getting the maximum number of books into the hands of troops. It was waged by the man whose reflexive instinct, after witnessing the horrors of combat, was to buy 17,000 books and return to the front to oversee their immediate distribution—even if this meant he could be punished for operating outside of ordinary channels of procurement (he was never reprimanded for this act). Trautman was fueled by no desire other than to give American troops the books they wanted to read.

As for Scott, there were no hard feelings. For years after the war ended, Scott wrote warm letters of congratulation to Trautman whenever the librarian's latest feats made the newspapers.[27]

* * *

Trautman's speech to the Council on Books in Wartime was shared with the press, and he became a literary celebrity. Ordinarily, Trautman shied from the limelight—even preferring that others take credit for the work of the Army Library Service, particularly if it meant greater cooperation and assistance from high-ranking military officials or publishers. He had publicly provided details of his European trip only to bolster his case for eliminating the publishers' royalty so more books would reach troops. Like the publishers, the public was spellbound by the details of Trautman's observations in Europe—and they were liberally reprinted in big city papers and small-town gazettes.[28] Knowing that there was a Ray Trautman in the Army, who bent over backward to cater to the emotional welfare of troops, provided solace to everyone at home who worried and wondered about their loved ones overseas.

All the media attention propelled Trautman to the top of his field. He was invited to give a prime-time radio interview about Army Library Service.[29] Major institutions like his alma mater Columbia were eager to have him speak to aspiring librarians and those already working in the field. He was asked to speak before the NYC Board of Estimate to argue against budget cuts to the New York and Brooklyn Public Libraries.[30] High-ranking members of the military showered accolades on his service. Even the head of the Special Services Division sent Trautman a letter praising his "accomplishments during the period of your recent temporary duty overseas," and congratulating him on "a mission well accomplished."[31]

Perhaps the most meaningful commendation came from the American Library Association president, Carl Vitz, whose speech at the annual convention in October 1944 had focused on the literary marvels one of their members was pulling off. Because Trautman was overseas at the time, he did not learn of the speech until after he returned home in

January 1945. Noting that the ALA had engaged in "important pioneer work" during World War I by creating the Library War Service, Vitz was deeply impressed by what Trautman's "wise, imaginative, and far-sighted direction" had made possible in World War II. Trautman supervised 600 librarians (many of whom were ALA members), was responsible for 2,000 libraries, and worked with a book-buying budget of more than $8 million per year. Between donated books, purchased hardcovers, and ASEs, Trautman had worked with more books, branches, and bookworms than any other librarian in the world.

As Vitz addressed the ALA's vast army of civilian librarians, he warned them that their work was about to get a lot more challenging. The Army had provided "an exposure to books [that] is unprecedented and will create unprecedented opportunity," Vitz said. But, he added, "We must be ready to measure up to this standard of service when our veterans return."[32] The Army had upped the ante on what quality library service looked like.

And Trautman had no plans to slow down. He was driven to continue building the best libraries that he could.

* * *

By April 1945, the war in Europe was coming to an end. After retaking the initiative following the Battle of the Bulge in January 1945, the Allies pushed their way forward toward Berlin. That troops in Europe would be "home alive in '45" seemed less an exercise of wishful thinking and more of a reality.[33]

However, April brought one final blow, with the death of Franklin Roosevelt. For years, his steady hand had navigated the nation through a devastating economic depression and then unified the nation as it went to war. It seemed to many an injustice that their commander-in-chief could not witness the peace for which he had fought so long and hard.[34]

The press reported that four servicemen received a cable from their mother, stating that their father had passed away in his sleep. "He did his job to the end, as he would want to do," Eleanor Roosevelt purportedly told her sons.[35] Soldiers interpreted the First Lady's message as their marching orders. "We have got to carry on just the way he would have wanted," one soldier said.[36] With fresh determination to claim victory, the country rededicated itself to fighting to the finish.

Trautman reflected on Eleanor and Franklin Roosevelt's attitude that books were democracy's armor. From Eleanor's early interest in providing books to Black service clubs to her participation in the Victory Book Campaign, and the president's pronouncement of Victory Book Day and speeches on the importance of books in democracy—the best tribute he could offer to the Roosevelts was continuing to get books into the hands of soldiers.

# 11

# A Job Well Done

> Anything derogatory I may have said in the past about librarians is hereby rescinded. Never did a bunch of book guardians do such a superb job.
>
> —Master Sgt. Fon W. Boardman[1]

On May 8, 1945, President Truman, Winston Churchill, and Joseph Stalin announced over the radio that the German government had surrendered unconditionally. The war in Europe was over.[2] For Trautman, this meant it was time to implement the plans he had sketched out during his European tour.[3] Written with an eye to the need for "adaptation to local circumstances," the *Guide for the Operation of Small Army Libraries* sounded nothing like a typical Army manual. Encouraging ingenuity and independence, it was filled with suggestions rather than rules. Army personnel serving as librarians in the ETO were urged to show "positiveness," "imagination," and "initiative."[4] The only unbending principle was conveyed in all caps: "NO LIBRARY PROCEDURES OR REGULATIONS SHOULD BE MADE WHICH WILL CURB THE USE OF BOOKS."[5]

By May 8, V-E Day, Trautman had selected 120 female librarians to establish new libraries across Europe.[6] Most of these women had proven their bona fides by managing Army libraries in the United States.[7] Having witnessed the conditions on his European tour, Trautman knew only the most enterprising and intrepid librarians would be suited to the challenges these libraries would face.[8] Unit librarians for small troop installations received between 100 and 1,000 volumes for their branch. For larger installations, meaning 3,000 or more troops, 2,000-volume libraries were established. To ensure that isolated detachments would not be left out, fifty bookmobiles, holding 1,500 volumes each, were shipped to Europe so troops scattered across more remote areas would still have a library connection.[9] Troops could either visit an Army library, or an Army bookmobile would visit them.

Meanwhile, there was still a war being waged in the Pacific, and Trautman was determined to get libraries established across the region. As he noted in a speech, the "extremely difficult logistical situation of the Western Pacific Theater of Operations... [causes] troops in that theater... to depend almost entirely on automatically issued ASEs and magazine sets," but it was the Library Branch's intention to oversee the construction of library buildings and fill them with reading materials.[10] For all islands occupied by the Allies, there were large numbers of troops who performed essential work at airstrips, supply depots, hospitals, and staging areas; they often experienced long hours of work followed by periods of downtime with little to do. Trautman wanted to develop stationary libraries across this region. Given that war supplies no longer needed to be shipped to the Pacific *and* the ETO, he reasoned that the Pacific would have roughly twice the shipping capacity for war matériel. MacArthur no longer had an excuse for refusing shipments of books.

To streamline the creation of libraries, he and others on his team developed several pre-made book kits. There was the Library Service's "PB Kit," consisting of a single crate crammed with 500 popular paperbacks, and an "RB Kit" containing 100 reference books such as dictionaries and encyclopedias.[11] As Trautman explained, these kits were "packed in a wooden case equipped with shelves, which serves as a bookcase when the lid is removed."[12] An "RB Library" was also developed, which combined the RB Kit with 400 popular fiction and nonfiction titles.[13] To launch a new library, one or more of these kits could be requested. Trautman intended to ship over 600,000 volumes to the Western Pacific, with at least one kit for every group of 500 men.[14] This way, combat troops would be awash in ASEs, and stationary troops would have libraries. He was planning for the long haul, believing, as most did, that the war with Japan would not end anytime soon. According to his diary, he placed a bet with another officer, wagering a bottle of top-shelf bourbon that V-J Day would not come until after March 1, 1946.[15] Thus Trautman spent much of the early summer of 1945 preparing to inundate the Pacific with books.

In early August 1945, he visited Army library facilities in California and surveyed the West Coast's infrastructure for shipping library supplies to the Pacific.[16] As he was drawing up plans, news spread that the United States had dropped an atomic bomb on Hiroshima, devastating the entire area. Days later, word came that a second bomb was dropped on Nagasaki.[17] News of the magnitude of damage caused by the bombs, and the staggering civilian death toll, made Trautman homesick for his own family. In a letter to Jane, he told her how much he wished she and Eric were with him. When he returned home, he would "do the shopping and clean up the basement," along with anything else that would make her happy. Their eighth wedding anniversary was later that month. He had already missed five years' worth of holidays, birthdays, milestones, and anniversaries. Hiroshima and Nagasaki were the latest reminders that life could be over in an instant. Trautman didn't want to miss another thing. Though he had no control over where the Army sent him and for how long, Trautman told Jane that he hoped he could make it to New York in time to celebrate their anniversary this year. "Maybe you better buy yourself a new dress for the occasion. If not for then—why not get a new dress anyhow for no reason except I love you very much."[18]

As it turned out, Trautman would have more to celebrate than his wedding anniversary. Behind the scenes, some of Trautman's superiors had been campaigning to boost his rank. In August 1945, Trautman learned he had become a full colonel.[19] Major General Joseph W. Byron, director of the Special Services Division and a longtime supporter, sent a handwritten letter to personally congratulate Trautman on his "well deserved" promotion.[20] A more effusive note arrived from Colonel

Frederick Warburg, the chief of the Army's Athletics and Recreation Branch. "Whether the news of your promotion caused the Jap[anese] to curl up is hard to prove. At any rate it caused much jubilation to your friends and admirers. Your eagles are so deserved and so obvious a recognition of the great service you and your staff have rendered the soldier that any congratulations are ridiculous."[21]

* * *

With Japan's declaration of peace on August 14, 1945, Americans in uniform stopped thinking of their return home as an "if" and instead as a matter of "when." Their focus shifted from surviving to living, and they began to think of replacing their military garb with civilian clothes. Ray Trautman was no different.

The Library Branch was churning out more reading material than ever before—over six million ASEs, several million comic books, tens of thousands of subscriptions to 125 different periodicals, and tens of thousands of hardcover and trade paperbacks each month. The program was at its pinnacle.[22] World War I had demonstrated that as the size of the Army shrank so, too, would the budget and attention given to Army libraries.[23] After the 1919 Armistice, Army library expenditures fell from $94,000 in 1921 to $44,000 in 1931, and they continued to decline until 1940, when the draft took effect.[24]

Trautman had been wholeheartedly invested in getting books and magazines to soldiers, but needs were shifting. As troops transitioned to veterans, they would leave Army libraries and seek books as civilians. He wanted to be involved in making sure that all people who wanted reading materials could obtain them—whether they were in or out of uniform.

He knew there was work ahead. Before the outbreak of war, forty-five million Americans—about 37 percent of the population—had no access to public libraries; if they read books, it was generally because they had the means to purchase them.[25] And for those who had a local public library, the percentage of the community that claimed borrowing privileges ranged from a high of 31 percent in California to a low of 2 percent in Mississippi.[26] Whether someone was a card-carrying library visitor often depended if their home was in close proximity to a public library. Trautman knew that these statistics didn't reflect the public's desire for books. When he had been an educational adviser with the CCC, he had served a community that lacked a public library but cherished the books and reading materials supplied in CCC camps. As Army chief librarian, he saw this eagerness on a far greater scale—to the tune of millions in uniform, many of whom hadn't touched a book as a civilian but dove into every ASE they could lay their hands on in the Army.

Trautman felt a duty to go where he could make the greatest difference. This meant leaving the Army and finding ways to serve the public's need for books and to spread the joy of reading.

Though he did not immediately disclose his decision, Trautman received a number of job offers—director of the San Francisco Public Library, an executive position at *Esquire* magazine, a management role at *Reader's Digest*.[27] It was an offer to become vice president and general manager of *Omnibook* that attracted him. From its inception in 1938, *Omnibook*'s goal was to expose the public to a wider range of ideas, opinions, stories, and histories by abridging bestselling books so that readers could sample several books in the time it would take to read one unabridged title. His job would involve expanding *Omnibook*'s circulation in the United States and internationally. He could use this role to reach parts of the country where books were an exception to daily life. Plus, *Omnibook*'s offices were in New York. After moving from Kentucky to New York to Baltimore to Arlington, and then back to New York, the Trautmans were eager to stay in one place. And the boost in salary—earning a princely $30,000 per year[28]—would come in handy as Ray and Jane wanted to expand their family. Trautman accepted with the proviso that the news be kept secret until he'd had a chance to tell his colleagues and friends of his decision to leave the Army.

First, however, came an invitation to the White House. It came from Frederic Melcher, publisher and editor of *Publishers' Weekly*, who had devoted his life to the world of books—recording the latest trends and developments for libraries, booksellers, authors, and publishers.[29] When the ASEs were first created, *Publishers' Weekly* tracked their success and predicted they would have a long-term impact on the American reading public.[30] Melcher knew it was Trautman's dogged ingenuity and fortitude that made the ASEs such a success, and he wanted to honor the Army's chief librarian by having him participate in the American Booksellers Association's (ABA) tradition of gifting books to the White House Library.

The history of this custom dated back to 1929, when John Howell, a publisher from San Francisco, had been a guest at President Herbert Hoover's inaugural ceremonies and learned that the president had had to borrow a book from a White House security guard because there were no books at the White House.[31] At the time, each president brought their personal library to the White House and packed their books for home upon departing office.[32] Howell relayed this story to the ABA, and a resolution was swiftly adopted to give President Hoover 500 current books on all subjects—including literature, history, travel, world affairs, biography, science, and fiction[33]—so that a permanent White House Library could be established.[34] The ABA planned to augment its first 500 volumes by gifting each presidential administration an additional set of books, chosen by a national committee of librarians, editors, publishers, and booksellers.[35] From the first donation, Melcher served on the committee that selected books and nominated individuals to take part in the White House ceremony.[36] Given Trautman's enormous influence on American reading habits and the growth of the book industry, Melcher wrote to Trautman in September 1945 to see if he would be interested in presenting President Truman with some of the 200 books the ABA was donating to the White House Library. "I should like very much to have you present at that formality, as it would add a great deal to the occasion if you could," Melcher wrote.[37] Trautman sent an immediate response humbly accepting.

On October 4, 1945, Trautman was one of seven people to visit the Trumans and gift the White House Library its next installment of books.[38] Many titles that had been made into ASEs were among the 200 titles that were donated, including *Strange Fruit*.[39] For President Truman, the gift of books was meaningful. Beginning with childhood,

"I always had my nose stuck in a book.... There were about three thousand books in the library downtown [in Independence, Missouri], and...I read them all, including the encyclopedias," Truman said.[40] To spend an afternoon at the White House, and have a chance to speak with Truman about their shared love of reading, was an apt bookend to Trautman's tenure as Army chief librarian.

Presenting the White House Library with a selection of books made Trautman reflect on another historic library. Since the late 1930s, President Roosevelt had dreamed of building a presidential library in which anyone could access his "'correspondence, papers, manuscripts, source material, log books, paintings, drawings, prints, works of art,'" and other material pertaining to his life and work.[41] Roosevelt envisioned his advisors and members of his administration donating their papers so that his library would contain "a body of material such as does not exist anywhere else."[42] Although presidential papers were ordinarily housed in the Library of Congress, Roosevelt proposed building a library in Hyde Park, New York, offering twelve acres of the Roosevelt property there—including the newly built library—to the federal government, and following the usual protocol of the United States Archivist taking receipt of the collection.[43]

So loathsome was this novel arrangement to House Republicans that in 1939 they voted against a bill that would authorize the government to take title to the Roosevelt property, many arguing that "such material should be preserved in Washington, if anywhere, along with other government records."[44] Republican Representative Harold Knutson of Minnesota said this would benefit "future statesman 'who can go there and look at them and see how not to run a government.'"[45] After many additional hours of occasionally bitter debate, the bill ultimately passed.[46] The Franklin D. Roosevelt Presidential Library and Museum became the first presidential library in the United States, and it has inspired the development of over a dozen presidential libraries since.[47]

In late 1945, Trautman contacted the director of the FDR Presidential Library to donate materials on behalf of the Army Library Service. President Roosevelt had played a key role in elevating the nation's consciousness about the importance of books during the war. Trautman believed that his library should house GI paperbacks and periodicals to reflect the former president's commitment to the idea that "books are weapons in the war of ideas."[48] To this day, they are available to researchers.

* * *

During the latter portion of October 1945, Trautman completed his Army separation paperwork and then began writing letters to everyone—leading publishers, high-ranking military officials, Army librarians, journalists, and notable civilians whose time, support, and assistance had contributed to the effectiveness of the Army Library Service.[49] Together they had faced challenges, shared sacrifices, and maintained an unwavering commitment to getting the job done. He wanted his letters to be personal rather than official.[50] "I expect to return shortly to civil life after serving for the last five years as Chief of the Army Library Service," one of Trautman's letters began. He then honored the unique work and assistance that had been provided. For example, in his letter to Harry Scherman, the president of the Book of the Month Club, Trautman expressed his "sincerest appreciation" for the "donation of thousands of Book of the Month Club subscriptions to Army posts in this country and overseas." Especially for those stationed in remote outposts, "they knew they could always count on receiving" these subscriptions. "As a bookman yourself, you don't need to be told what those books meant," Trautman said.[51]

Many who worked with him felt a need to tell Trautman what he meant to them. A good number counted themselves friends. Even publishers grew sentimental. The head of Curtis Publishing wrote, "We will miss you, Ray," and remarked how satisfying it was to work with Trautman to give magazines to "the men and women in our armed forces overseas."[52] Similarly, two of the top executives at Pocket Books wrote, "It has been a lot of fun working with you and you should be very proud of the tremendous job you did—building it up from nothing to the biggest book business in the world." They hoped to "continue our pleasant friendship."[53]

Magazine publishers, many of whom had originally balked at some of Trautman's demands, were suddenly overcome with nostalgia for their mini magazines. Henry Luce, whose magazine empire included *Time* and *Life*, had been furious when the Army Library Service initially sidestepped *Time* because of stalled price negotiations and, even more galling, worked with its competitor, *Newsweek*, to create the first "baby" edition for troops.[54] *Time*'s pony edition nonetheless became a staple in the Army's magazine sets, and an overseas edition of *Life* was also added.[55] As a token of thanks, Trautman received a handsome set of bound editions of the overseas edition of *Life*, with his name inscribed in gilt lettering on the front cover of each volume.[56] Postwar profits would more than make up for wartime disagreements. As Trautman had predicted, troops who had devoured the free magazines became subscribers in peacetime. The circulation rate for *Time* increased by 154 percent by the 1950s, and *Life*'s circulation almost doubled—from 3.2 million in 1941 to nearly 6 million.[57] The Army's worldwide distribution of the magazines also spawned international markets after the war.[58]

Similarly, Harold Ross, perhaps the worst complainer of them all, owed Trautman and the Army Library Service a huge debt of gratitude; the "peewee" edition of *The New Yorker* may have single-handedly ensured the longevity and profitability of the magazine. *The New Yorker*'s Jane Grant stated in her autobiography that because of Trautman's "untiring efforts" to get *The New Yorker* overseas, the magazine received the government's paper quota to print editions for the Army. *The New Yorker*, a weekly at home, began as a monthly magazine for troops in late 1943. The Army was testing the waters. Having branded itself as a magazine for "discriminating people," it was unclear whether troops would gravitate to a magazine whose icon—Eustace Tilley—sported a monocle and top hat.[59] They did. By March 1944, the peewee edition graduated to a weekly, and by the end of the war, Grant noted, "the 'pony' edition of *The New Yorker* had surpassed the parent *New Yorker* in circulation and brought it to the attention of new readers in many parts of the world."[60] When troops returned home, they subscribed to the magazine. As Ross reflected in October 1945, "There would be no *New Yorker* today if it were not for [Grant's]" insistence on making a "peewee" edition for the Army, and Trautman for giving the magazine the opportunity.[61] To show his appreciation, Ross arranged for the production of seven "limited edition" bound copies of the complete collection of *The New Yorker*'s peewee editions. An inscription lists the seven people who received copies. Among them, after President Roosevelt, George Marshall, and Chester Nimitz, was Ray Trautman.[62]

Even the Army's top brass shared their gratitude for Trautman's commitment to his work. Brigadier General Robert Cutler said that "it was a real source of satisfaction to work with a man, like yourself, who liked work and kept your eye on the ball."[63] Major General Joseph W. Byron wrote, "I want to add a personal word to say to you that the genuine single mindedness which characterized your work really made the library program successful. I count myself fortunate to have been associated in this work with men like yourself."[64] Many understood the far-reaching impact that the Army libraries had had on millions. Acting director of the Special Services Division, Francis R. Kerr, wrote, "The future historians of this war will record the part played by the Army Library Service throughout the emergency. To you for your splendid professional judgment, keen enthusiasm, and determination to see the job through should go most of the credit."[65]

While Trautman found all of this highly gratifying, he was moved more by the tokens and notes from those who had worked with him in the literary trenches. Colleagues reminisced how he would do nearly anything to make sure troops got reading materials. The staff of *Yank the Army Weekly*, a magazine put out by the Special Services Division and whose offices were next to the Army Library Service, recalled that he had saved the magazine. When it learned it had no paper to print on, Trautman spontaneously offered a huge stock of paper that had just arrived in an Army warehouse for the *Reader's Digest* servicemen's edition. He visited the warehouse, tracked down the paper, and modified invoice numbers and address labels so that some of the stock would be rerouted to *Yank*. The magazine was saved from disaster.[66] When a hardcover edition of the best stories from *Yank* was printed in 1945, one copy was set aside for Trautman. Every writer, illustrator, cartoonist, and photographer who passed through the New York office signed it.[67] Among those who added an inscription were bestselling author Marion Hargrove, whose *See Here, Private Hargrove* was sensationally popular with troops; artist George Baker, creator of the Sad Sack; the journalist Joe McCarthy, who ignored Douglas MacArthur's direct order to stay out of Hiroshima and documented the devastating aftermath of the atomic bomb; and dozens of others.

Cartoonists, in particular, were grateful for Trautman's open-mindedness in providing strips to troops when some people doubted their value. Dave Breger, who coined the term "GI Joe" and published his cartoons in *Yank* and *The Stars and Stripes*, showed his appreciation by giving Trautman an inscribed cartoon honoring the Army's battalions of bookworms.[68] It depicted two soldiers standing outside a bombed-out library; one of them appears to be standing guard as the other faces into the library, his elbows propped on a windowsill with a book in his hands. "Gee, I wish I had a library card—some swell books here!" reads the caption.[69]

Those who knew Trautman's work best were the librarians who had served under his direction. The service command librarians in the Army's Nine Corps Areas were the lesser-known stars in the Army Library Branch's constellation, and several felt a need to tell their chief what his support and vision meant to them. Capturing the sentiments in many letters from Army librarians was a note from Jed Taylor, the command librarian for the First Service Command, headquartered in Boston. "When you walked out of the office…there ended the most exciting, sparkling, and successful part of Army Library Service."[70] Ninth Service Command Librarian Xenophon Smith wrote Trautman, "As I look back upon it all now, I find a great deal of satisfaction in the accomplishments. While the library profession and the general public may never fully recognize them it is enough that you and I know what they are. [Y]our efforts may and should have a definite effect on the reading interests and habits of the entire world."[71]

A final letter that Trautman saved for the rest of his life came from the ALA, whose executive secretary, Carl Milam, had helped select Trautman to run the Army's libraries. It praised the incredible impact one intrepid librarian had made on the literary world. "All of us here at [ALA] Headquarters feel very strongly about how much the Army's Library Service has done, not only to meet the immediate needs of the Army, but to lay a foundation of reading interest for the future, which may greatly affect the library development of the country."[72] Trautman had not only changed the way the Army approached books, he had transformed a generation into readers and introduced them to libraries. Milam had no doubt the right man had been chosen for the job.

# 12

# Finding His Way

> A man's reading tastes won't change just because he's taken off his uniform.
>
> —Ray Love Trautman[1]

What job could possibly compare to being chief librarian of the US Army during World War II? It was a unique opportunity to bring together the titans of the book and magazine industries and formulate plans to send hundreds of millions of books and magazines to Americans in service—and mainly for the love of reading. The war also brought together the entire nation. On the home front, people had donated books, denounced book bans, and exercised their democratic freedom to read. There's been nothing like it before, and nothing like it since.

Although Trautman was no longer overseeing the project, the ASEs continued to be produced into 1947, serving the millions of occupation troops. For those being discharged, the need for portable paperbacks did not diminish simply because they would no longer wear a uniform. As they faced their return to civilian life—something they had dreamed about ever since they went to war—many troops suddenly felt suffocated by heavy expectations. Would they work? What career would they pursue? Would they go (or return) to school under the GI Bill—the Servicemen's Readjustment Act of 1944? Was marriage in the cards? Or children? Homeownership? To so many, civilian life felt overwhelming and complicated.

Under the stress of war, they turned to stories and books for an escape. Faced with serious decisions about their postwar lives, many instinctively reached into their pockets for an ASE. For some, this begged yet another question: Would these pocket-sized books still be available once they were out of uniform? Throughout the war, publishers received a stream of inquiries from troops asking to purchase ASEs for their homes, and the number of these letters only increased as they worried about their civilian book supply. "Will you pass along what information you can as to how I might obtain the complete library as my own," one private asked.[2] "Every dogface has a few Armed Services volumes on his 'shelf' and the wish 'I'd like to keep a couple of my favorites as souvenirs,'" one soldier commented before asking how he and his friends could obtain ASEs after the war.[3] "I would like to know if any of your books are for sale to members of the armed forces, and if so, the prices," a serviceman wrote from India.[4] "All my life I've wanted a library of good books but financial considerations have made it an impossibility," a private wrote from Germany. Assuming paperback ASEs would be more affordable than hardcovers, he asked for information on how to purchase a complete set.[5]

The council and military were contract-bound to keep the ASEs from being sold in the United States, and no ASEs would be available to veterans once they were discharged. Upon learning this, many troops hoarded the last ASEs they came across, read them on their way home, and saved these paperbacks. ASEs can still be found on bookshelves, in boxes of Army mementos, and at used bookstores.

All of this clamoring for pocket-sized paperbacks validated what Trautman and W. W. Norton had predicted in 1943: The ASEs created a new audience and a new market for books. As an officer who toured the Middle East, Greece, Turkey, and India in the summer of 1945 wrote, "The time will come when the publishers will discover that this project made readers of many men who might not have been so otherwise." The ASEs may have cost publishers their time and resources during the war but, "In the long run, publishers will not lose, although some may be unhappy because now there probably has been created a larger [demand] for cheap editions."[6]

By late 1945, publishers who had been staunch hardcover adherents had grown to embrace softcovers. When Trautman made his ASE prototype, the paperback industry in the United States was only a few years old and there were three companies printing them. By war's end, Penguin, Pocket Books, Avon, Popular Library, Dell, and Bantam were all printing softcover editions. And through the late 1940s, more paperback publishing companies and imprints were founded, including New American Library, Signet, and Mentor. When the war ended, the public's appetite for paperbacks was only beginning. In 1947, ninety-five million paperbacks were sold in the United States. By 1952, this number rose to 270 million. And by 1959, the public purchased more paperbacks than hardcovers.[7]

* * *

The paperback boom had not yet happened as Trautman began working at *Omnibook* in late 1945. Still, he saw limitless potential in an inexpensive magazine containing abridgements of four or five bestselling titles per issue, delivered in the identical format as the Army's overseas edition. With few paperback options for chart-topping books, veterans would likely gravitate toward *Omnibook* because it supplied the titles they wanted in a familiar wrapper.

When he started at *Omnibook* on November 20, 1945, Trautman's main initiatives were to expand circulation and attract new readers.[8] One project that would check both boxes was to distribute the magazine in areas of the nation that had limited access to books and magazines. In some states, particularly those with dispersed populations that were not congregated around a city center, library service was sparse. For example, in Oklahoma, Louisiana, Texas, New Mexico, Virginia, Idaho, Alabama, and Kentucky, more than 66 percent of the population had no library access.[9] Trautman had firsthand experience growing up in a small town and struggling to get reading material. He knew rural areas wanted books; they just didn't have the money, population, or means to get a library system built.[10]

Trautman looked upon his job to increase *Omnibook*'s circulation as an opportunity to reach those areas that needed reading materials the most. An *Omnibook* subscription in 1946 was $4 per year, or thirty-five cents per issue, and for that, a person received around sixty abridged books per year.[11] At this rate, practically anyone could start their own home library. But would rural communities subscribe? Turning to a place he knew well, he decided to use Mowrystown, Ohio, as a testing ground.

As Trautman worked out an approach, he thought of the National Youth Administration (NYA), a New Deal program that provided work to young Americans.[12] He recalled that the NYA had collaborated with the ALA to improve rural library service during the 1930s by distributing books to areas that lacked public libraries.[13] In some towns, NYA workers provided library service by bicycle. A NYA worker was assigned a route and visited every home to solicit book requests, then later would return to loan the desired titles usually obtained from a county library. Periodically, they would return to collect books and take new requests. It was a creative and successful program employing young people and providing library service to rural communities.[14] Could Trautman similarly hire young people in Mowrystown to go door to door and give away free copies of *Omnibook* and provide subscription information?[15] He ran the idea past a few marketing experts, but learned that *Coronet* magazine had tried something similar and it did not reap many new subscribers.[16] Based on this information, Trautman scrapped his youth employment idea and simply mailed free magazines, as he had done during the war.[17]

The other project Trautman worked on was expanding *Omnibook*'s international presence in parts of Europe.[18] The need for books and magazines was immense. Between bombings, arson, paper rationing, and censorship, the war had created a reading famine. European nations occupied by Nazi Germany had faced widescale destruction of books, libraries, and information. By 1945, it is estimated that the Nazis destroyed over 100 million books across Europe.[19] An October 1945 piece in *Publishers' Weekly* noted a "hunger for books in Europe, the hunger for our books and for British books, for any books from the countries which have had a free press, through the war, and could continue the production of the best output of its writers, its scientists and its thinkers."[20]

Publishers in Italy and Germany copied the ASE format and printed as many books as they could on limited supplies.[21] Recognizing the need for books, the US government and the Council on Books in Wartime worked to bring books to Europe. Each had a limited impact. Beginning in 1944, the Office of War Information produced ten titles in French under the imprint *Les Éditions Transatlantique*, including *America*, by Stephen Vincent Benét, *Benjamin Franklin*, by Carl van Doren, and *The Story of Dr. Wassell*, by James Hilton. Another ten titles were also produced in Dutch under the imprint *Uitgave 'Transatlantik'*.[22] Meanwhile, the Council on Books in Wartime produced "overseas editions," which were translations of American books, to serve areas of Europe that had been under Nazi occupation. In the end, however, only seventy-two titles were printed: twenty-two in English, twenty-two in French, twenty-three in German, and five in Italian.[23] There was much more work to do to get reading material to Europe.

There was no doubt in Trautman's mind that *Omnibook* could begin to fill this void. In late 1945, by arrangement with a printer in Stockholm, the first European edition of *Omnibook* rolled off the presses, containing three abridgements of popular American books. The first edition carried *A Tree Grows in Brooklyn*; Margaret Landon's 1944 fictionalized biography, *Anna and the King of Siam*; and Vicki Baum's 1943 novel *Hotel Berlin*, based on her escape from Nazi Germany.[24] Each month, an average of four new condensed books were included in each issue. Many Europeans were already familiar with the magazine thanks to American troops sharing their editions during the war. As one man living in Amsterdam wrote Trautman, "As long as the anglo-american troops were here I got your magazine regularly in my possession," and he was relieved that he could obtain the European edition now that the troops were gone.[25] This letter likely reminded Trautman of how much he enjoyed connecting books with readers. At *Omnibook*, it was rare to receive a letter like this one. During his years in the Army, each day brought a multitude of heartfelt letters from troops wishing to share their excitement about a book or magazine. Sitting at a desk and hatching schemes to build circulation was so distant from the work he loved most.

As Trautman began to wonder whether *Omnibook* was the right position for him, he received the unexpected news that he was being awarded the Legion of Merit, one of the highest honors the Army can confer, bestowed on those who "have distinguished themselves by exceptionally meritorious conduct in the performance of outstanding services."[26] General Joseph Byron, director of the Special Services Division during World War II, had recommended him.[27] In early 1946, Trautman received an engraved Legion of Merit Medal, along with this citation:

> Colonel Ray L. Trautman,... as Chief, Library Branch, Special Services Division, Army Service Forces, from November 1940 to November 1945, conceived, planned and organized the mass production of special light weight editions of books for distribution overseas and in Army hospitals within the United States. His achievements were a significant contribution to the maintenance of Army morale.[28]

Those who worked with Trautman felt that this recognition was more than well deserved.[29] It seemed only appropriate that the Army should acknowledge the man who, in the words of one newspaper, developed "the largest and most far-reaching publishing enterprise in history."[30]

This recognition only exacerbated the sense that he needed to do more for books and libraries. An opportunity came along when Brigadier General Russell B. Reynolds, the new chief of the Special Services Division, asked Trautman if he could help the Army Library Service with a potential budget crisis.[31] Reynolds explained that the proposed Army budget for 1947 (prepared in 1946) had eliminated funding for, among other things, salaries for library personnel.[32] Given Trautman's recent recognition for his library work, Reynolds hoped the former chief librarian could pull strings so that library service for occupation troops would not suffer. What Trautman said and did have been lost to time, but the Senate Appropriations Committee ultimately granted the Army Library Service the full funding it needed.[33] Reconnecting with the Army and the Library Branch made him nostalgic for his old job. Less than a year from being honorably discharged, Trautman applied to the Army Reserves. He would never be chief librarian again, but he could not resist staying involved.[34]

* * *

The Legion of Merit opened new doors to Trautman outside of the Army. As Milton Ferguson, the chief librarian of the Brooklyn Public Library, said in a letter, "Your efforts have made thousands of readers who will go freely into public libraries when they put on civilian clothes again."[35] Throughout 1946, public libraries and universities invited Trautman to advise them on how they could provide the same type of outstanding library service that he developed for troops in World War II.[36]

At a talk at the New York Public Library in February 1946, he suggested that librarians stop spending much of their time behind desks and glass barriers, and instead circulate among their patrons and discuss books with them. What made the Army Library Service so successful was its guiding principle to understand what a reader wanted and to connect them with the best book that fit their needs. With the Army, he faced millions of people who bragged about never having read a book in their lives. By making books easily accessible, providing a range of titles while prioritizing bestsellers and modern favorites, and keeping his finger on the pulse of reading habits by asking questions and talking with troops, Trautman had made books one of the most popular recreational offerings in the Army. He challenged librarians to do the same by creating libraries with an engaged staff who gave readers the books they wanted.[37]

Around the same time, Columbia University, his alma mater, invited Trautman to give a lecture to students enrolled in its School of Library Service.[38] On February 20, 1946, Trautman led a spirited discussion on his work with Army libraries and how books became a vital piece of equipment to millions of young men and women during the war. "Of course there were men who liked westerns and others who cared for Thomas Mann.... But it was more common for a serviceman to like both westerns and Thomas Mann," he admitted.[39] In his five years building the Army Library Service, one lesson was apparent to Trautman: The secret to stimulating an interest in reading was to connect people to books they'd truly enjoy.[40] With an estimated 15 percent increase in the size of the reading public since the war's end—based on book sales and library use—this new class of librarians could expect new challenges.[41]

At Columbia, Trautman championed the opportunities for civilian librarians to work at one of the hundreds of military libraries being established across Europe and the Pacific for occupation troops. The majority of his audience was female,[42] and Trautman noted that over 100 women librarians served in the European Theater in 1945, and that the Western Pacific was currently recruiting librarians to fill ninety-five positions.[43] For those wishing to explore the world, run their own small library, and be given an arena for creativity, nothing could compare to being an Army librarian. Trautman spoke with the genuine enthusiasm he felt about the work he was describing. His energy was contagious, his passion for reading and spreading the gift of books palpable. By all accounts, the audience left energized and inspired.

After his talk, Trautman was invited to have lunch with members of the Columbia faculty. Whether this had all been a test to see how well Trautman lectured and blended with academic life is unknown. He apparently made a favorable impression on Columbia, and teaching had made a favorable impression on Trautman. Carl White, the dean of the School of Library Service, was considering appointing Trautman to the faculty of its library school. At the time, White was developing an entirely new program for the School of Library Service, one that would strengthen the quality of instruction while also hiring new faculty to carry the school into the world of postwar librarianship.[44] Of the students expected to graduate in 1947, 106 were returning veterans (men and women), whose chief experience with libraries likely came from their years in the military.[45] Given the GI Bill, White expected hundreds of additional veterans to apply to the School of Library Service, in part because of the role books played in their lives while at war.[46] Trautman was an ideal candidate for a teaching job, but first White needed to build the new program he envisioned.

On July 24, 1947, Trautman and Jane welcomed their second child, Roger. While Trautman's salary at *Omnibook* made the expenses of a growing family manageable, he could not shake the feeling that what he wanted to do most was return to some form of library work. While he believed in the mission of *Omnibook*, he felt he had the capacity to make greater contributions than what one magazine afforded him.

When a letter from Columbia arrived in the spring of 1948, asking Trautman for his "reaction to a proposal to teach here, assuming that mutually agreeable arrangements could be reached as to rank and salary," Trautman was immediately tempted.[47] If he accepted, he would make about a third of his *Omnibook* salary,[48] but Dean White raised a salient point: "Positions at Columbia are conspicuous from the standpoint of the library profession, [and] this would be a good place for you to get back into the field."[49] As an academic, Trautman would have opportunities to research and write about pressing library needs and problems while proposing solutions. To teach the newest class of librarians—by taking them to libraries, exposing them to trailblazing role models, and using his experience—this was the type of hands-on work in which Trautman could thrive. He could make a real difference. Plus, an academic schedule would enable him to go on temporary active duty with the Army Reserve during the summer and continue to make an impact on the library program for troops. Teaching would allow him to get out from behind his desk and get his boots on the ground again. Trautman accepted.[50]

In July 1948, Dwight Eisenhower, now president of Columbia University, personally announced to the *New York Times* that Trautman would be teaching at Columbia after having "built the Army's library service into one of the world's largest publishing ventures."[51] The last time Trautman and Eisenhower had worked closely together was in the ETO when Eisenhower unwittingly sent Trautman into the Battle of the Bulge. These were rather more staid circumstances.

When Trautman's appointment to Columbia became public, many who knew him breathed a collective sigh of relief that he was returning to librarianship.[52] Warm letters came from leading executives across the publishing world, including Harcourt, Brace & Co., Farrar Straus, *Esquire* magazine, the American News Company, and *Newsweek*.[53] Many of them admired Trautman. Gibson McCabe, who became publisher of *Newsweek* after working with Trautman in producing the "Battle Baby" edition for troops during the war, wrote:[54] "I just heard of your change to become a black-garbed gentleman, and I presume that I am somewhat presuming in addressing you as Trautman. From here on in I guess I better get formal and say 'Dear Professor.' Then I can shine in reflected glory when I say 'I was talking to a friend of mine, a professor at Columbia, the other day...' and thereby lend stature to my remarks."[55]

Even those at *Omnibook* felt the move was a good one. As Victor Knauth, a part-owner of *Omnibook* and its treasurer, said: "You can imagine my delight... about your appointment at Columbia. It is... perfect and I congratulate you."[56]

# 13

# Back into the Field

> A library is more than books, stacks, indices and audits. It is a living thing, a dynamic social agency which reaches millions of persons, and profoundly influences the lives they lead.
>
> —Lt. Col. William A. Bishop, Chief of the Army Recreational Service[1]

As Trautman prepared for the classroom, he acknowledged that the Army Library Service of World War II had been an outlier. It was hard to imagine how or when a librarian would again be tasked with taking a fledgling, underfinanced system and building it into a global service that distributed tens of millions of books and magazines per month. What his students would most likely encounter were public libraries in their home or adopted community; those who patronized them were not facing life-or-death situations. *These* were the libraries that Trautman needed to grasp. And to do that, he turned to his local library. Living in Bronxville, a village measuring only one square mile—though "the finest square mile in the country" according to residents[2]—Trautman frequented the nearby Yonkers Public Library (YPL). In the late 1940s, Trautman joined the library's board of trustees and immediately was captivated by the challenges of maximizing the library's potential.[3]

One of the main problems facing the YPL was that it served a sprawling community, and its branches were often too far from people's homes. Beginning in 1930, it had attempted to ameliorate this situation by using a bookmobile—the first bookmobile in Westchester County, and the eleventh in the nation[4]—to bring, as one local newspaper put it, "mental nourishment to the outlying sections of Yonkers."[5] It was instantly popular. According to the article, "the number of children sitting on fences and on curbs, of adults pacing under the trees with an armful of books awaiting the arrival of the Yonkers Bookmobile is daily increasing." This experiment in mobile library service demonstrated how people desperately wanted books. "I've been worrying about you all afternoon," an eight-year-old exclaimed to the bookmobile's librarian as this young reader exchanged her last book for a new one.[6] With the bookmobile, the number of card-carrying book borrowers increased, as did circulation rates.

As the population of Yonkers climbed during the 1940s—it was affordable and an easy train ride into Grand Central Station—the bookmobile library service couldn't keep up with the demand.[7] What the YPL needed were more physical locations to supplement the work of the bookmobile, but there was no budget to purchase new buildings. Doing some digging, Trautman discovered that during the 1930s, the YPL had installed a small borrowing library at an office of the Otis Elevator Company to serve residents who lived too far from the main branch; it even had a full-time librarian whose salary was funded by the federal government's Works Progress Administration (WPA). However, when the WPA ended in the early 1940s, so did the Otis Elevator library branch. Trautman favored the idea of setting up small libraries in commercial buildings and wanted to see if he could revive this tradition without WPA funding.[8] With Trautman's encouragement, by late 1948 the YPL was negotiating the development of a small library book collection and deposit point inside the local Refined Syrups and Sugars plant. Meanwhile, Trautman investigated what neighborhoods in Yonkers needed better library access and whether any nearby commercial buildings would be willing to donate space for a recreational library.[9] In this way, a constellation of small libraries could be established across Yonkers without the expense of purchasing official library building space.

Since staffing seemed to be the main reason the Otis Elevator library outpost was closed, Trautman hatched an idea that might infuse the

YPL with more helpers. Remembering the days when he struggled to pay his tuition to study library science at Columbia, he proposed starting a fellowship program at the YPL so that aspiring librarians would be able to earn money and gain hands-on experience as they matriculated.[10] As a trustee, he was learning about the challenges a public library faced and believed the YPL could provide his students valuable experience—whether it was taking a shift driving the bookmobile, staffing a new satellite branch inside a commercial building, or working within the main library and interacting with readers.

Likely the most gratifying change that Trautman brought about in his first year as library trustee was nudging the YPL away from its exclusive use of hardcovers. Whether on the finite shelf space in its bookmobile, or in makeshift branch libraries in commercial buildings, the size of books would dictate how many could be made available. With the burgeoning paperback market—in major part due to his ASEs—it was possible to take advantage of their smaller format. The YPL had yet to break with tradition. This changed in November 1948, when the first forty-three paperbacks were added to the YPL's shelves; they disappeared swiftly. Trautman offered to donate paperbacks to supplement the library's holdings; the YPL's librarian immediately accepted.[11] The library's receptivity to paperbacks would come in handy. In December 1948, the YPL learned its budget had been cut by 5 percent, which would ordinarily require a reduction in acquisitions.[12] By purchasing paperbacks, which still cost a fraction of a hardcover, the library kept readers awash in new books despite a diminished budget.

Though he had gone from operating the largest library system on earth to acting as an advisor for his local library, Trautman's work as a YPL trustee invigorated him. He loved dealing with the everyday problems of a typical public library, sleuthing for creative solutions, and being involved in the minutiae of how to maximize a community's exposure to library books. He knew that when people had access to books, and there was a motivated librarian to guide them, a lifelong reader could be made. And that's what the work was all about.

* * *

During his first years at Columbia, Trautman taught a staple course to first-year students, Foundations of Librarianship, which surveyed the history of library development, techniques for the mass dissemination of information, book and magazine publishing, and incorporating technology into library work.[13] He also supervised "field projects," which were essentially independent studies that required each student to observe and research a particular library or practice and develop a paper about their findings.[14]

When summer arrived, Trautman went on active duty with the Army as a reserve officer. For the first few years in this role, Trautman was tasked with writing job descriptions for positions in the Army Library Service and writing performance evaluations.[15] Though he could have balked at performing such comparatively lowly administrative tasks, Trautman never looked at his work this way. Wherever his assistance was needed, he was glad to go.

To this end, in 1950 and 1951, Lt. Col. William A. Bishop, chief of the Army Recreational Service, assigned Trautman to investigate the cause of complaints about library service at Army installations up and down the West Coast. Bishop knew Trautman would give an objective appraisal and could distinguish between someone doing a bad job and someone struggling against the usual challenges.

Among the individuals Trautman needed to assess was the recently appointed chief librarian, Mildred Young, the first woman to occupy the Army Library Service's top role. After observing Young, conducting interviews, and inspecting operations he knew like the back of his hand, he reported that this choice of leader was "highly commendable." Trautman explained, "The director of the Army Library Service requires a specialized educational background plus several years of varied professional experience prior to Army Service."[16] Mildred Young (or Milly, as her friends called her), held a bachelor's degree from Huntingdon College in Alabama and a degree in library science from the University of North Carolina. From there, she sampled a variety of library work, first starting as a librarian in Chapel Hill, then as a high school librarian. After the United States declared war, she became a post librarian at

Camp Butner in North Carolina—a position where she distinguished herself for her skill and savvy. Young kept her library buzzing with popular books and commanded the help of the local Red Cross to host book drives when her Army book-buying budget fell short of troops' needs.[17] With the declaration of peace in 1945, she left Camp Butner and moved to New York, where she served as a book selector in the chief operations section of the Army Library Service until 1948.[18] After six years of Army library work, she earned the position of chief librarian and an office within the Adjutant General's wing of the Pentagon.[19]

Having crossed paths a few times during Young's Army career—they both attended an Army Library conference in Atlanta in 1943,[20] and briefly worked from the Army Library Service's New York City office in 1945—Trautman was aware of her reputation. Still, he was not one to play favorites or embellish. He just couldn't find anything to criticize. "You have in th[is] . . . Army Librarian . . . that essential combination of excellent Army library experience, good background, pleasing personality and a real interest in the mission of Special Services," he wrote in his formal evaluation of Young.[21] According to Trautman, the main problems the Army Library Service faced, as Bishop was "doubtless aware," was its insufficient funding and the attitudes of some high-ranking officers who minimized the importance of libraries.[22]

However, Young was a force. Early in her tenure, she went on a seventy-day tour of Army libraries overseas—surveying posts in Guam, Japan, and the Philippines—to observe how well they were functioning and collect the observations of the women librarians running them.[23] From Washington, she launched projects that Trautman's inner circle of librarians had devised during the war but were unable to execute. For starters, Young managed to gain approval for an official Army short story contest. While Trautman had been in Europe from October 1944 to January 1945—the Bulge trip—publishers had complained there was a shortage of modern titles to print as ASEs, and the Army Library Service's office in New York had proposed creating a short story competition so troops could submit their own work for publication in special ASE volumes.[24] Though Trautman favored the project, he struggled to obtain official approval for such a program. As chief librarian, Young also believed there was merit to the idea, and she managed to win the support of Army Chief of Staff Omar Bradley. In 1949, a War Department circular announced a short story contest for troops; those judged to have written the best stories would win cash prizes and see their work published in *Collier's Weekly* magazine and in a book produced by Rinehart and Company.[25] When the Army's official announcement of the contest was distributed, Young mailed a copy to Trautman with a note: "Dear Chief—I thought you might be interested in this new project of ours."[26] (For years, many Army librarians never dropped the habit of referring to Trautman as "Chief."[27]) Trautman was amazed that the idea had come to life.

A second initiative that Young undertook involved insignia. During World War II, Army librarians and Army hostesses wore the same patch—a semicircle of colorful panels that almost looked like an open book with its fanned pages edged in different colors. But librarians had to meet onerous educational qualifications—including an advanced degree in library service—and often had to have professional experience. This made their specialty quite different from that of Army hostesses.[28] While Army librarians performed technical work only within the Army Library branch, Army hostesses fulfilled a much broader mission of overseeing "a well-balanced program of off-duty [recreational] activities," including sports, live shows, crafts, and reading.[29] To be sure, both fulfilled critical morale work during the war, but many librarians felt they deserved their own insignia for their distinct and specialized jobs—just as men in the military had their own unit, division, or specialization patches.[30] Meanwhile, Army hostesses felt the term "hostess" suggested they were entertainers, chaperones, dates, or a number of other things they were not.[31] During Young's tenure, the Army Library Service was granted new insignia: a square white patch with blue lettering that read "Army Library Service."[32] In 1951, the term "Army Hostess" was replaced with "Army Service Club Director Personnel," and a blue-and-white patch reading "Army Service Club" became the official insignia for service club workers.[33] These distinct patches were badges of honor to those who wore them. Rather than have librarians and service club directors lumped together under a single insignia, apparently because both specialties were dominated by women, those who served in these unique roles felt their new patches provided a measure of dignity that they had previously been denied.

While he provided deserved praise for the job Young was doing as chief librarian, Trautman had saltier words to describe the conditions he observed on a tour of the libraries in the Sixth Army Headquarters—spread out on the West Coast, from California to Washington State.[34] He determined that the Sixth Army's chief of Special Services, a colonel, was responsible for violating Army regulations, reallocating library funding to other recreational activities that he preferred, and downgrading library positions so that credentialed staff would be paid less than they were supposed to earn. This colonel was also threatening to replace professional librarians with service club directors. According to Trautman, this colonel was "obsessed by three things listed in order of obsession: (a) Women (b) Pistol and rifle shooting to which he devoted half his time. . . . (c) Service Club directors—possibly part of (a) above." He recommended that this colonel be removed from his post because he was destroying both the library program in the Sixth Corps Area and morale. Trautman called a meeting and read his findings in the colonel's presence. When the colonel "tried to brush off my opinions . . . and indicated that he planned to make no changes," Trautman "thanked him for his time . . . and said that I had no choice but to turn in an adverse report."[35] After filing his report, Trautman was asked if he could soften his evaluation, and refused.[36] His recommendation of removal was sound.

Trautman's experience with the colonel was a sign of a larger problem: There were still plenty of people in the Army who demeaned books and believed troops had no interest in them. Immune to data and prejudiced by their own feelings, officers with an aversion for books—who failed to see reading as a part of military culture—had the power to strangle library service and override the professional expertise of Army librarians. There were too many examples to ignore. Fort Ord's library contained very little nonfiction because the Special Services officer in charge "doesn't believe in non-fiction," as Trautman wrote in his report.[37] At Camp Stoneman, California, under the pretense of budgeting, the librarian was allotted $50 per month to buy books for two separate libraries and her salary was slashed; at the same time, no one batted an eyelash when it came to approving a new $650,000 service club.[38]

Trautman was frustrated by these and many other examples of libraries being shortchanged. World War II had ended only a few years earlier, yet many military personnel had already forgotten how crucial books and magazines had been for millions of troops. Polls continued to show that most soldiers preferred entertainment that afforded them privacy and solitude rather than more time with those with whom they had marched, drilled, and cursed all day.

It was obvious to Trautman that the Army needed to recalibrate how it viewed entertainment and recreation, and someone needed to educate the new class of officers entering the Special Services Division about the critical role that libraries played in boosting and maintaining morale.

# 14

# New Frontiers

> What greater bulwark is there for democracy than a well-read, well-informed citizenry?
>
> —Rep. Kenneth Roberts,[1]

What do you get when you take a chaplain, private detective, police officer, magazine editor, traffic engineer, radio manager, movie executive, television director, social worker, lawyer, famous baritone (Edward Ansara), Broadway stage manager (James Wicker), nightclub comedian, television writer, advertising production manager, opera impresario and theater manager (Felix Salmaggi), band leader, conductor and composer (John Kander), and two librarians?[2] Ray Trautman's new Army outfit.

After he finished his academic responsibilities at Columbia in 1953, Trautman went on active duty with the Army, taking command of the 8970th Special Service Unit,[3] which was headquartered in Midtown Manhattan.[4] Since visiting the Sixth Army's installations on the West Coast and observing firsthand how some Special Services officers seemed to underestimate the value of books and libraries in favor of flashier entertainment, Trautman viewed the 8970th as a way to rectify matters. He set the tone. While this specialized force's mission was to train morale directors in the range of activities the Army offered—sports, music, movies, theater, and libraries—Trautman aimed to ensure that books would not be lost in this crowd of amusements. "Our job is to give them a curriculum that is important enough, and train them so well," he said, that the role of libraries in Special Services work—though one branch of many—would not be ignored. With the Korean War recently ended—in July 1953, just before Trautman began his work with the 8970th—large-scale programming was disfavored. Instead, the Army needed experts trained to provide small outposts "with a movie projector, a small library, and some recorded or live music."[5] Meeting forty-eight times per year, plus undergoing fifteen days of field training during the summer, Trautman shaped his kaleidoscope of specialists into a dynamic team.[6]

Described by an Army newspaper as the "only unit of its kind in either the Regular Army or the Army Reserve," nothing was ordinary about Trautman's battery of irregulars. For most Army units, a typical military field exercise might simulate battle conditions; troops would pursue an objective wearing a fifty-pound pack while crawling through mud under a canopy of barbed wire, bullets sailing a few feet above their heads, live grenades detonating, and TNT bursts punctuating the chaos.[7] The 8970th also faced multiple-day field exercises, but their mission was to maneuver recreational equipment—like crates of books and small musical instruments—across challenging terrain to deliver a morale boost to even the most remote locations.[8] They were trained in operating movie projectors, hosting theater programs, setting up stationary libraries, and organizing GI bands. They also underwent periods of intense classroom study and lecture, learning about the inner workings of all the recreational offerings, as well as supply procedures and administration.[9]

At the end of the unit's inaugural training cycle, Trautman expressed his gratitude to the group by handing each member a newly minted silver dollar. According to a local newspaper, "The colonel felt that the large and heavy coins would be tangible reminders to the men of his unit and their families of the 'weight of their responsibilities as Reservists,' and of the cost to the American taxpayer for their training."[10]

Trautman served in this role for several years, earning glowing evaluations. As the chief of the Special Services Division stated in a 1958 performance review: "This officer approaches his assignments with interest and enthusiasm and is able to apply good judgement and common sense to the solution of problems. His personal habits and code of ethics are beyond reproach." Although the chief recommended a promotion, Trautman himself waged a private campaign against it, worried that it would remove him from "front-line" training and wedge him behind a desk doing administrative work. He was content as a colonel who trained the most unusual unit in the Army.[11]

* * *

As a professor, Trautman was expected not only to teach but also to produce scholarship or make contributions to the field of library science through research or field studies.[12] In 1954, he published a book-length work on the history of the School of Library Service; it would be Trautman's only sole-author work.[13] In the 1960s, he coauthored a Spanish–English dictionary for library workers, the *Technical Dictionary of Librarianship* (*Diccionario Técnico de Biblioteconomía*), supplying English definitions for 3,000 technical library terms.[14] These projects only confirmed to Trautman that publishing books did not excite him. He instead gravitated toward projects that would allow him to investigate shortcomings in library service and develop practical solutions to increase book and library usage.

His first large-scale project involved a study of the library needs in the territory—and eventually state—of Alaska. This topic first crossed Trautman's path when he had been invited to attend the Army's March 1949 first global conference of command librarians. Hundreds of military librarians descended upon Washington, DC, to discuss the challenges and results they achieved in their unique stations.[15] When Mildred Hammond, the command librarian for Alaska, discussed her travails in founding Army libraries in one of the most rugged and unforgiving environments outside of a war zone, Trautman's ears perked up. When he had served as chief librarian, there were no Army libraries established in Alaska, and so he was unfamiliar with the discrete problems Alaska posed. Hammond detailed typical issues—shortage of library space, not enough books, and a ridiculously small budget. Making matters worse, Hammond confided that it was an exercise in "persistence" to convince some officers that many GIs liked to read, and not spend all their free time "drinking beer, or going to movies."

"Alaska is the last frontier," Hammond had declared. Twice the size of Texas, Alaska's population was spread thinly across thousands of miles of mountains, forests, and islands. "Where towns exist, they are small. Recreational facilities are extremely limited," she said. Alaska's beauty was matched by its challenges, and Hammond believed that more and better libraries were desperately needed—and not just for the Army.[16] By the time she had finished speaking, Trautman had determined to develop a plan for meaningful library service.

Not until Alaska approached statehood in the late 1950s did Trautman find an opportunity to conduct this study. In 1955, a piece of legislation known as the Library Services Bill was being considered by Congress. It would provide federal funding for the extension of public library services into rural areas—meaning any incorporated or unincorporated town with a population of less than 10,000 people.[17] Under the bill, each state could submit a library plan to the commissioner of education, and, if approved, would receive $40,000 per year for five years to spend on projects that would launch or improve free libraries in rural communities.[18] Although Alaska would not become a state until 1959, it was included under this bill.[19] This investment in libraries made Trautman think that new solutions to Alaska's library needs might be welcomed and implemented. He eagerly tracked the progress of the bill.

During congressional proceedings over the spring of 1955, a bleak picture emerged of libraries in the United States.[20] Legislators from Idaho, North Dakota, South Dakota, Mississippi, and West Virginia described how over half their constituents lacked public libraries; and in Nevada, Nebraska, Kansas, Oklahoma, Alabama, Kentucky, Florida, Virginia, and Maine, between one-third and one-half of each state's residents lacked library access.[21] Representatives from state after state explained that low-population areas suffered from a shortage of funding—not a deficit of desire—for libraries. Many re-employed the World War II argument that access to books and ideas was essential to maintaining democracy. "Every citizen should have access to the information a library affords," and "an informed citizenry is one of our best bulwarks of freedom and libraries serve a vital function in this area," Representative Griffiths of Michigan stated.[22]

Alabama Representative Carl Elliott, one of the bill's sponsors, laid out his case for why the federal government needed to invest in rural libraries. In Alabama, nearly one-third of the population had no access to public libraries, and another one-third had inadequate service. "Books, plus an effective means of getting them to the people, are desperately needed," Elliott said. For the price of a pack of chewing gum for each person in the United States, good library service could be provided nationwide. The expense was negligible, yet the cost of inaction was severe. "Life's first danger is an empty mind," argued Elliott. And while people across the United States were "prone to say, 'We live in the strongest nation on earth; we are building houses at the fastest rate in history; we own more automobiles than any other people,' we must not forget that man builds no structure which outlives a book."[23] After Elliott's speech, a number of representatives from other states spoke of nearly identical problems and favored universal library service, believing that every citizen should have an equal chance to enjoy books, improve their minds, and learn.[24] Many members of Congress had come to understand what Trautman knew all along: Libraries democratize information and opportunity.

As the Library Services Bill moved through Congress, Trautman prepared to take a sabbatical from his teaching responsibilities at Columbia in 1956 and planned to spend it conducting a study on rural library service, with a focus on Alaska. He began by making inquiries of Alaskan librarians and government officials to see if they were interested.[25] Practically everyone Trautman contacted—including the governor of Alaska, the president of the University of Alaska, government officials in Washington, the Territorial Library Board in Juneau, and Army friends who had Alaskan connections—favored his undertaking a study.[26] In 1956, Trautman flew to Juneau, where territorial librarian Dorothy Phelps provided a workspace at the newly opened Alaska Department of

Library Service.[27] Phelps was an energetic librarian, driven to meet the vast library needs of the territory.[28]

Though the records of Trautman's trip have not survived, the ways in which Alaskan library service expanded afterward bear his mark. When Alaska began receiving congressional funding under the Library Services Act for the 1958 fiscal year, the Alaska Department of Library Service immediately strengthened its presence in communities that had never seen a library book. To do this, Phelps turned to the mail (just as Trautman had done during World War II). Phelps did not initially mail library books; she boarded the mailboat—called *Expansion*—with crates of books and traveled across the Aleutian-Kodiak area, spending time at each port where there was a mail delivery so that she could establish contacts with locals and gather information for future efforts. As a result of this trip, 146 makeshift libraries were established. These unconventional branches were run by volunteers who housed and cared for the book collection provided by Phelps. They tracked book borrowing and returns, and they arranged with Phelps to periodically swap one compilation of books for another. As news spread about the provision of free library books, more outposts were established.[29]

Another mark was the creation of a library youth program. Borrowing ideas that were prevalent during the 1930s with the CCC and the National Youth Administration, students across rural communities in Alaska were offered extra-curricular credits for their help administering their community library program.[30] In this way, staffing issues could be alleviated, community members were given direct involvement in the functioning of their public library, and young people could begin developing an interest in books. When Wilfred Morin, a library extension specialist in the Library Services Branch of the US Department of Education, visited Alaska in 1958, he was heartened to see what a difference books made to these rural communities. "Through books," Morin wrote in a report, rural communities were not "so isolated.... The entire world is just within reach." "The books now come to them, bright in their plastic jackets, in the small, easily handled boxes, along with the fruit, vegetables, meat and livestock. Food and recreation for the body and for the mind... come along now on the *Expansion*."[31]

* * *

Trautman devoted himself to an array of library activities throughout the 1950s. Between his Army Reserve work, teaching at Columbia, writing a book, volunteering as a trustee for the Yonkers Public Library, and conducting a study of Alaska's library needs, he found he needed a place where he could clear his mind. He turned to a weekend retreat in the village of Greenville, located in Upstate New York, near the Hudson Valley. It consisted of a rustic farmhouse that had no electricity and hundreds of pristine acres surrounding it.

Beginning in the early 1950s, the Trautman family would pile into their car and drive north from Bronxville until they arrived at a small general store in Livingstonville, where they would buy kerosene, food, and other necessities. They drove to their land, parked their car on the side of the road (there was no driveway), and then hiked up a small mountain to reach the farmhouse. In the winter, Trautman left a toboggan at the foot of his land and loaded it with the family's supplies for the weekend. Then he would pull it up the long hill, often letting Eric and Roger (at least when they were smaller) hitch a ride. Trautman would make sure the coal oven in the cellar had a roaring fire, and their little homestead would turn into a cozy getaway from the winter chill. Always keeping busy, Trautman loved splitting firewood, and he always carried his double-bit axe with him anytime he was outside. When it was time to return home, the family would either hike to their car or take the toboggan back down the hill, where they would leave it tucked in the brush for their next trip. The whole experience brought Trautman back to his childhood—tending to the family farm, exploring the woods and streams in Mowrystown, Ohio. They were simpler times.[32]

As the years passed, Trautman revived some of the conservation projects from his years with the CCC. Expanding his property to embrace approximately 1,500 acres of woodland, he put in ponds, planted a garden, and tried to be a good steward of the land.[33] When he learned that

Rensselaer County, which neighbored his property, was undertaking a project to plant 63,000 trees provided by the State of New York Conservation Department, he wanted to be part of this concerted effort to reforest the area. According to the newspaper, residents who enrolled under the New York State Forest Practices Act could secure thousands of free trees and could even request the help of a forester to plant them.[34] Trautman immediately contacted the New York State Conservation Department to register and order seedlings for his property. Unable to wait for his registration to be approved, Trautman purchased 2,500 red pine seedlings, along with 2,500 white spruce trees, to plant across his land.[35] When Trautman received his official designation as a New York State tree farmer, he proudly displayed signs on his property to advertise his conservation work and inspire others to do the same.[36] This work was so important to him that Trautman even added "tree farmer" to his biography in *Who's Who*, placing it on equal footing with being a professor at Columbia University, colonel in the Army, and recipient of the Legion of Merit.[37]

Spending time in the countryside seemed to revive Trautman, and Jane loved the quiet and serenity. For decades, Jane had supported his career in more ways than he could possibly repay her. She played the part of a colonel's wife, raised their children as Trautman was absent on Army and library business, and understood Trautman's relentless passion to spread books and libraries into the farthest reaches of the world. Knowing how much she craved the countryside, Trautman wanted to give Jane the life she wanted. In 1957, they made the decision to make their permanent home in Greenville, New York, selling their house in Bronxville. Eric and Roger attended the Greenville public schools, Jane gardened and read, and Trautman commuted to New York when teaching at Columbia, living in an apartment near campus a few days each week.[38] For decades, Trautman escaped to this land—caring for it while savoring its peacefulness. Even as he advanced in age, these woodlands kept him spry; Trautman was known to walk for miles at a steady clip.[39] Visitors had a hard time keeping up with him.

* * *

As the 1950s came to a close, Trautman experienced several changes, small and large. In 1958, he resigned as trustee of the Yonkers Public Library, wishing to spend more of his time in Greenville while also committing his limited time to tackling more pressing book and library projects. He left the YPL knowing it had a dedicated group of trustees and librarians who would continue to reach new and established readers.[40]

The biggest adjustment came when Trautman received official notice that he had completed the allotted period of commissioned service and was required by law to either transfer to the Retired Reserve or request discharge from the Army.[41] Having recently been awarded the New York State Conspicuous Service Cross for his outstanding work in the US Army,[42] Trautman felt he still had more to contribute. He wrote directly to General G. H. Decker, the Army chief of staff, to request continued active engagement with the 8970th and in performing the Army library work he so loved. Trautman knew Decker well, for they had crossed paths at Fort Thomas in Kentucky when Trautman had been an educational adviser with the CCC in the late 1930s.[43] Decker replied to Trautman, noting that his time at Fort Thomas was "one of my most pleasant and rewarding assignments" and that he appreciated Trautman's warm words about his promotion to chief of staff. Nevertheless, Decker could not convey the news Trautman wanted to hear. Retirement was not meant to represent a "divorce…from the Army or its activities," Decker said. Rather, he hoped Trautman would "maintain a lively interest in the Army and its activities for the civilian communities."[44]

Trautman, however, had no interest in building ties between the Army and the community. His service had always been devoted to reading and libraries. If the Army—in which he had served for over three decades in various capacities—no longer had a place for him involving these things, he would look elsewhere.

Though he would rarely, if ever, wear them after his official retirement in 1961, for the rest of his life Trautman kept his heavy Army overcoat, Eisenhower jacket, service cap, and perfectly pressed dress uniform always at the ready.

# 15

# The Forgotten Readers

> From [those books], Roderick Rando, Peregrine Pickle, Humphrey Clinker, Tom Jones, the Vicar of Wakefield, Don Quixote, Gil Blas, and Robinson Crusoe, came out, a glorious host, to keep me company. They kept alive my fancy, and my hope of something beyond that place and time."
>
> —Charles Dickens, *David Copperfield*[1]

Following his retirement from the Army, Trautman wanted to dedicate himself to making a lasting impression in the library world. He had devoted years to projects that connected people to improved access to books. While the Library Services Bill helped bolster rural library service, there were other communities left in the literary dark: patients in mental health clinics, the imprisoned, adults with limited reading proficiency, and the sight impaired and blind. What were their needs, and how could books make a difference in their lives? For the next decade, Trautman pursued research projects delving into these communities so that he could understand them, and their reading habits, better. He prepared reports, ran experiments, and published his findings. Taking all that he had learned, he created a new course in the field of library science devoted to these "forgotten people."[2] If his students became sensitive to communities not ordinarily considered by libraries and librarians, they could guide the future.

In 1961, Trautman requested administrative approval from Columbia to develop a course he dubbed Institutional Libraries. Field studies would fuel the content. He planned to use his sabbatical in the fall of

1962 to begin to study what role books could play in clinics and prisons.[3] While society might write off some groups as lost causes, Trautman, for one, would not. He had experience in people underestimating his capabilities. Adversity, he knew, could make or break a person; if people had access to the right tools to work through it, Trautman believed they could come out on top. Books were those tools. But they had to be at hand, and any barriers needed to be broken.

What began as a basic idea would evolve into four major projects that formed the basis for a course and curriculum that opened eyes.

* * *

Trautman got a lucky break in 1961 when Stefan B. Moses, of the New York State Library, was asked to recommend a librarian who would be able to assist the Menninger Foundation in building libraries for its staff and patients. Moses insisted that Trautman would be the right person for the job.[4] Trautman was soon invited to the Menninger Foundation's campus in Topeka, Kansas, to tour its library facilities, meet with staff and librarians, and create a proposal for the rapid expansion of the foundation's libraries and holdings.[5]

The Menninger Foundation was founded in 1919 as a small, family-run psychiatry practice housed in a Kansas farmhouse. By the 1960s it had grown to an internationally renowned facility where patients were treated, students obtained professional training, and clinicians and experts conducted psychiatry research.[6] Karl Menninger had spent decades developing theories on how positive environmental changes (for Trautman, this obviously involved access to books) could yield benefits to those with poor mental or emotional health, as well as prisoners and neglected children.[7] Menninger's first book, *The Human Mind*, published in 1930, attracted an audience of laypeople by describing mental wellness in easy-to-understand terms and normalizing the fact that everyone faces difficulties. *The Human Mind* compared life to fishing, and how a fish hooked on a line had to fight to become free; but sometimes the strife became "too tough," and the fish became stuck. Similarly, he said, a person "struggles with his environment," and the hooks that "catch him." Some can figure out how to get unhooked; others simply can't. "His struggles are all that the world sees and it usually misunderstands them. It is hard for a free fish to understand what is happening to a hooked one." With help, Menninger believed, anyone could be freed.[8] Menninger's philosophy was that the key to becoming "unhooked" was to discover useful things to do and build.[9] The discovery of future potential could be sparked by anything—such as a conversation with "an attendant, or a gardener, or a maid, or a nurse." Psychiatry simply tried to direct a person toward that light.[10]

Menninger's philosophy resonated with Trautman, who developed a deeper recognition that, in many settings, people can't control their environment and have difficulty finding rays of hope. For those feeling trapped—whether that be in the form of a lengthy hospitalization, a substantial prison term, an inability to read and comprehend—Trautman believed—as he always had—that the right books could help open new worlds of possibility. Stories usher readers into new environments, and they return to their own circumstances with fresh perspectives. They could find means to heal, reconstruct their lives, and kindle a sense of purpose. Trautman had already experimented with some of these ideas when applying "bibliotherapy" in military hospital libraries during World War II. He was inspired to apply these ideas in other spaces.[11]

Trautman spent over two years as a consultant for the Menninger Foundation, developing its libraries as well as his own theories on the restorative qualities of books. By the end of his study, he had earned the admiration and gratitude of Karl Menninger.[12] Though they practiced different disciplines, they shared similar philosophies and harbored the same sympathies. An "omnivorous reader" himself, Menninger knew firsthand what power books had.[13]

* * *

With his study of the Menninger Foundation completed, Trautman had material for one unit of his course. He next turned to a population that was used to having "the book thrown at them." Trautman wanted books handed to them.

Even before he left the Menninger Foundation, Trautman began to develop ideas for his next project, involving America's prisons. Both he and Karl Menninger were interested in reconsidering what prisons could do, and both felt that opportunities for rehabilitation and healing were largely ignored.[14] To understand the problem fully, Trautman needed to go inside. Partnering with New York State, he examined the condition of prison libraries and developed guidelines to maximize their potential.

Trautman was persuaded that prisoners, and society at large, would benefit if incarceration provided opportunities for rehabilitation, enabling inmates to develop positive habits and skills that would continue to serve them after release. Many correctional facilities mainly served a custodial function; he was interested in exploring how prison libraries could do more.[15] He discovered that most prison library shelves were lined with musty tomes of donated, and unread, titles. These were mere gestures of a library. No effort was being made to provide books that would actually be useful. Trautman was troubled by the message this sent to prisoners: castoff books for people cast off by society.

From 1963 to 1964, Trautman investigated and prepared his findings and recommendations, which were consolidated into a 124-page guide, *A Plan to Provide Library Service to People in New York State Institutions*. Much of its focus was on providing quality books that would best serve the varied purposes and needs of the prisoners. Outdated books had to go. Acquisition policy should prioritize modern titles and popular periodicals, and an array of reading materials needed to meet all reading levels. Understanding that most prisoners would come to the library to find a source of escape, help, or self-study, it recommended that reading materials generally serve one or more of these functions: "recreation, information, social adjustment, mental health, job information, vocational training, and education."[16]

*A Plan to Provide Library Service* did no good unless it was implemented. After battling for funding, in 1967 Trautman secured a budget to create a model library at the Auburn State Prison, a maximum-security facility with 1,700 inmates, situated between Syracuse and Rochester.[17] The oldest prison facility in the state, Auburn was infamous for, as one newspaper account had it, a storied history in "escapes, bloody riots and forced labor." Its first prisoner uprising occurred in 1821 when inmates tarred and feathered a guard. Later years were marked by deadly brawls, arson, and daring jailbreaks.[18] Auburn's warden, J. Edwin LaVallee, nonetheless took a progressive approach to incarceration and trailblazed educational coursework so inmates could improve their minds and post-release job prospects.[19] When Trautman came aboard, half of all prisoners at Auburn were enrolled in classes. Admittedly biased, he believed the library could one-up the educational programming because a library could provide learning opportunities to *all* of Auburn's residents.

Trautman from childhood had embraced the adage, the "footstep of the farmer is the best fertilizer." Only by observing the conditions himself, and understanding the needs and people being served, could he formulate a plan and response.[20] He toured every nook of the facility—from cells to the exercise yard—as well as Auburn's two libraries: the School and Technical Library for those enrolled in coursework, and the Main Library, which was open to all. He circulated among prisoners and talked with them. He learned that inmates were interested in books, but that it wasn't easy to borrow the few titles worth the effort.

The School and Technical Library was so inefficient that it would be difficult to devise worse operating guidelines. An inmate had to follow eight detailed steps to borrow a book. "It is a wonder any inmate ever gets a book which he wants and needs," Trautman lamented. Inmates were not allowed to walk among the bookshelves to peruse titles or handle books inside the library. An inmate was permitted to enter the library to submit book borrowing paperwork to a staff member, and if the desired book was available, the inmate might walk out with it. Rather than offer the opportunity for exploration, prisoners were bound by mechanical procedures that distanced them from engaging with the full range of reading materials available. "Allow students (for the first time) to come to the library to browse, select their own books from the shelves, sit, study, consult reference books, and obtain information and guidance from the librarian," Trautman advised.

As for the Main Library, Trautman was shocked to learn that it was open for only ninety minutes each day: "45 minutes at noon and 45 minutes at supper." In addition, it consisted of books that were "gifts and cast-offs," and it was inconveniently located. As he browsed the selection, Trautman saw few titles that would stir any excitement. An inmate would have to hunt for the hidden library, arrive during the limited hours of operation, and quickly search for a figurative needle in a haystack if he wanted something tempting to read.

All of it needed to change. Trautman recommended the Main Library be moved to the centrally located recreation yard, and that operating hours extend to the "maximum time inmates are permitted in the yard."[21] Next, books in both libraries needed to be "drastically weeded," with many books discarded and replaced with thousands of paperbacks, in addition to at least 100 magazine and newspaper subscriptions. And both libraries needed to streamline borrowing privileges.

Once he had borrowed a book, an inmate needed conditions conducive to reading. The cells Trautman visited were dark and dingy, and he suggested that "a 100-watt light bulb and an individual tensor (high intensity) reading lamp should be issued to all who request them." Before anyone could balk over purchasing lamps, he noted that it was possible to make tensor lamps in the "Industry Shops" that were already in operation at Auburn. Trautman also recommended providing a basic set of books in each cell, such as "a Bible, a dictionary... thesaurus, Shakespeare, or a book or two on art, music, religion, philosophy, a craft, skill, hobby or occupation." This way, if a person wanted to turn to a book when the libraries were closed, they would always have a handful of titles at their disposal. And, perhaps thinking of how veterans wanted ASEs after they left war zones, he recommended that inmates "be encouraged to take them home upon release."

Lastly, to complement Auburn's robust educational opportunities, Trautman recommended that the prison add a new option for job training. "For inmates who are college graduates, and who indicate a serious vocational interest in librarianship, arrangements should be made to give them professional training through library school extension courses taught by Syracuse Library School instructors inside the institution." This could even lead to prisoners earning master's degrees in librarianship while incarcerated; not only would this enable them to serve as qualified institutional librarians within their facility while still serving their sentence, but they would have a degree and experience to market once they left prison and could become gainfully employed.[22]

Trautman's model library at Auburn showed what could—and should—be done in prisons across the United States. He incorporated his research into his Institutional Libraries course so future generations of librarians could carry his blueprints and put them to use wherever they could.

Trautman remained committed to studying all aspects of prison libraries and sharing his findings, both nationally and internationally. After completing *A Plan to Provide Library Service to People in New York State Institutions*, he spoke at the 1965 American Correctional Association (ACA) Congress of Correction, in which he laid out how prisons could better their book selection, train inmates to become library staff, and reduce recidivism and crime rates by supplying *good* libraries.[23] During the summer of 1971, he toured prisons, reformatories, bastilles, and jails in Germany, France, Italy, Switzerland, Austria, and Yugoslavia.[24]

* * *

Trautman's work on prison libraries reflected a lifelong belief, one rooted in early adulthood, that too many adults in the United States needed help building their reading skills. Data from the mid-1960s reported that a third of prisoners were functionally illiterate, meaning they could not read on a fifth-grade level.[25] Trautman could only assume that the percentage was just as high outside of prisons.

He set to work. First, he became a consultant for President Lyndon Johnson's anti-poverty program, Job Corps, which allowed young people who did not complete high school to enroll in a one-year program so they could learn a trade, get paid for their work, and gain an education.[26] The Job Corps borrowed several aspects of the CCC of the 1930s—there were even Job Corps centers specializing in conservation work situated at former CCC camps. As in his CCC days, Trautman's focus was on building good libraries. To do this, he needed to provide the right books. The reading proficiency of Job Corps enrollees was all over the map. Trautman needed to serve a wide range of reading needs on an extremely limited budget. Although the Job Corps considered hosting a book drive, Trautman dissuaded officials from pursuing this route. He knew from the Victory Book Campaign and his own recent work with prisons that donated books were too often poor quality. He reached out to the Book of the Month Club to secure discounted subscription rates so that popular books would line the shelves.[27] He also recommended that acquisition policy focus on obtaining books on a variety of reading levels while prioritizing books that played to a reader's tastes. This usually meant light, amusing, page-turning fiction.

Libraries across Job Corps camps flourished, and large numbers of young people developed a habit of reading. Some required tutoring and classes to improve their reading proficiency and comprehension. Job Corps libraries, though not all, assisted burgeoning readers by color-coding their books by difficulty level. In this way, enrollees could build their reading skills over time.[28]

While working with the Job Corps, it became clear to Trautman that too few books were suitable for adults building their reading abilities yet didn't insult their intelligence. To be part of the solution, Trautman became an editorial consultant at the McGraw-Hill publishing house; in this role, he helped adapt books for young adults and inexperienced readers.[29] Among the titles in the series were Jack London's *The Call of the Wild*, the short stories of Edgar Allan Poe, and—a book that was close to his heart—*Stories by Jesse Stuart*.[30] It was, after all, "children of the night" who would be reading these books. Each volume was abridged and illustrated, and the wording was occasionally adjusted to hit the right stride in difficulty. These were intended to be gateway books—stories that would build competency and confidence so that readers could work their way to more difficult material.

Just as with the ASE program, Stuart was thrilled to be part of the McGraw-Hill series. When Trautman sent him an advanced copy of

*Stories*, he wrote, "You are the good luck man of my lifetime!" Having spent years teaching and as a school principal, he was aware of the state of reading and felt Trautman's work—and maybe his—would make a difference. "This book and ones like it are sorely needed," Stuart said. "Not only the literates and semi-literates but also [those] who can and won't read books can read this one and, I believe, like it. The length is right.... And the the illustrations are magnificent," he added. Stuart asked to purchase fifty copies so he could send them to teachers he knew. "I know what this book will do," he said. "Wait and see. It's going to serve a big, big purpose."[31]

* * *

Trautman's final project with a "big purpose" developed in the late 1960s, when he attended the 1967 American Library Association's annual conference. He had been invited to speak on a panel about institutional library service with a focus on prisons. However, the panel that preceded his discussed accessibility in libraries and, in particular, the need to better serve those who were blind or visually impaired.[32] Representatives from the Braille Institute of America and the New York Library for the Blind discussed the pitiful selection of titles and the lack of industry-wide standards that prevented those with sight impairments from fully enjoying books and libraries. As one speaker put it, those with disabilities "should have the same opportunity for library services as others."[33] Trautman was so moved by the presentation that he returned to New York and proposed a collaboration with the National Accreditation Council for Agencies Serving the Blind and Visually Handicapped. Not only did he offer to create standards for the production of all literature for the visually impaired, but he secured funding to become project director of a multi-year study so he would have the means to leave no stone unturned.[34]

Based on data from the US Public Health Service, in the late 1960s, more than five million Americans were estimated to be visually impaired—meaning they had limited to no vision.[35] Their reading materials needed to be in braille, large-font, or audio formats. Each had its flaws.

For the year 1964, data showed that only 700 modern titles were printed in braille, compared to the approximately 28,000 titles that were published in "ink print text" that year.[36] Moreover, braille translations tended to contain inaccuracies, translation mistakes, and other errors affecting readability. Trautman thought it entirely unacceptable to give readers books with "typographical errors on every page," and he was especially concerned about the effect this had on the "visually handicapped child who is already seeking to develop tactile reading skills and whose fingers find the material confusing."[37]

As for large-type books, though mainstream publishers were beginning to cater to the growing market for large-print editions, they selected different font sizes and styles without regard to what actually produced the most legible materials for those with low vision.[38] And as for audio tapes and disks, many were produced by volunteers—not professionals—which resulted in readings that were too fast, muffled, or inarticulate; there was also a tendency for mispronounced words, which particularly infuriated Trautman. Listeners learned inaccuracies.[39] For Trautman—the man who had invented the Armed Services Edition because American soldiers needed tiny paperbacks so they could read at war—it was outrageous that five million Americans—around half of the number who had served in the armed forces in World War II—needed specialized books so they could read for the rest of their lives, and that so little had been done for them.

Trautman devoted part of his sabbatical leave from Columbia to study every facet of the problem. For large-print books, it was not a matter of simply increasing the font size. Tests were performed to determine what features created the most readable book for low-vision readers. Recommendations included using a font size so that "there are no more than six letters and spaces per horizontal inch," heavy typefaces (as opposed to thin lettering), double spacing, line widths of six inches or less, and using underlining for emphasis instead of italics. For paper, non-glare or dull finishes were required, the best hues were a creamy white or off-white (never bright white), and an opacity of at least 91 percent was needed to promote contrast and minimize "show through" on pages printed on both sides.[40]

For audio recordings, Trautman recommended the use of professional equipment and readers whenever possible. If a trained narrator could not be used, the reader needed at least to exhibit fluency and a strong command of language, use appropriate vocal inflection and rhythm, and maintain a good flow and pace. The goal was to create an audio version that would "approximate as closely as feasible the quality of the ink print text."[41]

While sighted people could benefit from both large-print and audio recordings, Trautman's study of braille materials was particularly detailed, perhaps because only those with knowledge of braille could ensure the accuracy, reliability, and useability of the books. While there were promising technologies being developed—such as a "video scanning device which produces braille-like touch signals directly from ink paper, and a machine which produces moving braille characters from magnetic tape"—the bottom line was that braille materials, however produced, had to be "faithful reproductions of the original ink text" and "accurately embossed."[42] To heighten useability, Trautman's study provided detailed standards as to the "size, height and spacing of dots and lines," as well as the paper weight that worked best for embossing.[43]

Finally, there was the quality and variety of reading materials. It was recommended that a central agency compile lists of all titles in braille and large type so that publishers could consult these lists and avoid the unnecessary duplication of a book that already existed in such a format. The other pressing challenge involved the scope of titles; too many braille and large-print books were in the public domain, which meant that the material was so old that the copyright had expired. Public-domain classics, important as they were to keep in print, did not supplant the need for modern bestsellers and new releases. Trautman's study took a hard stance: Were publishers unwilling to produce copies of popular books for the sight impaired, the "fair use" clause within copyright law would enable a nonprofit agency or governmental service to create a braille, large-print, or audio edition. And for libraries, copyright clearance by the Division for the Blind and Physically Handicapped of the Library of Congress was available for the transcription of a book into audio or braille form by volunteers.[44] "Blind and visually handicapped readers have an inalienable right to have access to reading materials available to the general public," Trautman's study concluded.[45]

Not only did Trautman utilize the information from his research for his new Columbia library course, but nearly 9,000 copies of the report were distributed across the United States. In addition, Trautman helped prepare a similar report for the US Office of Education.[46]

* * *

The classroom became Trautman's final frontier for his engagement in the world of books and libraries. He carried all of his discoveries, facts, and statistics back to Columbia to share with his students. Each class represented the future generation of librarians, and he was passing his torch to them, so they could carry forward the work of getting books into the hands of all who wanted to read them.

Trautman's course on institutional library service was among the first of its kind, and certainly the most comprehensive. He devoted his final years of teaching to perfecting its content and delivery, knitting together all of his research, experiences, and passion. It covered everything from the historical origins of libraries to practical problems, like securing funding for institutional libraries and the unique needs of different groups. He included units on correctional facilities, hospitals, the blind and visually impaired, young adults building their literacy skills, and the catchall of all other "unserved, poorly served, and forgotten people." The nation's "children of the night" had never been far from his mind. The course ended by considering the value of library service to these communities and the resources needed to ensure consistent progress in making more inclusive and better libraries for all.[47]

Trautman began his teaching career as a lecturer for survey courses, with 100 or more students. His course on institutional libraries was a discussion-based seminar, where students sat around a large conference table and traded ideas. He challenged them to consider the role of libraries in improving humanity, encouraged them to approach problems creatively, and set an example of how to listen to differing opinions and keep an open mind. As one student said, the course "raised my consciousness as to the value of a librarian in our present society" and nurtured an interest in "issues traditionally relegated outside the curriculum, such as problems of all oppressed . . . people."[48] When asked how their experience could have been bettered, one student in 1975 responded: "The Dean should cancel all classes of the summer session while Dr. Trautman conducts a consciousness raising workshop for all faculty members."[49]

* * *

In 1976, Trautman was appointed Professor Emeritus of Library Service. He would always be "a permanent member of the Columbia community," as a letter from William J. McGill, the university's president, informed him, though now he would do so from a position of retirement.[50] The news was bittersweet. Trautman would miss the classroom, his students, and the range of opportunities provided by his affiliation with such a respected institution. He packed his office in Butler Library—the decades of letters, photos, and mementos tenderly wrapped and placed in boxes. Wishing to keep yet another memento of his time at Columbia, Trautman asked the dean of the School of Library Service if he could purchase the well-worn wooden desk in his office. For $10, Trautman was granted permission to take his desk and the matching filing cabinet.[51] They accompanied Trautman for the rest of his life, and then were preserved by Trautman's eldest son, Eric. To Eric, his father's desk brought back fond childhood memories of going to work with his father, sitting together in Trautman's office where a small desk had been set up for Eric. Eric would read, color, and amuse himself with whatever diversions Trautman happened to supply as Trautman would sit at his large desk and hatch new schemes to spread books and libraries to all communities.[52]

* * *

Trautman's retirement was short-lived but filled with the things he loved best. He read, traveled, spent time with family, nurtured friendships, and enjoyed the outdoors. He devoted an entire day each week to letter writing, and his correspondence with Jesse Stuart, his closest friend, flourished. Their letters showed signs of their mortality. After multiple heart attacks and a stroke, Stuart wrote his oldest friend and confided how badly he wanted more time. "Give me a few more years to live, with my reserve already written and those I have to write, I'll do eight more [books]. Still a few more years," Stuart wrote, as if Trautman had the power to grant this wish.[53]

But neither had many more years. Though they did not express this thought explicitly, they managed to say goodbye to one another indirectly. "Ours has been a long and durable friendship," Stuart wrote to Trautman in one of his last letters.[54] "You've never let me down," Trautman replied.[55] Shortly after, Stuart had a sixth heart attack and stroke that left him partially paralyzed and unable to do the thing he loved most: write.[56] Powerless to send letters, Trautman entertained thoughts of visiting Stuart in Kentucky, as he had before.[57] However, in 1979, Trautman visited a VA Hospital after feeling unwell for several weeks. He was diagnosed with cancer of the small intestines and began treatment. The prognosis was not a promising one.

Though weary and ill, Trautman continued to seek ways to help others. When he saw a need, he couldn't resist doing something to fill it. It was this attitude that made Trautman an accredited IRS tax preparer in the last years of his life. In 1981, between cancer treatments, Trautman had been shopping at the local mall when he observed a tax-preparation business advertising its services for astronomical prices. Trautman returned to the mall with a card table and a sign stating he would prepare tax returns, free of charge, for anyone in need. This infuriated the tax business, which reported him for lacking the proper credentials to prepare other people's tax returns.[58] Two could play this game. Trautman immediately registered to take the Volunteer Income Tax Assistance Program Test offered by the IRS, and when he received his results, there was a handwritten note commending Trautman's unusually high score.[59] With his certification in hand, he returned to the mall with his card table and continued to offer free tax return assistance. Trautman prepared so many tax returns without charge that the Department of the Treasury invited him to a ceremony where he would be awarded a certificate for his service. He was too ill to attend. When the certificate arrived in the mail, a note from Joyce L. Robbins of the IRS was tucked inside. It stated, "Your unselfish caring has alleviated a great deal of anxiety and confusion for taxpayers who could not pay for tax assistance. Yours is one certificate that I really wanted to present personally." She hoped he would offer his services again the following year. "We sure need you."[60]

Undoubtedly Trautman would have helped if he had lived longer. On January 27, 1982, he passed away. He was seventy-four years old. Trautman's final act was to donate his body to medical research.[61] True to his nature, he died giving.

# Epilogue

> Be alert to the needs of subordinates and all those less fortunate than yourself and spare no effort to further their aims and aspirations. . . . Spend some time each week to help correct abuses—write letters of complaint. Take time to help others.
>
> —Ray Love Trautman[1]

Ray Trautman devoted his life to books because there was no greater gift he could share with others. As a child, he had discovered a love of reading, and it fueled a lifelong quest to make books and libraries available to all. Millions became readers because of his efforts. His time with the Civilian Conservation Corps during the New Deal revealed to him the full power of connecting books to emerging readers; he watched as new worlds of possibility opened for young men discovering books for the first time. During World War II, he waged battles in boardrooms and war zones as he supplied America's military with hundreds of millions of books, magazines, and comic books. His contemporaries marveled at the achievement, describing Trautman as the person who handled "more words than any other man in the world,"[2] ran "the largest and most far-reaching publishing enterprise in history,"[3] built "the world's largest library,"[4] and orchestrated "the largest giveaway of books besides the Gideon Bible."[5]

Whenever and wherever there were challenges to libraries and book circulation, Trautman strove to protect and enhance the freedom to read. In his view, no obstacle should keep books out of the hands of the public—not jail bars, book bans, vision impairments, long-term clinical care, low literacy, or rural poverty. He would think of the troops he had met in foxholes. They lived on ASEs with loose bindings, creased and scuffed covers, and pages splattered with mud and blood. Through them, troops found companions when feeling friendless, information when seeking answers, hope when all seemed lost, humanity in the face of cruelty, and a sense of joy and wonder while surrounded by bleakness. Trautman knew that soldiers needed books just as much as rifles and ammunition. Bullets might fight foes on a battlefield, but books could fight the enemies lurking within—ignorance, boredom, fear, hopelessness. And in life and war, those enemies could be the toughest to battle. He never knew what specific book—a classic, a work of fiction, a poetry collection—would stir a numbed heart or restore a weary soul; he just knew that reading had the capability of performing such miracles. Trautman believed that everyone should have access to a wide selection. This is why he wanted all communities to have a decent, functioning library, one with every kind of book stocked on its shelves.

Mainly because of serving as chief librarian of the US Army, Trautman made a lasting impact on the role of books in American life. While his influence was palpable in predictable ways—the exponential growth of the postwar paperback industry, for example—it also took surprising forms, such as making an impression on American home design. When veterans took advantage of government-guaranteed home loans under the GI Bill, a postwar surge in homeownership necessitated the construction of hundreds of thousands of new residences.[6] As housing developments mushroomed across the United States, middle-class living rooms included a ubiquitous new feature: built-in bookshelves.[7] Veterans, used to carrying ASEs in their pockets, could not imagine their civilian lives without books within arms' reach. Trautman's library service for troops had a postwar trickle-down effect across society. Veterans shared their love of reading with their families, inspiring spouses and children to develop a reading habit. For many people, to this day, a love of reading stemming from a World War II veteran continues to be passed down from one generation to the next.

As his time ran short, Trautman knew there was more work to be done and he would not live long enough to do it. In his final years, he counted on his students, throwing all of his energy into teaching. He hoped to raise awareness of the new reading frontiers he so wished to serve. If his students could see the opportunities that he did, Trautman hoped some would be inspired enough to carry the torch that he no longer could.

And we should do no less. Anyone inspired by his story can honor his legacy by reading, sharing books, supporting libraries, resisting book bans, serving the needs of "forgotten people" (those children of the night), remaining curious, and doing our part to spread the joy of reading. As Trautman would be the first to tell anyone, there's no greater gift to bestow than a love of books.[8]

# *Acknowledgments*

It has been such a joy to research and write this book that as I type these final thoughts, it is with both sadness because it marks the end of this journey, but also excitement because I can finally share this story.

This book would not exist if it were not for Eric Trautman, Ray's son. After he read *When Books Went to War*, he reached out to me and invited me to visit him. He generously shared stories about his father, and we remained friends for several years. The more he told me about the remarkable things his father did for books and libraries, the more I wanted to write this biography. When I mentioned this to Eric, he generously offered to share everything his father had saved. Luckily, being a librarian, Ray saved everything. Eric made available to me boxes and boxes of records, diaries, photo albums, books, magazines, and various ephemera. He also shared all he had from his mother, Jane, which included diaries, photos, and books. As I went through this material, I'd make lists of questions to ask Eric, and he patiently answered them. If it were not for Eric's willingness to share his memories and all of the materials his father and mother saved, this biography would not have been possible. I am deeply grateful and am honored to consider Eric a dear friend.

There are many other people I would like to thank for supporting and encouraging me as I have worked on this book. My family, Christopher and Beatrice Manning, have been so patient and understanding as I've traveled to visit Eric and visit archives, buried myself in books to learn every detail I could, and disappeared to my writing room to research, write, and edit this book. One of my favorite memories of this time was when Beatrice made a graphic novel of the story in Chapter 9, on the Battle of the Bulge. Her interest and enthusiasm energized me. Thank you.

Three people who gave me valuable feedback and suggestions on an early draft were my sister, Holly Guptill-Symonds; a former student, Anthony Geremonte; and my favorite history professor in college and friend, Professor Richard Hamm. Holly—it was so enjoyable to work with you on this, and I appreciate the care, skill, and time you put into your comments and questions. Your detailed feedback was incredibly helpful to me. Anthony—your enthusiasm and careful edits were especially helpful. I appreciate the thoughtful comments and ideas you shared. Also, thank you for your willingness to once again work with me on a book. And Professor Hamm (it's been twenty years since I've been in your classroom, and I still can't quite bring myself to call you Richard)—you helped me from the very beginning as my college thesis advisor, and this is now the fourth book of mine that you've read and edited. Your insight and suggestions, guided by your deep knowledge of history, were especially helpful. I cannot thank you enough.

A wonderful group of researchers and librarians assisted me in tracking down source material, and I am grateful for their help. Erica Ivins aided me with the John Alden Jamieson papers at Columbia University; her careful attention to the material and excellent sense of organization were a great help. It was a pleasure to once again work with Cara Setsu Bertram, who assisted me with the American Library Association archives at the University of Illinois Urbana-Champaign. Her knowledge of the archives is impressive, and she guided me to extremely helpful resources. I would also like to thank Tal Nadan, an extraordinary librarian who works in the archives at the New York Public Library. She was a huge help in working with the Victory Book Campaign records, *New Yorker* archives, and adjacent material to these collections that I would not have consulted without her advice.

I would also like to thank Jenny Emery Davidson and Martha Williams at the Community Library in Ketchum, Idaho, for inviting me to be a writer-in-residence at the historic Ernest and Mary Hemingway House and Preserve. It was such a pleasure to meet and discuss the importance of books and libraries, and I loved visiting the Community Library and the nearby Wood River Museum of History and Culture (a special thanks to Mary Tyson for an incredible exhibit tour). I am especially grateful for the opportunity to be a writer-in-residence; it was a dream come true to write in such an inspiring place. I completed drafts of Chapters 8 and 9 during my residency, which felt especially appropriate since Chapter 8 contains the attempt to ban Hemingway during World War II.

Once a draft of the book was complete, I had the good fortune of once again working with the best literary agent there is, E. J. McCarthy. It's been over ten years since we met, and I have loved working with him on every project during that time and hope we will have many more. I am so grateful for his expertise, passion, guidance, and excellent advice. He is so knowledgeable about the process and manages to make it so smooth and stress-free. He is also one of the nicest people I have ever met, and I could not enjoy working with him more. I am deeply appreciative of all the time he poured into this book and for being such a tremendous help.

To my team at Oxford University Press—what a pleasure it has been working with you! From my first conversation with Timothy Bent, I felt that I had met the perfect person for this book. As we went through the editing process, that impression was only confirmed. It has been such an incredible experience to work with him, and I cannot thank him enough for the time and care he put into revisions. His thoughtful comments and polishing have made the story shine. I would also like to thank Chelsea Hogue, who has been so helpful in answering my many questions and has skillfully guided the manuscript through the publication process. Additionally, Thomas Deva has been invaluable in moving this book through production, and I appreciate his assistance. And I am grateful for the sharp eyes and excellent edits by Keith Cline, who copyedited this book.

Last, but certainly not least, I would like to thank Kim Dower for her vision and enthusiasm for sharing this book with a wide audience. She has gone above and beyond, and I have been so impressed with her inspired ideas and tireless commitment. I am so grateful for her help.

# *Endnotes*

## FRONTMATTER

1. "To the Advisory Committee," providing excerpt of letter from overseas to John Farrar, dated November 1, 1943. Council on Books in Wartime Records, 1942–1947, Coll. No. MC038, 20th Century Public Policy Papers, Seeley G. Mudd Manuscript Library, Department of Rare Books and Special Collections, Princeton University Library (hereinafter Council Records).

## INTRODUCTION

1. Roscoe C. Blunt, Jr., *Inside the Battle of the Bulge* (Praeger, 1994), 52.
2. Bill Davidson, *Cut Off: Behind Enemy Lines in the Battle of the Bulge with Two Small Children, Ernest Hemingway, and Other Assorted Misanthropes* (Stein and Day, 1972), 82.
3. Col. R. Ernest Dupuy, *St. Vith Lion in the Way: The 106th Infantry Division in World War II* (Infantry Journal Press, 1949), 1, 16.
4. John Toland, *Battle: The Story of the Battle of the Bulge* (Random House, 1959), 28.
5. Dupuy, *St. Vith Lion in the Way*, 21.
6. Gerald Astor, *A Blood-Dimmed Tide: The Battle of the Bulge by the Men Who Fought It* (Dell, 1992), at 52.
7. Bill Fussell, *The Boys' Crusade* (Weidenfeld & Nicolson, 2004), 128–129.
8. Toland, *Battle*, 35.
9. Davidson, *Cut Off*, 28.
10. Molly Manning, Interview with Eric Trautman, June 14, 2022.
11. Manning, Interview with Eric Trautman, June 14, 2022.
12. Clip Boutell, "Authors Are Like People," *St. Louis Star-Times*, August 4, 1945, 11.
13. Cole, *The Ardennes*, 66; Manning, Interview with Eric Trautman, June 14, 2022.

## CHAPTER 1

1. Jesse Stuart, *Stories by Jesse Stuart* (adapted by Laurence Swinburne; editorial consultant, Ray L. Trautman) (McGraw-Hill, 1968), 75.
2. Clip Boutell, "Authors Are Like People: Fighting a Winning War with Words," *New York Post*, August 2, 1945, 23. Box 1, Folder 4, Clippings and Media, Ray L. Trautman Archival Materials, New York City (hereinafter RLT Materials).
3. US Bureau of the Census, 1910 US Federal Census, Ohio, Highland County, White Oak Township, District 0136, household of George H. Troutman [sic].
4. "Plan Series of Meetings," *Press-Gazette* (Hillsboro, OH), September 16, 1966, 1, 3; E. H. Diehl, *Diehl Families of America* (Privately printed by E. H. Diehl, February 1915), 166.
5. US Bureau of the Census, 1900 US Federal Census, Ohio, Highland County, White Oak Township, District 0131, household of Henry Trautman; "Mowrystown," *News-Herald* (Hillsboro, OH), March 7, 1901, 8.
6. "Old Mowrystown Band Pictured," newspaper clipping, n.d., no source, RLT Materials.

7. US Bureau of the Census, 1910 US Federal Census, Ohio, Highland County, White Oak Township, District 0136, household of George H. Troutman [sic].
8. US Bureau of the Census, 1920 US Federal Census, Ohio, Highland County, White Oak Township, District 0105, household of George H. Troutman [sic].
9. Jesse Stuart, *Beyond Dark Hills* (McGraw-Hill, 1938), 14–15, 26.
10. US Social Security Applications and Claims Index, 1936–2007, search under "Madalie Rose Trautman."
11. US Bureau of the Census, 1930 US Federal Census, Kentucky, Campbell County, City of Dayton, District 0024, household of George H. Trautman.
12. US Bureau of the Census, 1910 US Federal Census, household of George H. Troutman [sic].
13. "Whiteoak School News," *Press Gazette* (Hillsboro, OH), October 4, 1940, 7.
14. Highland County Library, "History + Funding," https://www.highlandco.org/history.
15. US City Directories, Norwood City Directory 1934, 465 (Wilson F.).
16. *Educational Directory: 1929* (US Department of the Interior, Bureau of Education Bulletin, 1929), 1, https://babel.hathitrust.org/cgi/pt?id=umn.31951000864302l&seq=227&q1=%24700.
17. *Crops and Markets* (United States Department of Agriculture, 1929), 120, https://babel.hathitrust.org/cgi/pt?id=mdp.39015082286868&seq=11.
18. "Real Estate Transfers," *Dayton Daily News*, November 17, 1921, 23; US City Directories, *Williams' Cincinnati Directory* (The Williams Directory Company, 1924), 1624.
19. Ray L. Trautman, "Personal Data Transcript," RLT Materials.
20. Rutherford Platt, *The Manual of Occupations* (G. P. Putnam's Sons, 1929), 223–224, https://babel.hathitrust.org/cgi/pt?id=uc1.%24b297640&seq=7.
21. "New Union Central Life Insurance Building, Cincinnati, Ohio" (Valentine-Souvenir, Co., n.d.) (postcard).
22. "The Union Central Building: Fourth Avenue – Vine Street – Baker Street, Cincinnati, Ohio," (Union Central Life Insurance Co., 1913), https://digital.cincinnatilibrary.org/digital/collection/p16998coll15/id/40628.
23. "'Shorty, Human Fly of Skyscraper, Likes to Flirt with Death; Shuns Auto Perils," *Cincinnati Post*, August 5, 1921, 8.
24. Emma L. Fetta, "Boredom Is Banished from Isolated Country Districts by Books Circulated Through County by Public Library," *Enquirer* (Cincinnati, OH), April 22, 1923, 91.
25. "New Safety Plane Perfected by Dayton-Wright Co.," *Dayton Daily News*, September 23, 1922, 1.
26. Charles Dickens, *David Copperfield* (Modern Library, 2000).
27. T. S. Eliot, *The Waste Land and Other Poems* (Barnes and Noble Classics, 2005).
28. "Increase of Graduates Shown," *Cincinnati Enquirer*, June 6, 1925, 8; Ray L. Trautman, "Personal Data Transcript."
29. Ronald Schaffer, "The War Department's Defense of ROTC, 1920–1940," *The Wisconsin Magazine of History* 53, no. 2, (Winter 1969–1970): 109, https://www.jstor.org/stable/4634503?read-now=1?read-now=1.
30. Jesse Stuart, *Beyond Dark Hills* (McGraw-Hill, 1938), 36, 62.
31. Molly Manning, Interview with Eric Trautman, December 15, 2022.
32. Stuart, *Beyond Dark Hills*, 95.
33. Stuart, *Beyond Dark Hills*, 96.
34. Stuart, *Beyond Dark Hills*, 96–98.
35. Stuart, *Beyond Dark Hills*, 97, 100.
36. Trautman, "Personal Data Transcript."

37. James F. Hopkins, *The University of Kentucky: Origins and Early Years* (University of Kentucky Press, 1951), 78–81.
38. Molly Manning, Interview with Eric Trautman, February 7, 2022.
39. "Ecology of Floracliff," https://floracliff.org/the-sanctuary/.
40. Ray L. Trautman, Scrapbook, RLT Materials.
41. Ray L. Trautman, "Personal Data Transcript," New York City, 1939, RLT Materials.
42. Trautman, "Personal Data Transcript," 1939.
43. Ray L. Trautman, Resume (dated April 20, 1932), New York City, 1939, RLT Materials.
44. "Graduates," *Kentucky Post*, August 30, 1931.
45. Trautman, "Personal Data Transcript," 1939.
46. "University of Kentucky Commencement Exercises Summer Session," August 19, 1932 (graduation program, Lexington, KY), RLT Materials.
47. Capt. William A. Cunningham, Letter to Whom It May Concern, August 20, 1932, RLT Materials.
48. "Heads Book Store," *Lexington Herald*, September 20, 1932, 11.
49. J. Winston Coleman, Jr., Letter to Ray L. Trautman, February 18, 1977, RLT Materials.
50. "Book Shop Is Sold," *Lexington Herald-Leader*, February 1, 1933, 7.
51. Ray Trautman, Review of *Yankee Bookseller*, by Charles E. Goodspeed, RLT Materials.
52. Pardoe Martin, Letter to Ray Love Trautman, November 11, 1932, RLT Materials.
53. "Lexington Youth to Train for Air Corps," *Lexington Herald-Leader*, February 17, 1933, 3; Work Projects Administration, *Randolph Field* (Devin-Adair Company, 1942), 43.
54. "Book Shop Is Sold," 7.
55. A. P. Sullivan, Letter to Ray Love Trautman, January 25, 1933, RLT Materials.
56. Dr. Bruce Ashcroft, "We Wanted Wings: A History of the Aviation Cadet Program" (HQ AETC Office of History and Research, 2005), 23–24.
57. Ernest T. Pyle, "West Point of the Air," *Modesto Bee* (Modesto, CA), June 15, 1930, 25.
58. Pyle, "West Point of the Air," June 15, 1930.
59. James D. Givens, Memorandum To: Incoming Students, February 1, 1933, RLT Materials.
60. Ashcroft, "We Wanted Wings," 24; Work Projects Administration, *Randolph Field*, 26.
61. Beirne Lay, *I Wanted Wings* (Harper & Brothers, 1937), 47.
62. Work Projects Administration, *Randolph Field*, 43.
63. Lay, *I Wanted Wings*, 65.
64. Work Projects Administration, *Randolph Field*, 44.
65. Manning, Interview, December 15, 2022.
66. "Named National Director of Army Library Service," *Baltimore Sun*, November 27, 1940, 11.
67. "Named National Director of Army Library Service," November 27, 1940.
68. Ray L. Trautman, Letter to Hud, May 18, 1933, RLT Materials.
69. Named National Director of Army Library Service," November 27, 1940.
70. Trautman, "Personal Data Transcript," 1939.
71. Alfred Emile Cornebise, *The CCC Chronicles: Camp Newspapers of the Civilian Conservation Corps, 1933–1942* (McFarland & Company, 2004), 11–12.
72. Cornebise, *The CCC Chronicles*, 9.
73. "$6,000,000 Going Out to Families of C.C.C.," *New York Times*, July 31, 1933, 13.
74. Cornebise, *The CCC Chronicles*, 10, 13.
75. Alfred Booth, Memo to Ray L. Trautman Re: Promotion, August 24, 1934, RLT Materials.
76. "Abstract of Clinical Record in the Case of 1st Lt. Ray L. Trautman Company 547, Noble, Kentucky"; see also "Proceedings of Disposition Board, Walter Reed General Hospital," September 20, 1935, concerning Ray L. Trautman.

77. Molly Manning, Phone Interview with Eric Trautman, December 19, 2022; see also Ray L. Trautman, "Personal Data Sheet, 434 West 120 St. New York City," created 1939, RLT Materials.
78. T. M. Chambliss, Memo to Headquarters Tenth Infantry, November 13, 1935, RLT Materials; see also John A. Salmond, *The Civilian Conservation Corps, 1933–1942* (Duke University Press, 1967), chap. 6.
79. "Personal Data Sheet, Ray L. Trautman, 434 West 120 St. New York City," created 1939.
80. "Personal Data Sheet, Ray L. Trautman, 434 West 120 St. New York City," created 1939.
81. James T. Golden, Jr., "Library Executives Give Hits on Bureaus; Departmental Work to Aid Readers Is Cited," *Cincinnati Enquirer*, January 29, 1940, 5.
82. Chalmers Hadley, Letter to Ray L. Trautman, August 2, 1939, RLT Materials.
83. Howard W. Oxley, Letter to Ray L. Trautman, April 23, 1936, RLT Materials.
84. Ray L. Trautman, Letter to Mr. Chalmers Hadley, August 9, 1939, RLT Materials.
85. "Statistics," *South Bend Tribune* (South Bend, IN), August 22, 1937, 25.
86. Ray L. Trautman, "A Community Survey of Boone County, Kentucky, and Its Largest Town, Walton," RLT Materials.
87. Trautman, "A Community Survey."
88. Trautman, "A Community Survey."
89. C. S. Marsh, "New Outlooks in the CCC," *New York Times*, June 3, 1934, 4.
90. Trautman, "A Community Survey."
91. Fetta, "Boredom Is Banished," 91.
92. See, e.g., Ray L. Trautman, "1938 Directory of Kentucky Libraries," RLT Materials.
93. Letter to Miss Lena B. Nofeier (incomplete), September 22, 1938, RLT Materials; Trautman, "A Community Survey."
94. John A. Salmond, *The Civilian Conservation Corps*, chap. 2.
95. Trautman, "A Community Survey."
96. "Personal Data Sheet, Ray L. Trautman, 434 West 120 St. New York City," created 1939.
97. "Personal Data Sheet, Ray L. Trautman, 434 West 120 St. New York City," created 1939.
98. Ray L. Trautman, Letter to Dr. Howard W. Oxley, February 18, 1939, RLT Materials.
99. Howard W. Oxley, "The CCC for American Youth," *The Phi Delta Kappan* 26, no. 6, (February 1942): 253.
100. Howard W. Oxley, Letter to Ray L. Trautman, February 27, 1939, RLT Materials.
101. Cornebise, *The CCC Chronicles*, 17.

## CHAPTER 2

1. Dickens, *David Copperfield*, 3.
2. Jane Trautman, Diary, 1938–1939, September 13, 1938 entry.
3. Trautman, Diary, November 7, 1939 entry.
4. Trautman, Diary, September 17–18, 1938 entries.
5. Ray L. Trautman, Letter to the Dean of School of Library Service, July 18, 1939, RLT Materials.
6. Edith Fairchild, Letter to Ray L. Trautman, July 14, 1949, RLT Materials.
7. Ray L. Trautman, Letter to Professor F. L. D. Goodrich, librarian, July 18, 1939, RLT Materials.
8. Trautman, Letter to the Dean, July 18, 1939.
9. Ray L. Trautman, Letter to Miss Fihe, July 19, 1939, RLT Materials.
10. Charles F. Gosnell, Letter to Ray L. Trautman, July 26, 1939, RLT Materials.

11. "Opening a New College," *Brooklyn Eagle*, October 28, 1937, 14.
12. Gosnell, Letter to Ray L. Trautman, July 26, 1939.
13. Charles F. Gosnell, Letter to Ray L. Trautman, August 2, 1939, RLT Materials.
14. Ray L. Trautman, Letter to Chalmers Hadley, August 9, 1939, RLT Materials; see also "Klapper Quits Post at Queens College," *New York Times*, April 20, 1948, 30.
15. Paul Klapper, Letter to Ray L. Trautman, August 7, 1939, RLT Materials.
16. Trautman, Letter to Miss Fihe, July 19, 1939.
17. Ray L. Trautman, Memorandum, Subject: Resignation from Assignment as Camp Educational Adviser, August 8, 1939, RLT Materials.
18. Ray L. Trautman, Letter to Miss Fihe, August 9, 1939, RLT Materials.
19. Trautman, Diary, August 30–September 1, 1939 entries.
20. Trautman, Diary, September 2, 1939 entry.
21. Trautman, Diary, September 3, 1939 entry.
22. "Big Throng at Fair Ignores Gray Sky," *New York Times*, September 2, 1940, 18.
23. "Program for Today at the World's Fair," *New York Times*, September 10, 1940, 26; "The Fair's Huge Exhibit Area," *New York Times Guide to the World's Fair*, May 5, 1940, 5.
24. "Fun: The Great White Way," *New York Times Guide to the World's Fair*, May 5, 1940, 17.
25. "Program for Today at the World's Fair," September 10, 1940; "If You Are Interested In—," *New York Times Guide to the World's Fair*, May 5, 1940, 23–26.
26. Trautman, Diary, September 10, 1939 entry.
27. Trautman, Diary, September 10, 1939 entry.
28. Trautman, Diary, September 3, 1939 entry.
29. Trautman, Diary, September 4, 1939 entry; Trautman, Letter to Miss Fihe, August 9, 1939; "Personal Data Sheet, Ray L. Trautman, 434 West 120 St. New York City," created 1939.
30. Gosnell, Letter to Ray L. Trautman, July 26, 1939.
31. Gosnell, Letter to Ray L. Trautman, July 26, 1939.
32. School of Library Service, Columbia University, Post-Graduate Employment Information (cardboard half-sheet), dated as seeking employment on or after August 15, 1940, RLT Materials.
33. Chalmers Hadley, Letter to Ray L. Trautman, August 2, 1939, RLT Materials.
34. Ray L. Trautman, "Metal Airplane Construction," 1940 bibliography assignment, RLT Materials.
35. Ray Trautman, *A History of the School of Library Service* (Columbia University Press, 1954), 41.
36. Trautman, *A History of the School of Library Service*, 41.
37. Trautman, Letter to Mr. Chalmers Hadley, August 9, 1939.
38. Jane Trautman, Diary, January 1–9, 1939 entries.
39. Jane Trautman, Diary, November 7, 1939 entry.
40. Jane Trautman, Diary, November 7, 1939 entry.
41. Jane Trautman, Diary, November 7, 1939 entry.
42. Pale green postcard regarding *Trees of Heaven* by Jesse Stuart, 1940, RLT Materials.
43. See, e.g., Mrs. Norman Johnson, postcard to Americana Trautman, February 27, 1939, RLT Materials.
44. Works Progress Administration, *New York City Guide* (Random House, 1939), 122; Richard F. Shepard, "Survivors of Book Row," *New York Times*, April 27, 1984, 70.
45. Marvin Mondlin and Roy Meador, *Book Row: An Anecdotal and Pictorial History of the Antiquarian Book Trade* (Carroll & Graf Publishers, 2004), xiv.

46. Mondlin and Meador, *Book Row*, xv.
47. Mondlin and Meador, *Book Row*, xv, xvii.
48. "Correspondence Book," labeled on inside page as "Ray L. Trautman Book Accounts," RLT Materials.
49. "Correspondence Book," 28–29, 89, 100.
50. "Correspondence Book," 100–101.
51. Ray L. Trautman, Letter to Mr. Hiram H. Parke, August 22, 1939, RLT Materials; Arthur Swann, Letter to Ray L. Trautman , September 6, 1939, RLT Materials.
52. "Personal Data Sheet, Ray L. Trautman, 434 West 120 St. New York City," created 1939.
53. "Correspondence Book," 89.
54. Peter Monro Jack, "A Fine Romantic Panorama of Hill-Country Life," *New York Times*, October 21, 1934, 38.
55. Marion Strobel, "Miss Strobel Pays Homage to New Poets," *Chicago Tribune*, December 15, 1934, 12.
56. "Mountaineer Turns Poet of Rolling Mill," *Greenup News*, October 26, 1934, 3.
57. Jesse Stuart, Letter to Ray L. Trautman, October 17, 1934, Jesse Stuart Correspondence, RLT Materials.
58. Jesse Stuart, Letter to Ray Trautman, July 2, 1940, Jesse Stuart Correspondence, RLT Materials; see also "Just A-Travelin' with Jesse," *Russell Times* (Russell, KY), November 10, 1939, 15.
59. Robert Van Gelder, "The Road Up for Jesse Stuart," *New York Times Book Review*, June 2, 1940, 14.
60. Ray L. Trautman, Letter to Florence W. Bowers, March 2, 1940, Jesse Stuart Correspondence, RLT Materials.
61. Pale green postcard regarding *Trees of Heaven* by Jesse Stuart, 1940.
62. "Jesse Stuart's Kentucky Novel," *New York Times Book Review*, January 2, 1940, 1, 14.
63. David Dick, *Jesse Stuart the Heritage* (Plum Lick Publishing 2005), 119.
64. Forrest C. Pogue, *George C. Marshall: Ordeal and Hope, 1939–1942* (Viking Press, 1966), 2.
65. Otto D. Tolisschus, "Last Warsaw Port Yields to Germans," *New York Times*, September 29, 1939, 1.
66. Pogue, *Ordeal and Hope*, 2.
67. Pogue, *Ordeal and Hope*, 18.
68. Pogue, *Ordeal and Hope*, 18–19; G. H. Archambault, "France to Mourn," *New York Times*, June 25, 1940, 1.
69. "Sweeping Drive Launched Against Holland, Belgium, Luxembourg as 'Safeguard,'" *Indianapolis Star*, May 10, 1940, 1.
70. "Belgium Admits German Advance," *Philadelphia Inquirer*, May 12, 1940, 6 (occupied Luxembourg); "Holland Surrenders to Nazis," *Pasadena Post*, May 20, 1940, 1 (Holland, Netherlands); Samuel Dashiell, "Minister Describes Bitter Last Meeting with King," *Los Angeles Times*, May 29, 1940, 1 (Belgium).
71. Percival Knauth, "Nazi Bugle Blares Tidings to World," *New York Times*, June 25, 1940, 4.
72. "President Says Labor Is Still Short of Goal," *Chicago Daily Tribune*, September 12, 1940, 8.
73. "Text of the President's Address Asking for a Great Defense Fund," *New York Times*, May 17, 1940, 10; "FDR's Fifty Thousand Airplanes," *Air and Space Forces Magazine*, June 1, 2009.

74. Doris Kearns Goodwin, *No Ordinary Time* (Simon & Schuster Paperbacks, 1994), 194–195; "President's Call for Full Response on Defense," *New York Times*, December 30, 1945, 6.
75. "Personal Data Sheet, Ray L. Trautman, 434 West 120 St. New York City," created 1939.
76. "The Late Enoch Pratt," *New York Times*, September 20, 1896, 16.
77. May Irene Copinger, "Training for a Library Career," *Baltimore Sun*, May 18, 1930, 14.
78. Ray L. Trautman, Letter to Pauline J. Fihe, June 8, 1940, RLT Materials.
79. Selective Training and Service Act of 1940, 76 PL. 783, 54 Stat. 885 (September 16, 1940).
80. "Draftees Hailed by Roosevelt as Hope of Peace," *Brooklyn Daily Eagle*, October 16, 1940, 1.
81. Trautman, Letter to Pauline J. Fihe, June 8, 1940.

## CHAPTER 3

1. Pierce Butler, ed., *Books and Libraries in Wartime* (University of Chicago Press, 1945), 57.
2. "Bibliothecal," *Philadelphia Inquirer*, October 7, 1876, 2.
3. Christine Czuryle, "26,000 American Library Association Began in Melvil Dewey's Desk in Boston," *Palladium-Item and Sun-Telegram* (Richmond, IN), July 19, 1963, 12.
4. Theodore Wesley Koch, *Books in the War* (Houghton Mifflin, 1919), 5–6; Frank P. Stockbridge, "Books, Books, Books, Demanded by Our Fighting Men," *New York Herald*, November 10, 1918, Sec. 6, p. 7.
5. Czuryle, "26,000 American Library Association Began in Melvil Dewey's Desk in Boston."
6. Koch, *Books in the War*, 6–7.
7. *War Library Bulletin*, May 1919, 16 (advertisement reproduced from *The Stars and Stripes*, May 2, 1919).
8. John Jamieson, *Books for the Army* (Columbia University Press, 1950), 13.
9. *War Library Bulletin*, June 1918, 1.
10. *Service with Fighting Men*, Vol. I (Association Press), 175.
11. Jamieson, *Books for the Army*, 15.
12. Butler, *Books and Libraries in Wartime*, 53–66.
13. Ray L. Trautman, Letter to the Adjutant General's Office, November 1, 1940, RLT Materials.
14. Jamieson, *Books for the Army*, 20–21.
15. Jamieson, *Books for the Army*, 15, 17.
16. "Dickerson Appointed Successor to Rush," *Indianapolis Star*, August 29, 1928, 1, 2.
17. Jamieson, *Books for the Army*, 15, 17, 21; "Dickerson Quits as Library Head," *Indianapolis Star*, September 27, 1944, 1.
18. "Carl Milam, 78, Librarian, Dead," *New York Times*, August 28, 1963, 27; "Carl Milam Gets in the Limelight," *Democrat-Herald* (Newkirk, OK), April 19, 1923, 12.
19. "Carl Milam, 78, Librarian, Dead," 27.
20. Jamieson, *Books for the Army*, 21.
21. Jamieson, *Books for the Army*, 21–22.
22. Jamieson, *Books for the Army*, 23.
23. Boutell, "Authors Are Like People," *New York Post*, August 2, 1945, 23.
24. Jamieson, *Books for the Army*, 23.
25. Jamieson, *Books for the Army*, 21–23.
26. Jamieson, *Books for the Army*, 23.

27. Special Orders No. 273, War Department, Washington, DC, November 19, 1940, ¶ 81, RLT Materials.
28. Jamieson, *Books for the Army*, 23.
29. "Named National Director of Army Library Service," *Baltimore Sun*, November 27, 1940, 11.
30. Jamieson, *Books for the Army*, 24.
31. Gen. George C. Marshall, *Report on the Army, July 1, 1939 to Jun 30, 1943* (The Infantry Journal, 1943), 23.
32. "Services for the American Soldier," May 1942, 13. John Alden John Alden Jamieson Papers, Rare Book and Manuscript Library, Columbia University Library (hereinafter John Alden Jamieson Papers); Jamieson, *Books for the Army*, 25.
33. Jamieson, *Books for the Army*, 26.
34. "Program: Conference of Morale Officers, February 25 to 28 [1941] inclusive," John Alden Jamieson Papers.
35. Jamieson, *Books for the Army*, 29.
36. Carl H. Milam, Postal Telegraph to Colonel Henry H. Pfsil, Morale Division, December 11, 1940, RLT Materials.
37. "Library Associating Meeting Opens Today," *Chicago Tribune*, December 27, 1940, 15.
38. Lt. Col. J. H. Hillis, letter to Carl H. Milam, December 23, 1940, American Library Association Archives, 020460a_007.
39. L. L. Dickerson, letter to Carl Milam, December 11, 1940, American Library Association Archives, 020460a_007.
40. Carl Milam, Letter to L. L. Dickerson, December 23, 1940, American Library Association Archives, 020460a_007.
41. "National Defense and the Library," *ALA Bulletin* 35, no. 1 (January 1941): 5; "Proceedings, Midwinter Conference, American Library Association, Council Meetings," December 28–29, 1940, Drake Hotel, Chicago, Illinois, 43–45, https://alair.ala.org/handle/11213/7820.
42. "Proceedings, Midwinter Conference, American Library Association, Council Meetings," 44–45.
43. Jamieson, *Books for the Army*, 28.
44. Jamieson, *Books for the Army*, 28.
45. Jamieson, *Books for the Army*, 29.
46. H. I. Phillips, "The Once Over," *Washington Post*, July 9, 1944, B4; see also "Victory Gift Books," *Brooklyn Citizen*, December 7, 1942, 19 (prices for books ranging from $2 to $4).
47. James Roosevelt with Bill Libby, *My Parents: A Differing View* (Playboy Press Book, 1976), vii, 20.
48. Goodwin, *No Ordinary Time*, 27.
49. Goodwin, *No Ordinary Time*, 28, 135.
50. Pogue, *George C. Marshall*, 115–116.
51. Goodwin, *No Ordinary Time*, 178.
52. Pogue, *George C. Marshall*, 115–116.
53. Morris J. MacGregor, Jr., *Integration of the Armed Forces 1940–1965* (Center of Military History United States Army, 1981), 24, 33.
54. Goodwin, *No Ordinary Time*, 522 (Eleanor Roosevelt's attitude); Morris J. MacGregor, Jr., *Integration of the Armed Forces 1940–1965* (Center of Military History United States Army, 1981), 18.

55. Joseph P. Lash, *Eleanor and Franklin: The Story of their Relationship, Based on Eleanor Roosevelt's Private Papers* (W.W. Norton & Co., 1971), 529–530.
56. Pogue, *Ordeal and Hope*, 115–116.
57. "The Freedmen's Bureau," *Brooklyn Daily Eagle*, October 23, 1867, 3; Lash, *Eleanor and Franklin*, 524; Pauli Murray, *Pauli Murray: The Autobiography of a Black Activist, Feminist, Lawyer, Priest, and Poet* (University of Tennessee Press, 1989), 65–68.
58. "This list of books on the Negro was submitted to this office by Howard University and is reproduced for the possible assistance of those charged with the selection of books for colored service clubs," list of titles, RLT Materials.
59. "This list of books on the Negro was submitted to this office by Howard University."
60. Eleanor Roosevelt, Invitation to Lieut. Ray L. Trautman for Garden Party, Tuesday, May. 13, 1941, RLT Materials.
61. General Marshall, "Informal Greetings," delivered at the Conference of Morale Officers, February 25, 1941, 2. John Alden Jamieson Papers.
62. "Program: Conference of Morale Officers, February 25 to 28 [1941] inclusive."
63. Jamieson, *Books for the Army*, 28 (traveling libraries), 39 (publisher book discounts), 63 (Book of the Month Club donations).
64. Ray L. Trautman, Letter to the Adjutant General, March 11, 1941, RLT Materials.
65. Jan-Pieter Barbian, *The Politics of Literature in Nazi Germany: Books in the Media Dictatorship*, trans. Kate Sturge (Bloomsbury Academic, 2013), 23–25.
66. Barbian, *The Politics of Literature in Nazi Germany*, 22–24.
67. Frederick T. Birchall, "Nazi Book-Burning Fails to Stir Berlin," *New York Times*, May 11, 1933, 1.
68. Birchall, "Nazi Book-Burning," 12.
69. Birchall, "Nazi Book-Burning," 12.
70. Barbian, *The Politics of Literature in Nazi Germany*, 24–25.
71. Christopher P. Loss, "Reading Between Enemy Lines: Armed Services Editions and World War II," *Journal of Military History* 67, no. 3 (July 2003): 817.
72. Jonathan Rose, ed., *The Holocaust and the Book* (University of Massachusetts Press, 2008), 1.
73. Flora B. Ludington, "Books and the Sword—Symbols of Our Time," *ALA Bulletin* (May 1943), 147–148, 152.
74. "Army Morale: It Must be Kept High to Turn Soldiers into Good Fighters," *Life*, December 23, 1940, 55.
75. "National Defense: A Problem of Morale," *Time*, August 18, 1941, 35–36.
76. Marian Satterthwaite Carnovsky, "What Are the Draftees Reading?" *Saturday Review of Literature*, September 13, 1941, 4.
77. Carnovsky, "What Are the Draftees Reading?", 14–15.
78. "Library Told to Halt USO Book Drive," *Athol Daily News*, December 6, 1941, 1.
79. "Library Has Book Gifts Before Drive," *Athol Daily News*, November 29, 1941, 1.
80. Jamieson, *Books for the Army*, 55.
81. "Book Drive for Camp Libraries Starts Next Mon.," *Daily Calumet*, July 19, 1941, 1; Jamieson, *Books for the Army*, 59.
82. "Modesto Book Drive for Service Men Set," *Stockton Daily Evening Record*, October 11, 1941, 4.
83. "1,700 Books Sent to Camp Upton Boys," *Newsday* (Nassau Edition), November 28, 1941, 17.

84. Jamieson, *Books for the Army*, 58.
85. "Book Drive for the Naval Air Station," *Cocoa Tribune* (FL), October 30, 1941, 3.
86. Jamieson, *Books for the Army*, 60.
87. "Frederick Osborn, a General, 91, Dies," *New York Times*, January 7, 1981, B12; Frank Lorimer and Franklin Osborn, *Dynamics of Population* (Macmillan, 1934), 348.
88. Barry Alan Mehler, "A History of the American Eugenics Society, 1921–1940) (Ph.D. dissertation, University of Illinois, Urbana, 1988), 223, 227–229, 244.
89. "Frederick Osborn, a General, 91, Dies.
90. Ray L. Trautman, War Department Office of the Chief of the Morale Branch Memorandum, October 8, 1941, American Library Association Archives, 020460a_001 (book drive correspondence).
91. F. H. Osborn, Draft Letter to Carl H. Milam, October 1, 1941; Trautman, War Department Office of the Chief of the Morale Branch Memorandum, October 8, 1941.
92. Trautman, War Department Office of the Chief of the Morale Branch Memorandum, October 8, 1941.
93. "Final Reports, Victory Book Campaign, 1942–1943." Victory Book Campaign Records, Manuscripts and Archives Division, New York Public Library, Astor, Lenox, and Tilden Foundations. Box 1, Folder 27.
94. "Final Reports, Victory Book Campaign, 1942–1943."
95. "Book Drive Starts Jan. 12; 10,000,000 Volumes Expected for Use in Army, Navy Posts," *New York Times*, December 25, 1941, 22.

## CHAPTER 4

1. Eleanor Roosevelt, "My Day," *San Francisco News*, January 5, 1943, 14.
2. "The Tragedy at Honolulu," *Time*, December 15, 1941, 19, 22–23.
3. "The Tragedy at Honolulu," 19.
4. Frank L. Kluckhohn, "Unity in Congress," *New York Times*, December 9, 1941, 1.
5. "Our Declaration of War," *New York Times*, December 12, 1941, 1.
6. "Roosevelt Tells Boston Crowd of Defense Record; Hits Martin, G. O. P," *Boston Globe*, October 31, 1940, 8.
7. George Gallup, "Poll Shows Public for 60-Hour Week," *New York Times*, February 1, 1942, 36; George Gallup, "Gallup Poll Fids Public is Agreeable to Ratioing as a Necessary Move," *New York Times*, January 24, 1942, 8; George Gallup, "Draft of Women Favored in Poll," *New York Times*, January 9, 1942, 17.
8. George Gallup, "Roosevelt Gains in Public Esteem," *New York Times*, January 28, 1942, 17.
9. Ray L. Trautman, Note on RLT Letterhead, May 6, 1976, RLT Materials.
10. John Hall Stewart, *A Documentary Survey of the French Revolution* (Macmillan, 1951), 672–673, https://sites.pitt.edu/~syd/nap.html#:~:text=Soldiers%2C%20you%20are%20naked%2C%20ill,fertile%20plains%20in%20the%20world (Napoleon).
11. "Address by the King," *New York Times*, September 4, 1939, 4.
12. Tacitus, *Life of Cnaeus Julius Agricola c.98 CE*, transl. Alfred John Church and Williams Jackson Brodribb, ¶ 30, https://sourcebooks.fordham.edu/ancient/tacitus-agricola.asp.
13. Trautman, Note on RLT Letterhead, May 6, 1976.
14. "'You'll Win' F.D.R. to Irish AEF," *New York Daily News*, March 31, 1942, 9.
15. Charles T. Lucey, "GOP Protests Letter Given to Soldiers," *Pittsburgh Press*, September 5, 1944, 15.

16. "Memo for Files," attached to letter "To Members of the United States Army Expeditionary Forces." Roosevelt, Franklin D. Papers as President, Official File 25, Box 7. Franklin D. Roosevelt Presidential Library, Hyde Park, New York.
17. Trautman, Note on RLT Letterhead, May 6, 1976.
18. "Biographical Information" for Althea Hester Warren, Victory Book Campaign Records, Manuscripts and Archives Division, New York Public Library, Astor, Lenox, and Tilden Foundations.
19. Martha Boaz, *Fervent and Full of Gifts: The Life of Althea Warren* (Scarecrow Press, 1961), 96.
20. Boaz, *Fervent and Full of Gifts*, 95–96.
21. "City Gives Books for Service Men," *New York Times*, January 13, 1942, 17.
22. Boaz, *Fervent and Full of Gifts*, 99.
23. Marshall, *Report on the Army*, 98.
24. Marshall, *Report on the Army*, 98–99.
25. "City Gives Books for Service Men," 17.
26. "Willkie Is Donor in Book Campaign," *New York Times*, January 27, 1942, 19.
27. "Willkie Is Donor in Book Campaign," 19.
28. Margaret K. Gilbert, "Soldiers' Reading," *American Library Association Bulletin* 35, no. 12 (December 1941): 711.
29. Boaz, *Fervent and Full of Gifts*, 98.
30. "First Million Books Are Ready," *Paris News* (TX), March 8, 1942, 2.
31. Mrs. Cornelius Beeckman, "Books You Don't Want to Part with Are the Books That You Should Give," *Herald-News* (Passaic, NJ), February 13, 1943, 11.
32. Jamieson, *Books for the Army*, 59.
33. "Not an Attic-Cleaning," *Bangor Daily News*, January 6, 1943, 8.
34. "No Fun in Attics for Soldiers," *Brattleboro Reformer*, January 2, 1943, 4.
35. "Elsa Maxwell's Column," *St. Louis Star-Times*, January 8, 1943, 16.
36. Roosevelt, "My Day," January 10, 1942, https://www2.gwu.edu/~erpapers/myday/displaydocedits.cfm?_y=1942&_f=md056079; Roosevelt, "My Day," April 17, 1942, https://www2.gwu.edu/~erpapers/myday/displaydoc.cfm?_y=1942&_f=md056162.
37. "Give Good Books . . . Give More Books," 1943 brochure for the Victory Book Campaign, https://sos.oregon.gov/archives/exhibits/ww2/Documents/life-books5.pdf.
38. "Saturday Review's Norman Cousins, 75," *Chicago Tribune*, December 2, 1990, 50.
39. Eric Pace, "Norman Cousins, 75, Dies; Edited the Saturday Review," *New York Times*, December 1, 1990, 31.
40. Pace, "Norman Cousins, 75, Dies," 31.
41. Norman Cousins, "Design for Giving," *Saturday Review of Literature*, February 7, 1942.
42. Norman Cousins, Letter to Eleanor Roosevelt, March 25, 1942, RLT Materials.
43. Cousins, Letter to Eleanor Roosevelt March 25, 1942.
44. "Roosevelt Makes Victory Book Plea," *New York Times*, April 15, 1942, 18.
45. "Roosevelt Makes Victory Book Plea," 18.
46. "Victory Book Day," *New York Times*, April 17, 1942, 16.
47. "War Book Drive Goes On," *New York Times*, September 14, 1942, 13.
48. Eleanor Roosevelt, Letter to General Osborn, April 7, 1942, RLT Materials.
49. F. H. Osborn, Letter to Eleanor Roosevelt, n.d., RLT Materials.
50. "Captain Trautman Here at Convention as Guest," *Monroe Morning World* (LA), April 19, 1942, 2.

51. E. C. Hoge, Travel Orders No. 48, to Captain Ray L. Trautman, May 6, 1942, RLT Materials.
52. *Final Reports, Victory Book Campaign 1942–1943* (ALA, American Red Cross, USO, 1944), 12, John Alden Jamieson Papers.
53. Final Reports, Victory Book Campaign 1942–1943, 12.
54. W. A. B., Letter to the Wichita VBC, March 5, 1952, VBC Records.
55. "Batista Hails Tie to U.S.," *New York Times*, October 11, 1941, 5.
56. "U-Boats Destroy Five More Ships," *New York Times*, March 15, 1942, 1.
57. Matt Blitz, "The True Story of Ernest Hemingway's Favorite Bar," *Food & Wine*, June 22, 2017, https://www.foodandwine.com/travel/bars/ernest-hemingway-favorite-bar-true-story.
58. "Marital Tragedy," *New York Times*, October 31, 1926, 35.
59. "An American Storyteller," *Time*, December 13, 1954, 72; A. E. Hotchner, *Papa Hemingway: A Personal Memoir* (Random House, 1966), 121–122.
60. "An American Storyteller," December 13, 1954, 71.
61. Hotchner, *Papa Hemingway*, 9–10.
62. Herbert Gorman, "How Men Have Fought and Died," *New York Times Book Review*, November 8, 1942, Sec. 6, p. 1; Ernest Hemingway, ed., *Men at War: The Best War Stories of All Time* (Crown Publishers, 1942).
63. "Code of Wartime Practices for the American Press" (US Government Printing Office, 1943 ed.).
64. Theodore F. Koop, *Weapon of Silence* (University of Chicago Press, 1946), 33.
65. Code of Wartime Practices for the American Press," 1–4, New Yorker records. Manuscripts and Archives Division. The New York Public Library. Astor, Lenox, and Tilden Foundations; *Military Intelligence Military Censorship* (FM 30–28) (Government Printing Office, 1944); *Censorship Regulations for United States Navy* (Government Printing Office, 1943); "When You are Overseas These Facts Are Vital," War Department Pamphlet No. 21–1 (Government Printing Office, July 29, 1943).
66. *Military Intelligence Military Censorship* (FM 30–28), 16.
67. Hemingway, *Men at War*, xiii, xxxi.
68. Roosevelt, "My Day," August 17, 1942, https://www2.gwu.edu/~erpapers/myday/displaydoc.cfm?_y=1942&_f=md056266.
69. Koop, *Weapon of Silence*, 205.
70. Roosevelt, "My Day," August 17, 1942, https://www2.gwu.edu/~erpapers/myday/displaydoc.cfm?_y=1942&_f=md056266.
71. Ernie Pyle, *Here Is Your War* (Pocket Books, 1944), 34.
72. Hemingway, *Men at War*, gallery proof, 1 (stamped September 16, 1942 by the Commonwealth of Australia War Supplies Procurement).
73. Clive Howard and Joe Whitley, *One Damned Island After Another* (University of North Carolina Press, 1946).
74. John C. McManus, *The Deadly Brotherhood: The American Combat Soldier in World War II* (Presidio Press, 1998), 94.
75. E. B. Sledge, *With the Old Breed at Peleliu and Okinawa* (Ballantine Books, 2007), 235.
76. Geoffrey Perret, *Old Soldiers Never Die: The Life of Douglas MacArthur* (Random House, 1996), 394.
77. Butler, *Books and Libraries in Wartime*, 54 (chapter by Lt. Col. Ray L. Trautman, "Books and the Soldier").

78. McManus, *The Deadly Brotherhood*, 87.
79. Adelaide, Interview with Ray L. Trautman (n.d., but after war ended, before Trautman left Library Branch), RLT Materials.
80. Adelaide, Interview with Colonel Trautman, n.d.
81. Jamieson, *Books for the Army*, 109.
82. "Captain Trautman Here at Convention as Guest," 2.
83. David Paul Nord, Joan Shelley Rubin, and Michael Schudson, eds., *A History of the Book in America, Vol. 5: The Enduring Book Print Culture in Postwar America* (University of North Carolina Press, 2009), 43.
84. Nord, Rubin, and Schudson, *A History of the Book in America*, 43–44.
85. Adelaide, Interview with Ray L. Trautman, n.d.
86. Adelaide, Interview with Ray L. Trautman, n.d.
87. Jamieson, *Books for the Army*, 105.
88. Jamieson, *Books for the Army*, 8 n. 3; Pogue, *Ordeal and Hope*, 114.
89. "Overseas Supply: Interview with Major Harmon," n.d., John Alden Jamieson Papers.
90. Perret, *Old Soldiers Never Die*, 287.
91. William Manchester, *American Caesar: Douglas MacArthur, 1880–1964* (Little, Brown and Company, 1978), 3.
92. Manchester, *American Caesar*, 23.
93. Manchester, *American Caesar*, 6, 120, 324.
94. Perret, *Old Soldiers Never Die*, 45–46.
95. Perret, *Old Soldiers Never Die*, 120.
96. Perret, *Old Soldiers Never Die*, 122.
97. Frederick Osborn Papers. Folder "Osborn-Diaries-1943-45, Typescript," January 17, 1944 entry, 15–26, American Philosophical Society Archives.
98. "Overseas Supply: Interview with Major Harmon," n.d.
99. Manchester, *American Caesar*, 6.
100. Molly Manning, Interview with Eric Trautman, May 22, 2023.
101. Jamieson, *Books for the Army*, 292 n. 1.
102. Jamieson, *Books for the Army*, 128.

## CHAPTER 5

1. "Pat," Letter to Council on Books in Wartime, n.d. Council Records.
2. Nord, Rubin, and Schudson, *A History of the Book in America*, 43–44.
3. Jamieson, *Books for the Army*, 143.
4. Copy of letter from "Somewhere in the Philippines," February 2, 1945, Council Records.
5. Theodore Preston, *Magazines in the Twentieth Century* (University of Illinois Press, 1956), 58.
6. Preston, *Magazines in the Twentieth Century*, 59.
7. Elinor Kendall Evans, "Reading Interests of the American Soldier," Camp Blanding, Florida, May 1943, 2, John Alden Jamieson Papers.
8. Fon W. Boardman, Jr., "Of Books and the GI," *Publishers' Weekly*, April 6, 1946, 1949.
9. Goodwin, *No Ordinary Time*, 355–359.
10. "Bear by the Tail," *Marshfield News-Herald* (WI), June 19, 1942, 4.
11. Brendan Gill, *Here at the New Yorker* (Da Capo Press, 1997), 167.
12. Ray L. Trautman, "Career Management Branch Copy," May 16, 1949, Army Records.

13. Jamieson, *Books for the Army*, 133.
14. "The Army's First Purchase of Magazines for Overseas Men," addressed to Mrs. Armstrong, Hugh Rogers, Direct Washington Wire, July 3, 1943, RLT Materials.
15. "Francis Pratt, 72, Ex-*Time* Sales Aide," *New York Times*, December 27, 1975, 20.
16. "Francis Pratt, 72, Ex-*Time* Sales Aide," 20.
17. "The Army's First Purchase of Magazines for Overseas Men."
18. Molly Manning, Interview with Eric Trautman, June 8, 2024.
19. Jamieson, *Books for the Army*, 136.
20. Jamieson, *Books for the Army*, 129.
21. "Newsprint Saving Put Up to Papers," 18.
22. "War Production Board," *New York Times*, January 23, 1942, 18.
23. Edward W. Morrison, "Tank, Jeeps and Planes Roll from Assembly Lines," *Dayton Daily News*, April 19, 1942, 10.
24. Jamieson, *Books for the Army*, 133; New York Office memo. To Mr. Ross from Trunx, June13, 1944. New York Public Library, New Yorker Records.
25. "Praise the Lord and Pass the Ammunition; A Plea for Book Paper," *Chicago Daily News*, May 26, 1943.
26. Jamieson, *Books for the Army*, 129, 132–133.
27. "Magazines and Paper Rationing," *The Virginian-Pilot* (Norfolk, VA), January 29, 1943, 6.
28. Harry Evans, "Knight Errant," *Family Circle*, April 14, 1944, 11.
29. "Eric Knight Won Fame with Novel," *New York Times*, January 22, 1943, 10.
30. "Screen News Here and in Hollywood," *New York Times*, February 8, 1943, 15.
31. Isaac Anderson, "Books and Authors," *New York Times*, August 2, 1942, Sec. B, p. 10.
32. Paul I. Wellman, "Like Hero of His Novel, Eric Knight Found Something Worth Fighting For," *Kansas City Star*, January 23, 1943, 10.
33. "Major Eric Knight Reported Killed in Crash En Route to Africa; Taught at S.U.I.," *Iowa City Press-Citizen*, January 21, 1943, 11.
34. James Marlow and George Zielke, "Boys at Front Are Kept Posted on Home News," *Daily Herald* (Mississippi Coast), September 21, 1943, 3.
35. Paul Fussell, *The Boys' Crusade* (Weidenfeld & Nicolson, 2004), 15.
36. "A Short Guide to Great Britain" (War Department, 1942), RLT Materials.
37. "Send V-Mail to the Boys," *Keansburg News* (NJ), April 2, 1943, 6.
38. V-Mail *Newsweek*, Developed by U.S. Army Library Service, January 18, 1943.
39. *Newsweek*, January 18, 1943 ("Special Edition for the Armed Forces," marked "sample"), RLT Materials.
40. Alfred E. Clark, "Maxwell M. Geffen Is Dead at 84; Publisher of Specialty Magazine," *New York Times*, October 13, 1980, B7.
41. *Omnibook*, December 1938, back cover.
42. *Omnibook*, December 1938, back cover.
43. Charles B. Driscoll, "New York Day by Day," *York Dispatch* (PA), July 18, 1946, 4; "New Magazine Out Today," *New York Times*, November 1, 1938, 20.
44. Driscoll, "New York Day by Day," 4; Richard Match, "The Art of Condensing," *New York Times Book Review*, May 28, 1944, 27.
45. *Omnibook*, December 1938.
46. *Omnibook*, November 1942.
47. *Omnibook*, May 1943.

48. "*Omnibook* Changes to Pocket Size Uniform with Army Edition," *Publishers' Weekly*, May 8, 1943, 1821.
49. Jane Grant, *Ross, The New Yorker and Me* (Reynal & Co., 1968), 262.
50. Thomas Kunkel, *Genius in Disguise: Harold Ross of the New Yorker* (Random House, 1995), 45–46.
51. *The Spiker*, December 25, 1917, 8 (editorial staff listed).
52. "'Censored' Story Has Two Sides," *The Spiker*, August 1918, 4.
53. Kunkel, *Genius in Disguise*, 43–44, 46–48.
54. Grant, *Ross, The New Yorker and Me*, 262.
55. H. W. Ross, Letter to Messrs. Shawns, Lebrano, Geraghty, Cook, Peppe, September 13, 1943; H. W. Ross, Letter to Shuman, October 19, 1943, The New Yorker Magazine Records, ca. 1924–1984. Manuscripts and Archives Division, New York Public Library, Astor, Lenox, and Tilden Foundations.
56. Kunkel, *Genius in Disguise*, 118.
57. See *The New Yorker War Cartoons* (Special Edition for the Armed Forces, 1945); *The New Yorker Cartoons with the Talk of the Town* (Special Edition for the Armed Forces, 1945).
58. Jamieson, *Books for the Army*, 133.
59. *The Saturday Evening Post*, May 1945 Overseas Edition.
60. "Post Yarns Souvenir Set of Thirty-Six Booklets" (Curtis Publishing, 1944–1945).
61. Jamieson, *Books for the Army*, 134.
62. Jamieson, *Books for the Army*, 134–135.
63. Jamieson, *Books for the Army*, 131.
64. "Army Library Service," n.d., John Alden Jamieson Papers.
65. Robert G. Mason, Letter to Special Service Supply Division, August 15, 1944, John Alden Jamieson Papers.
66. Capt. James C. Farmer, Letter, John Alden Jamieson Papers.
67. Lt. Otto Kinzel, *USS Iowa*, Letter, John Alden Jamieson Papers.
68. Frank E. Bartholomew, Letter, John Alden Jamieson Papers.
69. Edward D. Howatt, Letter, John Alden Jamieson Papers.
70. Arthur Tozar, Letter, John Alden Jamieson Papers.
71. "Authors in Forum on Wartime Books," *New York Times*, May 14, 1942, 17; Robert O. Ballou and Irene Rakosky, *A History of the Council on Books in Wartime* (Country Life Press, 1946), 3.
72. "Authors in Forum on Wartime Books," 17.
73. "Authors in Forum on Wartime Books," 17.

## CHAPTER 6

1. Franklin Roosevelt, Letter to W. W. Norton, December 1, 1942, reprinted in Ballou and Rakosky, *A History of the Council on Books in Wartime*, i.
2. Goodwin, *No Ordinary Time*, 372; Marshall, *Report on the Army*, 239.
3. "Victory Book Campaign," June 1946, John Alden Jamieson Papers.
4. Pogue, *George C. Marshall*, 155.
5. "Victory Book Campaign," June 1946.
6. "Army to Purchase Books for Troops," *New York Sun*, May 12, 1943.
7. Sam Lazerow, Note, John Alden Jamieson Papers.
8. "4,632,283 Books Contributed to Armed Forces," *Elizabethton Daily Star* (TN), May 19, 1943, 2.

9. ASE prototype, RTL Materials.
10. Jamieson, *Books for the Army*, 144.
11. "Obituary H. Stahley Thompson," *New York Daily News*, March 19, 1970, 84; "Stahley Thompson, Publishing Aide, 61," *New York Times*, March 18, 1970, 47.
12. Jamieson, *Books for the Army*, 144.
13. Jamieson, *Books for the Army*, 147.
14. Jamieson, *Books for the Army*, 144.
15. Jamieson, *Books for the Army*, 145.
16. "Council to Begin Delivery of Armed Services Editions," *Publishers' Weekly*, September 11, 1943, 902.
17. *Editions for the Armed Services, Inc., A History* (Editions for the Armed Services, n.d.), 6–7.
18. Molly Manning, Interview with Eric Trautman, December 12, 2022.
19. John C. O'Brien, "Eric Knight and 34 Others Are Killed in Plane Crash," *Philadelphia Inquirer*, January 22, 1943, 3.
20. "Eric Knight Won Fame with Novel," *New York Times*, January 22, 1943, 10.
21. Ballou and Rakosky, *A History of the Council on Books in Wartime*, 11.
22. Ballou and Rakosky, *A History of the Council on Books in Wartime*, 3–4, 42.
23. Edmond Taylor, *The Strategy of Terror*, rev. ed. (Pocket Books, 1942), 62.
24. Christopher P. Loss, "Reading Between Enemy Lines: Armed Services Editions and World War II," *Journal of Military History* 67, no. 3 (July 2003): 826.
25. See, e.g., Ballou and Rakosky, *A History of the Council on Books in Wartime*, 11.
26. "8,000,000-Man Army: Stepping Up the Draft," *United States News*, May 22, 1942, 11.
27. Butler, *Books and Libraries in Wartime*, 54 (chapter by Ray L. Trautman, "Books and the Soldier").
28. Maxell, "Elsa Maxwell's Column," 16.
29. Flint Whitlock, *The Rock of Anzio* (Westview Press, 1978), 40.
30. Ralph Thompson, "A Report on Reading Overseas," *New York Times Book Review*, August 13, 1943, BR6.
31. Whitlock, *The Rock of Anzio*, 39; see also "Heart-Shield Bible," *Binghamton Press* (NY), March 5, 1943, 27.
32. Molly Manning, Interview with Eric Trautman, February 15, 2022.
33. "Minutes of the Executive Committee Meeting," February 10, 1943, Council Records.
34. Ballou and Rakosky, *A History of the Council on Books in Wartime*, 5.
35. "Minutes of the Executive Committee Meeting," February 10, 1943, Council Records.
36. "Minutes of the Executive Committee Meeting," February 17, 1943, Council Records.
37. "Army Air Forces Conferences Information Sheet," February 6, 1943, RLT Materials.
38. Ray L. Trautman, "1944 Ready Reference Diary," January 4, 1944 entry.
39. Ray L. Trautman, Letter to Mrs. Ray L. Trautman, postmarked February 23, 1943, RLT Materials.
40. Ray L. Trautman, Letter to Jane, n.d., aboard the *Southerner*, RLT Materials.
41. "Minutes of the Executive Committee Meeting," February 17, 1943.
42. Nord, Rubin, and Schudson, *A History of the Book in America*, 43.
43. "Minutes of the Executive Committee Meeting," February 17, 1943.
44. "Minutes of the Executive Committee Meeting," March 3, 1943, 2, Council Records.
45. Jamieson, *Books for the Army*, 145.
46. "Minutes of the Executive Committee Meeting," March 3, 1943, 2; Austin Stevens, "Notes on Books and Authors," *New York Times Book Review*, January 17, 1943, BR9.

47. "W. W. Norton Dead; Book Publisher, 54," *New York Times*, November 9, 1945, 15.
48. John Jamieson, *Books for the Army*, 146–147, 150.
49. "Minutes of the Executive Committee Meeting," March 17, 1943, Council Records.
50. "Minutes of the Executive Committee Meeting," March 24, 1943, Council Records.
51. *A History, Together with the Complete List of 1324 Books Published for American Armed Forces Overseas* (Editions for the Armed Services, n.d.), 14.
52. *Editions for the Armed Services, Inc.*, 14.
53. *Editions for the Armed Services, Inc.*, 14.
54. Jamieson, *Books for the Army*, 86.
55. Jamieson, *Books for the Army*, 146.
56. *See* Leonard Q. Ross, *The Education of Hyman Kaplan* (A-1, Armed Services Edition, 1943), inside back cover (listing the A-series ASEs).
57. "Minutes of the Executive Committee Meeting," June 8, 1943, 2, Council Records.
58. "Minutes of the Executive Committee Meeting," June 8, 1943, 2; Ballou and Rakosky, *A History of the Council on Books in Wartime*, 73.
59. "Navy Librarian," *Waco News-Tribune* (TX), December 2, 1935, 3.
60. "Navy Librarian," *Tyler Courier-Times* (TX), December 1, 1935, 14.
61. "Minutes of the Executive Committee Meeting," June 8, 1943, 2; Ballou and Rakosky, *A History of the Council on Books in Wartime*, 73.
62. Frank S. Adams, "As Popular as Pin-Up Girls," *New York Times Book Review*, April 30, 1944, BR18.
63. Molly Manning, Interview with Eric Trautman, July 5, 2022.
64. Anita R. Schiller, "Characteristics of Professional Personnel in College and University Libraries" (Library Research Center Graduate School of Library Science, University of Illinois, May 1968), 45–46, table 3.
65. "Navy Librarian," December 1, 1935, 14.
66. *Editions for the Armed Services, Inc.*, vii.
67. L.U., memorandum P.V.D.S., June 11, 1945, Council Records.
68. Ray L Trautman, Western Union telegram to Miss Isabel DuBois, November 27, 1946.
69. Ballou and Rakosky, *A History of the Council on Books in Wartime*, 74.
70. Special Orders No. 306, November 2, 1943, RLT Materials.
71. "Books in Wartime," *Yank the Army Weekly*, October 29, 1943, 21.

## CHAPTER 7

1. Betty Smith, *A Tree Grows in Brooklyn* (Harper Perennial 1992), 145.
2. Butler, *Books and Libraries in Wartime*, 54.
3. Sgt. Ralph Thompson, "A Report on Reading Overseas," *New York Times Book Review*, August 15, 1943, BR6.
4. Thompson, "A Report on Reading Overseas," BR6.
5. Paul McPharlin, "Soldiers Who Read," *Publishers' Weekly*, September 11, 1943, 904.
6. McPharlin, "Soldiers Who Read," 905.
7. McPharlin, "Soldiers Who Read," 906.
8. "Minutes of the Executive Committee Meeting," December 22, 1943, 2, Council Records.
9. 2nd Lt. Robert R. Rodgers, Letter to Council on Books in Wartime ("From an Army Hospital in England," copy), January 30, 1945, Council Records.
10. Letter from "a Private overseas," n.d., Council Records.
11. *Editions for the Armed Services, Inc.*, 28.

12. Letter signed "Sidney" from "somewhere at sea," n.d., Council Records.
13. Adams, "As Popular as Pin-Up Girls," BR1.
14. "A List of the First 774 Books Published for American Armed Forces Overseas" (Editions for the Armed Services, n.d.), 4.
15. Letter signed "Sidney" from "somewhere at sea," n.d.
16. Harold Strauss (reviewer), "A Czech Patriot," *New York Times Book Review*, October 25, 1942, 80.
17. Stefan Heym, Letter to Lt. Col. Ray L. Trautman, November 12, 1943, RLT Materials.
18. Jesse Stuart, Letter to Ray L. Trautman, April 13, 1943, RLT Materials.
19. "Books—Authors," *New York Times*, October 12, 1943, 23.
20. Jesse Stuart, *Taps for Private Tussie* (Editions for the Armed Services, G-188).
21. Jesse Stuart, *Head O'W-Hollow* (Editions for the Armed Services, Inc., 888).
22. Jesse Stuart, Letters to Ray L. Trautman, April 13, 1943; May 9, 1943, RLT Materials.
23. Adams, "As Popular as Pin-Up Girls," BR1.
24. Jack Goodman, *The Fireside Book of Dog Stories* (Editions for the Armed Services, No. A-30).
25. Eric Knight, *Lassie Come-Home* (Editions for the Armed Services, F-156); Eric Knight, *Sam Small Flies Again* (Editions for the Armed Services, G-187).
26. "Merry Christmas to you all," n.d., card from Jere Knight, tucked inside John Bunyan, *The Pilgrim's Progress* (Peter Pauper Press, n.d.), RLT Materials.
27. MM Geffen, Western Union Telegram to Mrs. Ray Trautman, Garfield Memorial Hospital, RLT Materials.
28. Alonzo G. Grace, et al., *Educational Lessons from Wartime Training* (1948), 17.
29. Grace, *Educational Lessons from Wartime Training*, 46–47.
30. Grace, *Educational Lessons from Wartime Training*, 51–52, 57.
31. Charles Glass, *Soldiers Don't Go Mad* (Penguin Press, 2023), xv.
32. Caroline Alexander, "The Shock of War," *Smithsonian* (September 2010).
33. Erin Blakemore, "How PTSD Went from 'Shell-Shock' to a Recognized Medical Diagnosis," *National Geographic*, June 16, 2020, https://www.nationalgeographic.com/history/article/ptsd-shell-shock-to-recognized-medical-diagnosis?loggedin=true&rnd=1690566818481.
34. Matthew J. Friedman, "PTSD: National Center for PTSD," US Department of Veterans Affairs, https://www.ptsd.va.gov/professional/treat/essentials/history_ptsd.asp.
35. Erin Blakemore, "How PTSD Went from 'Shell-Shock' to a Recognized Medical Diagnosis," *National Geographic*, June 16, 2020, https://www.nationalgeographic.com/history/article/ptsd-shell-shock-to-recognized-medical-diagnosis?loggedin=true&rnd=1690566818481.
36. Blakemore, "How PTSD Went from 'Shell-Shock' to a Recognized Medical Diagnosis."
37. Edward D. Ball, "Patton Defended Soldier-Slapping," *New York Times*, November 5, 1947, 15.
38. Benjamin Rush, *Letters of Benjamin Rush*, Vol. 2 (Princeton University Press, 1951), 1064; Terry Shepherd and Lynn B. Iles, "What Is Bibliotherapy?" *Language Arts* 53, no. 5 (May 1976): 569.
39. Beverly Sigler Edwards, "The Therapeutic Value of Reading," *Elementary English* 49, no. 2 (February 1972): 215.
40. Boutell, "Authors Are Like People," *St. Louis Star-Times*, August 4, 1945, 11.
41. "A List of the First 774 Books Published for American Armed Forces Overseas," 3.

42. *A History of the Council on Books in Wartime*, 81. (Internal quotations omitted.)
43. "Stewart Due Back in 1st Liberty Film," *New York Times*, November 5, 1945, 13.
44. Ray L. Trautman, Letter to Philip Van Doren Stern, February 19, 1945, Council Records.
45. J. B., Letter to the Chairman of the Council on Books in Wartime, January 4, 1945, Council Records.
46. Sgt. H. H., V-Mail to the Editions for the Armed Forces, December 21, 1944, Council Records.
47. "A List of the First 774 Books Published for American Armed Forces Overseas," 4.
48. E. B., Letter to Rosemary Taylor, July 17, 1944, Council Records.
49. D. C., Letter to "Mrs. Jones," May 20, 1944, Council Records.
50. Elinor Kendall Evans, "Reading Interests of the American Soldier," Camp Blanding, Florida, May 1943, 2, John Alden Jamieson Papers.
51. Adams, "As Popular as Pin-Up Girls," BR18.
52. A. J. Liebling, "Cross-Channel Trip-I," *New Yorker*, July 1, 1944, 42.
53. Adams, "As Popular as Pin-Up Girls," BR18.
54. Marshall, *Report on the Army*, 239.
55. Ray L. Trautman, Letter to Postell, December 15, 1944, RLT Materials.
56. Ray L. Trautman, Letter to Postell, December 15, 1944.
57. Ray L. Trautman, Letter to Postell, December 15, 1944.
58. "Minutes of the Executive Committee Meeting," October 6, 1943, Council Records.
59. "Books for Prisoners of War," *Publishers' Weekly*, May 22, 1943, 1970.
60. "Books for Prisoners of War," 1970.
61. "Letters [n.d.] to 'Dearest 'Mum,'" *Prisoners of War Bulletin* 2, no. 7 (July 1944): 8.
62. "Letters" from Zentusuji War Prison Camp, Japan, June 1943, *Prisoners of War Bulletin* 2, no. 7: July 1944): 8.
63. "Minutes of the Executive Committee Meeting," October 6, 1943, Council Records.
64. "Minutes of the Executive Committee Meeting," January 14, 1944, Council Records.
65. Jamieson, *Books for the Army*, 155–156.
66. "The Serious-Minded 'Funnies,'" *Toronto Daily Star*, January 18, 1943, 6.
67. Maxwell, "Elsa Maxwell's Column," 16.
68. "Says Boys Overseas Want Comic Strips," *Lebanon Daily News* (PA), September 9, 1943, 15.
69. "Comics A Help," *Parsons Sun* (KS), January 17, 1945, 6.
70. See, e.g., Dave Breger, "Private Breger," *The Stars and Stripes*, September 29, 1944, 2; Milton Caniff, "Male Call," *The Stars and Stripes*, October 2, 1944, 6; Bill Mauldin, "Up Front with Mauldin," *The Stars and Stripes*, October 2, 1944, 8.
71. Martin Blumenson, ed., *The Patton Papers, 1940–1945* (Houghton Mifflin Company, 1974), 624.
72. Bill Mauldin, *The Brass Ring* (W. W. Norton, 1971), 262–264.
73. Edward M. Seay, "Army Librarian Defends G. I. Interest in Comics," press release, n.d., RLT Materials.
74. *Overseas Comics* prototype, RLT Materials.
75. "Comics for Overseas G.I.s," *St. Louis Star-Times*, June 26, 1944, 4.
76. Roger V. Devlin, "The Rambler," *Tulsa Tribune*, August 16, 1944, 11.
77. Jamieson, *Books for the Army*, 134–135.
78. Jamieson, *Books for the Army*, 136.
79. Jamieson, *Books for the Army*, 33.

80. Ray L. Trautman 1944 Diary, February 6–9, 11–12 entries.
81. Certificate of personal property shipped, March 27, 1944, RLT Materials; Finance Office, U.S. Army, Bill of $17.50 to Ray L. Trautman, March 28, 1944, Washington, DC, RLT Materials.
82. Maxwell, "Elsa Maxwell's Column," 16.

## CHAPTER 8

1. Evans, "Reading Interests of the American Soldier," 2, John Alden Jamieson Papers.
2. "Book Burning by Nazis Hit," *Arizona Republic*, May 11, 1943, 8.
3. Steve Broder (artist), "Books Are Weapons in the War of Ideas" (poster) (Office of War Information, 1943).
4. "Ten Years Ago: The Nazis Burned These Books" (poster) (Office of War Information, 1943).
5. "Book News from the Public Library," *Ottawa County News*, July 9, 1943, 4.
6. "International List of Authors Whose Books Have Been Banned and Burned in Nazi-Germany," *The Saturday Review of Literature*, May 8, 1943, 6.
7. "ETO Chapter—Censorship," John Alden Jamieson Papers; Scott Donaldson, "Protecting the Troops from Hemingway: An Episode in Censorship," *The Hemingway Review* 15, no. 1 (1995): 87+. *Gale Academic OneFile* (accessed December 8, 2025), link.gale.com/apps/doc/A17915329/AONE?u=nysl_oweb&sid=googleScholar&xid=b3163152.
8. Ernest Hemingway, *Selected Short Stories* (Editions for the Armed Services, Inc., 1943), 29–30, 34–35.
9. Hemingway, *Selected Short Stories*, 64–65, 69–71.
10. Donaldson, "Protecting the Troops from Hemingway," 87+.
11. "ETO Chapter—Censorship."
12. Charles G. Bolte, *The New Veteran* (Reynal & Hitchcock, 1945), 14.
13. "ETO Chapter—Censorship."
14. Roscoe C. Blunt, Jr., *Foot Soldier: A Combat Infantryman's War in Europe* (Sarpedon, 2001), 64.
15. See *Loving v. Virginia*, 388 U.S. 1 (1967).
16. Lillian Smith, *Strange Fruit* (Reynal and Hitchcock, 1944).
17. William du Bois, "Searing Novel of the South," *New York Times Book Review*, March 5, 1944, B1.
18. 91 Cong. Rec. 8803 (1945, September 20) (statement of Senator Theodore Bilbo September 20, 1945).
19. "Boston Bans a Novel," *New York Times*, March 21, 1944, 17.
20. "Author DeVoto Buys 'Strange Fruit' as Cambridge Test Case," *Boston Globe*, April 4, 1944, 23.
21. "'47 Pulitzer Historian DeVoto Expert on Western Culture," *Kingsport News* (TN), June 20, 1948, 27.
22. Boston Globe, "Author DeVoto Buys 'Strange Fruit.'"
23. "Police Ban on Novel to be Tested in Court," *Hartford Courant*, April 5, 1955, 5.
24. "Boston Author and Store Test Police Censorship," *Berkshire County Eagle*, April 5, 1944, 9; *Commonwealth v. Isenstadt*, 318 Mass. 543 (1945).
25. "Boston Booksellers Discontinue Sale of 'Forever Amber,'" *Boston Globe*, October 19, 1944, 8.
26. "The Best Sellers of 1944," *Publishers' Weekly*, January 20, 1945, 223.

27. Capt. M. C., Letter to the Council on Books in Wartime, December 23, 1944, Council Records.
28. "Books Furnished Troops in the Pacific Theater," November 8, 1945, John Alden Jamieson Papers.
29. "Books Furnished Troops in the Pacific Theater."
30. "Books Furnished Troops in the Pacific Theater."
31. "Books Furnished Troops in the Pacific Theater."
32. "Boston Banned Four Books," *Boston Globe*, January 10, 1945, 4.
33. Jamieson, *Books for the Army*, 88.
34. Thomas F. O'Connor, "The National Organization for Decent Literature: A Phase in American Catholic Censorship," *Library Quarterly* 65, no. 4 (1995): 386.
35. "Magazines Banned by the National Organization for Decent Literature," "Books Furnished Troops in the Pacific Theater," Jamieson Papers.
36. "Magazines Banned by the National Organization for Decent Literature."
37. O'Connor, "The National Organization for Decent Literature," 396.
38. O'Connor, "The National Organization for Decent Literature," 400–401.
39. Raymond L. Trautman, Handwritten Letter to Paul Postell, envelope postmarked November 22, 1944, RLT Materials.
40. R. W. W., Letter to the Armed Services Editions, July 21, 1944, Council Records.
41. S/Sgt. Ken Eldredge, Letter to John Steinbeck, July 20, 1945, RLT Materials.
42. O'Connor, "The National Organization for Decent Literature," 401–402.
43. O'Connor, "The National Organization for Decent Literature," 402.
44. Ruth Benedict and Gene Weltfish, *The Races of Mankind* (Public Affairs Committee, 1944).
45. Benedict and Weltfish, *The Races of Mankind*, back cover; "Race Booklet Not Banned by Army," *Gazette and Daily* (York, PA), January 31, 1944, 2.
46. Ruth Benedict and Gene Weltfish, *The Races of Mankind*, 1–31.
47. Benedict and Weltfish, *The Races of Mankind*, 18; Jamieson, *Books for the Army*, 213.
48. Benedict and Weltfish, *The Races of Mankind*, 18.
49. Benedict and Weltfish, *The Races of Mankind*, 17–18.
50. Jamieson, *Books for the Army*, 213; 90 Cong. Rec. 4413 (Sen. May 12, 1944).
51. Jamieson, *Books for the Army*, 213.
52. "Race Booklet Not Banned by Army," *Gazette and Daily*, 2.
53. "Race Booklet Not Banned by Army," 2.
54. Helen Lombard, "That Pamphlet About the Races," *Daily Oklahoman*, March 7, 1944, 10.
55. "Book Extolling Mind of Negro Barred to Army," *Chicago Tribune*, March 6, 1944, 10.
56. "Prejudice Wins a Round," *Troy Record* (NY), March 13, 1944, 14.
57. "Adam and Eve (with Navels) Irk Congress," *Austin American-Statesman*, April 27, 1944, 15.
58. Jamieson, *Books for the Army*, 213.
59. "House Group Closes Books on Racial Equality Pamphlet," *Paris News* (TX), March 6, 1944, 1.
60. 90 Cong. Rec. 4413 (Sen. May 12, 1944).
61. Jamieson, *Books for the Army*, 213.
62. 90 Cong. Rec. A2927 (1944).
63. 90 Cong. Rec. 4413 (Sen. May 12, 1944).

64. Bergen Evans, *The Natural History of Nonsense* (Vintage Books, 1958), 8–9.
65. "Prejudice Wins a Round," *Troy Record*, 14.
66. "Education," *Time*, January 31, 1944, 31 (Pony Edition).
67. "Letters," *Time*, February 28, 1944, inside cover (Pony Edition).
68. Benedict and Weltfish, *The Races of Mankind*, inside front cover.
69. "YM, YW, Plan Banquet with Langston," *The O'Collegian* (Stillwater, OK), November 16, 1945, 1.
70. "'Races of Mankind' Exhibit," *The New York Age*, October 13, 1945, 5; "Study Proving Oneness of Races on Display," *New Pittsburgh Courier*, December 22, 1945, 2.
71. Jamieson, *Books for the Army*, 215.
72. 89 Cong. Rec. 9800 (Sen. November 22, 1943).
73. 90 Cong. Rec. 623 (1944).
74. 89 Cong. Rec. 9632 (1943); U.S. Const. Art. I, Sec. 4, Cl. 1.
75. 90 Cong. Rec. 717 (1944).
76. 58 Stat. 136, Title V § 22 (April 1, 1944).
77. 90 Cong. Rec. 720 (1944).
78. 90 Cong. Rec. 719 (1944).
79. Kelly Phillips Erb, "For Election Day, a History of the Poll Tax in America," *Forbes*, November 5, 2018, https://www.forbes.com/sites/kellyphillipserb/2018/11/05/just-before-the-elections-a-history-of-the-poll-tax-in-america/?sh=64c134874e44.
80. 90 Cong. Rec. 725 (1944).
81. Act of Apr. 1, 1944, Pub. L. No. 78–277, 58 Stat. 136, § 311(a).
82. 58 Stat. 136, Title V § 22 (April 1, 1944).
83. 58 Stat. 136, Title V §§ 22(2)(b) (April 1, 1944).
84. 58 Stat. 136, Title V §§ 24 (April 1, 1944).
85. Tom O'Connor, "Win Concessions on Book Gag," *Gazette and Daily* (York, PA), July 22, 1944, 3.
86. Jamieson, *Books for the Army*, 223.
87. Jamieson, *Books for the Army*, 223–224.
88. Jamieson, *Books for the Army*, 224.
89. Jamieson, *Books for the Army*, 226.
90. Jamieson, *Books for the Army*, 226.
91. Jamieson, *Books for the Army*, 224, 226.
92. "Thought Control," *Time*, July 17, 1944, 26 (Pony Edition).
93. "Thought Control," *Time*, 26.
94. First Supplemental National Defense Appropriation Bill for 1944: H.R. 3598, 660.
95. First Supplemental National Defense Appropriation Bill for 1944: H.R. 3598, 661.
96. First Supplemental National Defense Appropriation Bill for 1944: H.R. 3598, 662–663.
97. *See* Henry C. Cassidy, *Moscow Dateline 1941–1943* (Armed Services Edition B-50), 207.
98. First Supplemental National Defense Appropriation Bill for 1944: H.R. 3598, 665, 667.
99. First Supplemental National Defense Appropriation Bill for 1944: H.R. 3598, 667–668.
100. First Supplemental National Defense Appropriation Bill for 1944: H.R. 3598, 666.
101. "Army Denies Ban on 'Wilson' Movie," *New York Times*, August 13, 1944, 15; "Ban on Books by Army and Navy Is Opposed by Literary Council," *New York Times*, June 18, 1944, 29.
102. N. C., "Censoritis," *The Saturday Review of Literature*, July 1, 1944, 19, RLT Materials.

103. "For Immediate Release," (press release, n.d.), first sentence beginning: "The Council on Books in Wartime, in a resolution sent today to the President, Postmaster-General, Secretaries of War and the Navy, Speaker of the House of Representatives, and the President of the Senate, protested the restriction on book distribution to the armed forced under the Soldiers' Vote Act." Council Records.
104. William L. Shirer, "Propaganda Front," *Boston Globe*, July 16, 1944, 68.
105. William L. Shirer, "If He Can Fight, Vote U.S. Soldier Merits Treatment as Adult," *Washington Post*, July 16, 1944.
106. "The Taft Censorship Must Be Lifted," *Courier-Journal* (Louisville, KY), August 8, 1944, 4.
107. Dorothy Thompson, "On the Record—Taft Law Outrages Servicemen," *Cleveland Plain Dealer*, July 10, 1944, 4.
108. "Bungling Ban," *Detroit Free Press*, July 3, 1944, 6.
109. D. A. Moore, "Why Forbid Our Fighters to Read Valuable Books?" *Fresno Bee*, July 20, 1944, 22.
110. "More Title V," *Globe News*, September 22, 1944, 2.
111. Editorial, *Globe News*, August 5, 1944, 5.
112. Charles T. Lucey, "GOP Protests Letter Given to Soldiers," *Pittsburgh Press*, September 5, 1944, 15.
113. Lucey, "GOP Protests Letter Given to Soldiers," 15.
114. Richard L. Simon, Letter to Raymond L. Trautman, July 19, 1944, RLT Materials.
115. Robert Cutler, Memorandum to Commanding General, Army Service Forces, December 7, 1944, RLT Materials.
116. Robert Cutler, Letter to Raymond L. Trautman (in envelope), November 23, 1945, RLT Materials.

## CHAPTER 9

1. Dante Alighieri, *Inferno* (transl. Robert and Jean Hollander) (Anchor Books, 2000), Inferno I, lines 1–6.
2. Secret, Subject: Movement Orders, both dated October 12, 1944 (left corner) and October 17, 1944 (right corner), RLT Materials; Secret Memorandum Subject: Amendment of Movement Orders, Thru Deputy Director Special Service Division, to Officers Involved, October 21, 1944, RLT Materials.
3. "Paris Frees Itself," *New York Times*, August 24, 1944, 18.
4. Flora B. Ludington, "Books and the Sword—Symbols of Our Time," *ALA Bulletin* (May 1943), 151.
5. Ludington, "Books and the Sword," 151.
6. Ludington, "Books and the Sword," 148.
7. Ludington, "Books and the Sword," 148.
8. Ray L. Trautman, Letter to Bronxville Savings & Loan Assn, October 19, 1944; Ray L. Trautman, Letter to Mrs. George B. Hall, Bronxville Lodge, October 19, 1944; Ray L. Trautman, Letter to Mrs. Elizabeth "Betty" MacCloskey, October 20, 1944, RLT Materials.
9. Ray L. Trautman, Letter to Mrs. Elizabeth "Betty" MacCloskey, October 20, 1944.
10. Molly Manning, Interview with Eric Trautman, April 27, 2022.
11. Dwight D. Eisenhower, *Crusade in Europe* (Doubleday, 1948), 238.

12. Cornelius Ryan, *The Longest Day, June 6, 1944: The Climactic Battle of World War II* (Simon & Schuster Paperbacks, 1994), 254.
13. Trautman, Handwritten Letter to Postell, envelope postmarked November 22, 1944; Ray L. Trautman, Letter to Postell & Staff, n.d. (from Paris, before November 11, 1944 response letter), RLT Materials.
14. Trautman, Handwritten letter to Postell, envelope postmarked November 22, 1944.
15. Ray L. Trautman, Letter to Col. Warburg, October 28, 1944, RLT Materials.
16. Ray L. Trautman, Letter to Postell & Staff, n.d. (from Paris, before November 11, 1944 response letter).
17. Minutes of the Executive Committee Meeting, Council on Books in Wartime, Inc., December 13, 1944, Council Records.
18. Pvt. G. G., Letter to Thomas Y. Crowell, Co., September 20, 1944, Council Records.
19. JAJ, PEP, RF, Letter to "Dear Colonel," November 11, 1944, RLT Materials.
20. "Soldiers in Art Contest," *Daily Herald* (Gulfport and Biloxi, MS), January 31, 1945, 2; see also *Soldier Art* (Editions for the Armed Services, 739, 1945).
21. Ray L. Trautman, Letter to Postell, December 15, 1944, RLT Materials.
22. Minutes of the Executive Committee Meeting, December 13, 1944.
23. Trautman, Letter to Postell, December 15, 1944.
24. Ray L. Trautman, Letter to "Chief" (envelope says it's to Paul Postell), envelope postmarked November 12, 1944.
25. Trautman, Letter to "Chief," November 12, 1944.
26. Trautman, Letter to "Chief," November 12, 1944.
27. Andrew A. Beveridge, Susan Weber, and Sydney Beveridge, "Librarians in the United States from 1880-2009," Oxford University Press Blog, June 11, 2011, https://blog.oup.com/2011/06/librarian-census.
28. Mattie E. Treadwell, *United States Army in World War II Special Studies: The Women's Army Corps* (Office of the Chief of Military History Department of the Army, 1954), xi, 770–771.
29. Treadwell, *United States Army in World War II Special Studies*, xii.
30. Trautman, Letter to "Chief," November 12, 1944.
31. John Lardner, "Stories About WAACS in North Africa False, Lardner Declares," *Evening Star* (Washington, DC), June 10, 1943, A-11.
32. E. B. Potter, *Nimitz* (Naval Institute Press, 1976), 287.
33. Trautman, Letter to Postell, December 15, 1944, p. 3.
34. Letter to Postell & Staff, n.d. (from Paris, before November 11, 1944 response letter).
35. Jean de Brunhoff, illus., *A.B.C. de Babar* (*Editions du Jardin des Modes*, 1934), RLT Materials.
36. Ray L. Trautman 1944 Diary, November 23–30, December 1–3 entries.
37. Trautman, Letter to Postell & Staff, n.d. (from Paris, before November 11, 1944 response letter.
38. *Guide for the Operation of Small Army Libraries* (European Theater of Operations, Special Services, US Army, April 15, 1945).
39. Trautman, Letter to Postell, December 15, 1944.
40. Edward G. Huey, Restricted memo to Officers Concerned, December 13, 1944, RLT Materials.
41. Manning, Interview with Eric Trautman, June 14, 2022; John Toland, *Battle: The Story of the Bulge* (Random House, 1959), 3.

42. Toland, *Battle*, 27–28.
43. Ray L. Trautman, Letter to "Dear Military Personnel," from Gay Paris, December 15, 1944, RLT Materials.
44. Ray L. Trautman, French Xmas Card to Jane, n.d., RLT Materials.
45. Cash Sales Slip, Paris QM Sales Store, December 16, 1944, RLT Materials; Martin King, *The Battle of the Bulge: Hitler's Final Gamble in Western Europe* (Arcturus Publishing Limited, 2019), 44 (First Army in Spa).
46. Toland, *Battle*, 15.
47. Gerald Astor, *A Blood-Dimmed Tide* (Dell Publishing, 1992), 33.
48. Toland, *Battle*, 19–20.
49. Toland, *Battle*, 21.
50. Neill, *Infantry Soldier*, 167.
51. Astor, *A Blood-Dimmed Tide*, 73.
52. Toland, *Battle*, 21.
53. Neill, *Infantry Soldier*, 174.
54. King, *The Battle of the Bulge*, 107.
55. Astor, *A Blood-Dimmed Tide*, 82.
56. Neill, *Infantry Soldier*, 116.
57. Astor, *A Blood-Dimmed Tide*, 83.
58. Col. R. Ernest Dupuy, *St Vith Lion in the Way* (Infantry Journal Press, 1949), 25.
59. Astor, *A Blood-Dimmed Tide*, 21.
60. Neill, *Infantry Soldier*, 81.
61. Neill, *Infantry Soldier*, 170.
62. Trautman, Letter to Postell, December 15, 1944.
63. Hugh M. Cole, *The United States Army in World War II, The European Theater of Operations, The Ardennes: Battle of the Bulge* (Office of the Chief of Military History Department of the Army), 429.
64. Bill Davidson, *Cut Off* (Stein & Day Publishers, 1972), 23.
65. Davidson, *Cut Off*, 26–27.
66. Neill, *Infantry Soldier*, 91, 285.
67. Toland, *Battle*, 110.
68. Manning, Interview with Eric Trautman, June 14, 2022.
69. Manning, Interview with Eric Trautman, June 14, 2022.
70. Manning, Interview with Eric Trautman, June 14, 2022.
71. Manning, Interview with Eric Trautman, June 14, 2022.
72. Toland, *Battle*, 39.
73. Manning, Interview with Eric Trautman, June 14, 2022.
74. Blunt, *Inside the Battle of the Bulge*, 9.
75. Blunt, *Inside the Battle of the Bulge*, 77; *see also* Hugh M. Cole, *U.S. Army in World War II, European Theater of Operations, The Ardennes: Battle of the Bulge* (Washington, DC: Office of the Chief of Military History, Department of the Army, 1965), 379, 126.
76. Manning, Interview with Eric Trautman, June 14, 2022.
77. King, *The Battle of the Bulge*, 221.
78. Ray L. Trautman, Letter to Jane Trautman, December 23, 1944, RLT Materials.
79. Ray L. Trautman, Letter to "Dear Office," December 23, 1944, RLT Materials.
80. Blunt, *Inside the Battle of the Bulge*, 45.
81. Molly Manning, Interview with Eric Trautman, November 4, 2021.

82. Astor, *A Blood-Dimmed Tide*, 158–159; Manning, Interview with Eric Trautman, November 4, 2021.
83. Les G. Carpenter, "Pad and Pencil," *Danville Morning News* (PA), 4.
84. Letter to "Dear Office" from RLT, December 23, 1944.
85. Boutell, "Authors Are Like People," *St. Louis Star-Times*, August 4, 1945, 11.
86. Boutell, "Authors Are Like People, *St. Louis Star-Times*, August 4, 1945, 11.
87. Ray L. Trautman, Handwritten Letter to Postell, Paris, December 30, 1944, RLT Materials.
88. Ray L. Trautman, Handwritten Letter to Postell, December 30, 1944.
89. Trautman, Letter to "Dear Military Personnel," December 15, 1944.
90. Manning, Interview with Eric Trautman, June 14, 2022.
91. Ray L. Trautman, Handwritten Letter to Postell, December 30, 1944.
92. Army Qualification Card, for Trautman Ray Love, RLT Materials.

## CHAPTER 10

1. Pfc. Dennis R. Gilliam, "Pay Dirt" c/o Ann Ronne.
2. M. M. Geffen, To Eric Ray Trautman, December 20, 1943, RLT Materials.
3. Jere Knight, Notecard to Eric Trautman, n.d., RLT Materials.
4. Paul E. Postell, Letter to Jane Trautman, November 6, 1944, RLT Materials.
5. *The Special Service Company: FM 28–105 War Department Basic Field Manual* (War Department, January 5, 1945), 28–31.
6. Jamieson, *Books for the Army*, 109.
7. Jamieson, *Books for the Army*, 110.
8. Susan Klein, Letter to Col. Trautman, April 30, 1945, RLT Materials.
9. Jamieson, *Books in the Army*, 113.
10. Jamieson, *Books in the Army*, 117.
11. Jamieson, *Books in the Army*, 116.
12. Williams Boyd Sinclair, *Confusion Beyond Imagination: That Old Happy Morale*, Vol. 8 (Joe F. Whitley, 1990), 3.
13. Pfc. John Heneghan (somewhere in India), Letter to Mrs. Bowles, April 30, 1944, Council Records.
14. Bill Sloane, Letter from Chungking, December 23, 1943, Council Records.
15. John C. Nebo, Letter to Editions for the Armed Services, Inc., March 29, 1946, Council Records.
16. Jamieson, *Books for the Army*, 145.
17. S. Spencer Scott, Memo to Executive Committee, August 29, 1944, Council Records.
18. Minutes of the Executive Committee Meeting, Council on Books in Wartime, September 6, 1944, Council Records.
19. Scott, Memo to Executive Committee, August 29, 1944, 2.
20. Minutes of the Executive Committee Meeting, September 6, 1944.
21. "Armed Services Editions: Excerpts from Letters Received by the Center for the Book from Authors of Armed Services Editions," Library of Congress (prepared for February 17, 1983, Armed Services Editions 40th Anniversary Event).
22. "Fighting Men Need More Books Says Librarian," *The State* (Columbia, SC), February 11, 1945, 14.
23. Col. Trautman's Speech, February 1, 1945, Council Records.
24. Minutes of Executive Committee Meeting, February 24, 1945, Council Records.

25. Minutes of Executive Committee Meeting, May 2, 1945, Council Records.
26. Minutes of Executive Committee Meeting, May 16, 1945, Council Records.
27. S. Spencer Scott, Letter to Ray L. Trautman, July 9, 1948, RLT Materials.
28. Les G. Carpenter, "Pad and Pencil," *Danville Morning News* (PA), 4; "Fighters Want Books," *Billings Gazette* (MT), February 9, 1945, 4; "Books Rate High Among Soldiers," *Time-Mail* (Bedford, IN), February 8, 1945, 5; "Journalettes," *McComb Daily Journal* (McComb, MS), February 14, 1945, 2; "Upsurge of Yank Reading," *Lexington Herald* (KY), February 18, 1945, 27.
29. Raymond L. Trautman, Letter to Bennet Cerf at Random House, February 3, 1945, RLT Materials.
30. Francis R. St. John, Letter to Raymond L. Trautman, April 12, 1946; Morris Hadley, Letter to Raymond L. Trautman, May 2, 1946; Milton James Ferguson, Letter to Raymond L. Trautman, April 12, 1946, RLT Materials.
31. F. R. Kerr, Memorandum to Raymond L. Trautman, February 3, 1945, RLT Materials.
32. Carl Vitz, "The Time to Plan Is Always Now," *ALA Bulletin*, October 15, 1944, 408–409.
33. Paul Fussell, *Wartime* (Oxford University Press, 1989), 257.
34. Arthur Krock, "President Roosevelt Is Dead; Truman to Continue Policies; 9th Crosses Elbe, Nears Berlin," *New York Times*, April 13, 1945, 1.
35. "White House Statement," *New York Times*, April 13, 1945, 3.
36. Gene Currivan, "Generals and GI's Mourn Late Chief," *New York Times*, April 14, 1945, 6.

## CHAPTER 11

1. Boardman, "Of Books and the GI," 1949–1950; see also "Columbia Reorganizes Sales and Ad Departments," *Publishers' Weekly*, March 16, 1946, 1621.
2. Goodwin, *No Ordinary Time*, 620.
3. Boutell, "Authors Are Like People," *St. Louis Star-Times*, August 4, 1945, 11.
4. *Guide for the Operation of Small Army Libraries* (Special Services, US Army, April 15, 1945), 5.
5. *Small Army Libraries: TM 28-305 War Department Technical Manual* (United States Government Printing Office, November 1944), 1.
6. Boutell, "Authors Are Like People," *St. Louis Star- Times*, August 4, 1945, 11.
7. "Material for Colonel Trautman's Talks—11 February 1946," RLT Materials.
8. "Material for Colonel Trautman's Talks—11 February 1946."
9. "Material for Colonel Trautman's Talks—11 February 1946."
10. "Material For Colonel Trautman's Talks—11 February 1946."
11. Jamieson, *Books for the Army*, 98.
12. Butler, *Books and Libraries in Wartime*, 59.
13. Jamieson, *Books for the Army*, 98.
14. "Material For Colonel Trautman's Talks—11 February 1946."
15. Diary of Ray L. Trautman, 1944, February 29, 1944 entry.
16. Ray L. Trautman, letter to Hotel St. Francis, August 2, 1945, RLT Materials.
17. Sidney Shalett, "New Age Ushered," *New York Times*, August 7, 1945, 1; W. H. Lawrence, "2D Big Aerial Blow," *New York Times*, August 9, 1945, 1.
18. Ray L. Trautman, Letter to Jane Trautman ("Hello Darling"), August 9, 1945, Fort Ord, California, RLT Materials.
19. Special Orders No. 190, August 9, 1945, RLT Materials.

20. Maj. Gen. Joseph W. Byron, Letter to "My dear Trautman," August 23, 1945, RLT Materials.
21. "Frederick M. Warburg, 75, Dies; Investment Banker, Sportsman," *New York Times*, July 11, 1973, 44.
22. Boutell, "Authors Are Like People," *St. Louis Star-Times*, August 4, 1945, 11.
23. Jamieson, *Books in the Army*, 16–18.
24. Jamieson, *Books in the Army*, 18.
25. Louis R. Wilson, *The Geography of Reading* (University of Chicago Press, 1938), 14.
26. Wilson, *Geography of Reading*, 107.
27. Manning, Interview with Eric Trautman, December 15, 2022.
28. Manning, Interviews with Eric Trautman, November 4, 2021; July 5, 2022.
29. "Melcher, 83, Dies; Long a Publisher," *New York Times*, March 11, 1963, 9.
30. "Armed Services Editions Planned by Council on Books," *Publishers' Weekly*, May 22, 1943, 1966–1967.
31. "Plan Library for President," *San Bernardino County Sun*, April 20, 1929, 3.
32. "Booksellers to Donate Library to White House," *Great Falls Tribune* (MT), April 19, 1929, 1; "The White House Library," *Miami News*, June 11, 1929, 4 (detailing the size of former president's libraries that were installed and then removed, including Coolidge, Wilson, and then Hoover).
33. "Books for the White House," *Holyoke Daily Transcript-Telegram* (MA), April 12, 1930, 12.
34. "Book Men Start White House Library with 500 Volumes," *Stockton Daily Evening Record* (CA), April 19, 1929, 15.
35. "Plan Library for President," April 20, 1929, 3; "New Selection of Books Presented to White House Library," *Publishers' Weekly*, October 6, 1945.
36. "Books for the White House," 12.
37. Frederic G. Melcher, American Booksellers Association, Letter to Ray L. Trautman, September 22, 1945, RLT Materials.
38. "Seventy-Five Years of Bookselling," *New York Times Book Review*, May 25, 1975, 23.
39. "Two Hundred Titles Published Since 1941 Supplementing the Collections Presented in 1930, 1934, 1937, and 1941," *Publishers' Weekly*, October 6, 1945, 1661.
40. Merle Miller, *Plain Speaking: An Oral Biography of Harry S. Truman* (Berkley Publishing, 1974), 24.
41. "President Starts Archives Project," *New York Times*, December 23, 1938, 15.
42. "President Pushes His Archives Plan," *New York Times*, February 5, 1939, 4.
43. "House Republicans Block Bill to Set Up a Hyde Park Library for Roosevelt Data," *New York Times*, June 6, 1939, 1.
44. "House Republicans Block Bill to Set Up a Hyde Park Library for Roosevelt Data," 1.
45. "House Votes Hyde Park Library 221 to 124; Republicans Sharply Attack President," *New York Times*, July 14, 1939, 1.
46. "House Votes Hyde Park Library 221 to 124," 1.
47. "Presidential Libraries," National Archives Foundation, https://archivesfoundation.org/presidential-libraries/.
48. Ray L. Trautman, Letter to Fred W. Shipman, director FDR Presidential Library, September 12, 1945; Edgar B. Nixon, Letter to Paul E. Postell, September 20, 1945. FDR Presidential Library, Printed Materials, Box 501, U.S. Army Special Services Division.
49. Ray L. Trautman, Memo 605–45, War Department, October 12, 1945, RLT Materials.

50. Ray L. Trautman, Letter to Richard Simon, November 1, 1945. Council Records.
51. Ray L. Trautman, Letter to Harry Scherman, November 7, 1945, RLT Materials.
52. E. Huber Ulrich, Letter to Ray L. Trautman, November 27, 1945, RLT Materials.
53. Wallis E. Howe, Jr., Letter to Ray L. Trautman, November 7, 1945, RLT Materials; Harry Gilroy, "Pocketbooks, Inc., Marks 25 Years," *New York Times*, June 19, 1964, 28.
54. "The Army's First Purchase of Magazines for Overseas Men," addressed to Mrs. Armstrong, Hugh Rogers, Direct Washington Wire, July 3, 1943, RLT Materials.
55. Paul Postell, Letter to Ray L. Trautman, November 30, 1944; Trautman, Letter to Postell, December 15, 1944, RLT Materials.
56. Ray L. Trautman, Letter to E. R. Baker, Jr., *Life*, November 8, 1946, RLT Materials.
57. Peterson, *Magazines in the Twentieth Century*, 55.
58. Robert S. Strother, Letter to Ray L. Trautman, November 20, 1945, RLT Materials.
59. Peterson, *Magazines in the Twentieth Century*, 248.
60. Grant, *Ross, The New Yorker and Me*, 262–263.
61. Thomas Kunkel, ed., *Letters from the Editor: The New Yorker's Harold Ross* (Modern Library), 276.
62. *The New Yorker Overseas Edition*, n.d.; *The New Yorker War Cartoons* (Limited Editions, n.d.).
63. Robert Cutler, Letter to Ray L. Trautman (in envelope), November 23, 1945, RLT Materials.
64. Letter signed by Joseph W. Byron (top) and Joe N. Dalton (bottom) to Ray L. Trautman, February 17, 1945, RLT Materials.
65. F. R. Kerr, Letter to Ray L. Trautman, November 28, 1945, RLT Materials.
66. Molly Manning, Interview with Eric Trautman, February 27, 2022.
67. *The Best from Yank* (E. P. Dutton & Co., 1945), frontispiece (dedication to Col. Ray L. Trautman, with dozens of signatures).
68. Patricia Brown, "Breger, Creator of GI Joe Cartoon, Is Dead," *Sunday Record* (Hackensack, NJ), January 18, 1970, 19.
69. Framed Dave Breger cartoon inscribed to Trautman, "Gee, I Wish I had a library card."
70. Jed H. Taylor, Letter to Ray L. Trautman, December 4, 1945, RLT Materials.
71. Xenophon Smith, Letter to Ray L. Trautman, December 12, 1945, RLT Materials. (Internal quotation marks omitted).
72. Julia Wright Merrill, Letter to Colonel Ray L. Trautman, November 5, 1945, RLT Materials.

## CHAPTER 12

1. Douglas Gilbert, "Foxhole Bookworms Went Highbrow" (possibly *World-Telegram*, but this is a clipping), n.d., RLT Materials.
2. Pfc. Irwin Firus, Letter to "Sir," February 20, 1945, Council Records.
3. Cpl. Wm. Carpenter Good, Letter, July 9, 1944, Council Records.
4. Frank J. Wrobel, Letter, December 11, 1944, Council Records.
5. Firus, Letter to "Sir," February 20, 1945.
6. Letter to Miss Irene Rakosky (copy), September 1945, Council Records.
7. Nord, Rubin, and Schudson, *A History of the Book in America*, 43–45.
8. "You Meet Such Interesting People," *Publishers' Weekly*, November 10, 1945, 2146, RLT Materials.
9. Louis R. Wilson, *The Geography of Reading*, 14, table 2.

10. "The Equal Chance: Books Help to Make It!" (American Library Association, 1936), booklet, 7.
11. See, e.g., *Omnibook*, February 1946, i.
12. Betty and Ernest K. Lindley, *A New Day for Youth: The Story of the National Youth Administration* (Viking Press, 1938), 3–4.
13. Constance Bement, "WPA Library Service to New Areas," *Bulletin of the American Library Association* 32, no. 193 (March 1938): 939; Marion Humble, *Rural America Reads* (American Association for Adult Education, 1938), 13.
14. Humble, *Rural America Reads*, 14.
15. A. L. Blinder, Letter to Ray L. Trautman, July 19, 1946, RLT Materials.
16. Blinder, Letter to Ray L. Trautman, July 19, 1946.
17. "Mowrystown RFD Use for Test Mailing," clipping, n.d., RLT Materials.
18. "You Meet Such Interesting People," *Publishers' Weekly*, November 10, 1945, 2146.
19. Jonathan Rose, ed., *The Holocaust and the Book*, 1.
20. Frederic G. Melcher, "Editorial: Europe Hungry for Books," *Publishers' Weekly*, October 13, 1945, 1755.
21. See, e.g., D. H. Lawrence, *La Vergine E Lo Zingaro* (Arnoldo Mondadori Editore, n.d.); Oscar Wilde, *The Canterville Ghost* (Franz Cornelsen Verlag, 1948).
22. John B. Hench, "Propaganda, American War Books, and the Dilemmas of Translation, 1944-1946," *The Princeton University Library Chronicle* 71, no. 2 (Winter 2010): 151–167.
23. Ballou and Rakosky, *A History of the Council on Books in Wartime*, 83–93, app. D.
24. "First European Edition of *Omnibook* Published," *Publishers' Weekly*, October 20, 1945, 1842.
25. Herm. Wordragen, Letter to *Omnibook*, April 1, 1946, RLT Materials.
26. 77 P.L. 671, 56 Stat. 662, Sec. 2(b) (July 20, 1942).
27. William T. Ramsay, Memorandum to Col. Ray L. Trautman, February 19, 1946, RLT Materials.
28. Citation for Legion of Merit, official citation, embossed "official" golden seal, n.d., RLT Materials.
29. John Farrar, Letter to Ray L. Trautman, April 15, 1946, RLT Materials.
30. "Legion of Merit Given R. L. Trautman," *Bronxville Reporter*, February 21, 1946, 1, RLT Materials.
31. Russel B. Reynolds, Letter to Ray L. Trautman, n.d. (but must be from 1946–1947), RLT Materials; Jamieson, Letter to Ray L. Trautman, August 31, 1951.
32. Reynolds, Letter to Ray L. Trautman, n.d. (but must be from 1946–1947); Ray L. Trautman, letter to Gen. Reynolds, October 9, 1946, RLT Materials. Jamieson, letter to Ray L. Trautman, August 31, 1951.
33. Jamieson, *Books for the Army*, 275.
34. "Application for Appointment and Statement of Preferences for Reserve Officers," August 22, 1946, RLT Materials.
35. Milton James Ferguson, Letter to Ray L. Trautman, November 8, 1945, RLT Materials.
36. Esther Johnston, supervisor of branches at New York Public Library, Letter to Ray L. Trautman, February 8, 1946, RLT Materials.
37. Butler, *Books and Libraries in Wartime*, 65–66; "*Omnibook* Executive Is Speaker Before Librarians," n.d., for release at will, RLT Materials.
38. Dorothy W. Curtiss, Letter to Ray L. Trautman, February 7, 1946, RLT Materials.
39. Willa Martin, "GIs' 'Exposure' to Literature Betters U.S. Reading Habits," *Standard Star* (New Rochelle, NY), March 22, 1946, 13.

40. "*Omnibook* Executive Is Speaker Before Librarians," n.d.
41. Gilbert, "Foxhole Bookworms Went Highbrow," n.d.
42. Trautman, *A History of the School of Library Service Columbia University*, 44.
43. "Material For Colonel Trautman's Talks—11 February 1946." Jamieson, Letter to Ray L. Trautman, August 31, 1951.
44. Trautman, *A History of the School of Library Service Columbia University*, 53–54.
45. Trautman, *A History of the School of Library Service Columbia University*, 56.
46. Trautman, *A History of the School of Library Service Columbia University*, 62.
47. Mildred Melcher, Letter to Ray L. Trautman, June 2, 1948, RLT Materials.
48. Manning, Interview with Eric Trautman, July 5, 2022.
49. Mildred Melcher, letter to Ray L. Trautman, June 2, 1948.
50. Carl White, Letter to Ray L. Trautman, July 1, 1948, RLT Materials.
51. "Appointed at Columbia," *New York Times*, July 18, 1948, 42.
52. Victor W. Knauth, Letter to Ray L. Trautman, August 4, 1948, RLT Materials.
53. Scott, Letter to Ray L. Trautman, July 9, 1948; Roger W. Straus, Jr., Letter to Ray L. Trautman, July 9, 1948; Abe Blinder, Letter to Ray L. Trautman, July 13, 1948; Vice Pres. American News Company, Inc. (signature unreadable), Letter to Ray L. Trautman, July 20, 1948; Gibson McCabe (*Newsweek*, advertising manager), Letter to Ray L. Trautman, August 4, 1948, RLT Materials.
54. Milt Freudenheim, "Gibson McCabe. 89, Ex-Newsweek Publisher," *New York Times*, August 9, 2000, C18.
55. McCabe, Letter to Ray L. Trautman, August 4, 1948.
56. Knauth, Letter to Ray L. Trautman, August 4, 1948.

## CHAPTER 13

1. Lt. Col. William A. Bishop, chief, Army Recreational Service, "Speech Presented at the World-Wide Conference of Command Librarians Held in the Office of the Chief of Special Services," March 1949, RLT Materials.
2. "Expansion Is Considered," *Daily Argus* (Mount Vernon, NY), November 30, 1927, 12.
3. "Ray L. Trautman," *Herald Statesman* (Yonkers, NY), February 19, 1947, 1.
4. "Bookmobile Will Visit Upstate Communities, Showing Self Off and Boosting Tercentennial," *Herald Statesman* (Yonkers, NY), August 26, 1946, 1.
5. "Eager Response in Outlying Sections Met by Bookmobile," *Herald Statesman* (Yonkers, NY), July 17, 1930, 9.
6. "Eager Response in Outlying Sections Met by Bookmobile," 9.
7. "Library and Sugar Firm Confer on 'Book Deposit' at Refinery," *Herald Statesman* (Yonkers, NY), November 24, 1948, 2.
8. "Library and Sugar Firm Confer on 'Book Deposit' at Refinery," 2.
9. "Library and Sugar Firm Confer on 'Book Deposit' at Refinery," 2.
10. "Fellowship Asked," *Daily Times* (Mamaroneck, NY), April 28, 1947, 6.
11. "Library and Sugar Firm Confer on 'Book Deposit' at Refinery," 2.
12. "Library Board Revises Budget to Meet Cuts," *Herald Statesman* (Yonkers, NY), December 18, 1948, 1.
13. "Appointed at Columbia," *New York Times*, July 18, 1948, 42.
14. Trautman, *A History of the School of Library Service Columbia University*, 62, 60.
15. Ray L. Trautman, Memorandum to Chief, Army Recreational Service, June 29, 1949, RLT Materials; Edward F. Witsell, "Job Descriptions for Professional Library Positions," memo, October 31, 1950, RLT Materials.

16. Trautman, memorandum to Chief, Army Recreational Service, June 29, 1949, RLT Materials.
17. "Books Donated for Soldiers," *Durham Sun*, December 5, 1944, 5; Dorothy Ethlyn Cole, ed., *Who's Who in Library Service* (Grolier Society, 1955), 544.
18. Cole, *Who's Who in Library Service*, 544.
19. Cole, *Who's Who in Library Service*, 544.
20. "Camp Librarians Will Attend Atlanta Meet," *Durham Sun*, April 16, 1943; "Conference Army Librarians Fourth Service Command, Apr. 22, 23, 24, 1943, Atlanta, Georgia," program, RLT Materials.
21. Trautman, Memorandum to Chief, June 29, 1949.
22. Trautman, Memorandum to Chief, June 29, 1949.
23. "Army Library Inspection Ends," *Honolulu Star-Advertiser*, October 9, 1949, 30.
24. JAJ, PEP, RF, Letter to "Dear Colonel," November 11, 1944, RLT Materials.
25. Omar N. Bradley, Department of the Army, Circular No. 37 (Mar. 18, 1949).
26. Mildred Young (signed Milly), Memo Routing Slip to Ray L. Trautman, n.d. (but attached is March 18, 1949, Circular No. 37 from War Department), RLT Materials.
27. Paul E. Postell, Letter to Raymond L. Trautman, "Dear Chief," June 8, 1948, RLT Materials.
28. Memorandum for Chief, Army Recreational Service, Subject: "The Wearing of Army-Air Force Hostess-Librarian Uniforms by Other Army Recreational Service Personnel," n.d., RLT Materials.
29. "An Introduction to the Army Service Club Program," Department of the Army Pamphlet No. 21–59 (Government Printing Office 1954), 2–6.
30. *The Officers' Guide* (Military Service Publishing, 1942), 138–139 (pull-out "Typical Insignia United States Army").
31. "An Introduction to the Army Service Club Program," 14, 16–17.
32. "Clothing Requirements for Hostesses and Librarians Going to Japan, Korea, Philrycm (Philippines and Okinawa) MARBO (Iwo Jima, Saipan, Guam)," n.d., RLT Materials.
33. "An Introduction to the Army Service Club Program," 14, 29.
34. Memorandum for Chief, Special Services, AGO, D/A, Subject: Army Library Activities, Sixth Army, n.d. (but mentions in first paragraph a letter order amended June 8, 1950, concerning a visit to California in May 1950), RLT Materials.
35. Memorandum for Chief, Special Services, AGO, D/A, Subject: Army Library Activities, Sixth Army, n.d.
36. Interview by Molly Manning with Eric Trautman, February 8, 2022.
37. Memorandum for Chief, Special Services, AGO, D/A, Subject: Army Library Activities, Sixth Army, 18.
38. Memorandum for Chief, Special Services, AGO, D/A, Subject: Army Library Activities, Sixth Army, 16–17.

## CHAPTER 14

1. 102 Cong. Rec. 7588 (Rep. Roberts, May 7, 1956).
2. "8970th ARU Is Only Unit of Kind," *Pine Needles* (Camp Drum, NY), August 26, 1955, RLT Materials. Same information in "Recreation Unit Trains at Camp," *Watertown Daily News*, August 26, 1955, RLT Materials.
3. "Trautman Heads Reserve Unit Planning Recreation," *Herald Statesman* (Yonkers, NY), August 27, 1953, 26.

4. Organization 8970 ORTSU Special Services Unit Training Center (T/D No. 12–8970), n.d., RLT Materials.
5. "Committee to Formulate an M-Day Training Program," minutes of meeting, January 16, 1956, signed by Maj. Zinke, p. 3, RLT Materials.
6. "8970th ARU Is Only Unit of Kind," August 26, 1955.
7. Alonzo G. Grace et al., *Educational Lessons from Wartime Training* (American Council on Education, 1948), 26.
8. "8970th ARU Is Only Unit of Kind," August 26, 1955.
9. Training Schedule of 8970th ARTSU Special Services Unit Training Center, for April 1–June 30, 1955, RLT Materials.
10. "To Be Paid Reservists in Hard Cash," *Asbury Park Press* (Asbury Park, NJ), September 3, 1957, 3.
11. Manning, Interview with Eric Trautman, June 8, 2024.
12. Columbia University, Letter to Ray L. Trautman, January 10, 1949, RLT Materials.
13. Trautman, *A History of the School of Library Service Columbia University.*
14. Beatriz Massa de Gil, Ray Trautman, and Peter Goy, *Diccionario Técnico de Biblioteconomía: Español Ingles* (Technical Dictionary of Librarianship) (F. Trillas, 1965), 5–6.
15. Bishop, "Speech Presented at the World-Wide Conference of Command Librarians Held in the Office of the Chief of Special Services," March 1949.
16. Mildred A. Hammond, "United States Army in Alaska," March 1949, RLT Materials.
17. 84 P.L. 597, 70 Stat. 293, 84 Cong. Ch. 407, Sec. 9(e) (Jun. 19, 1956).
18. 84 P.L. 597, 70 Stat. 293, 84 Cong. Ch. 407 (Jun. 19, 1956).
19. 84 P.L. 597, 70 Stat. 293, 84 Cong. Ch. 407, Sec. 9(a) (Jun. 19, 1956).
20. "Federal Aid for Library Service in Rural Areas," House of Representatives, Subcommittee of the Committee on Education and Labor, May 25, 1955, comments by Rep. Griffiths (Michigan), 18–19.
21. "Federal Aid for Library Service in Rural Areas," House of Representatives, Subcommittee of the Committee on Education and Labor, May 25, 1955, "A Problem for the Nation" chart, 27.
22. "Federal Aid for Library Service in Rural Areas," House of Representatives, Subcommittee of the Committee on Education and Labor, May 25, 1955, comments by Rep. Griffiths (Michigan), 21.
23. "Federal Aid for Library Service in Rural Areas," House of Representatives, Subcommittee of the Committee on Education and Labor, May 25, 1955, comments by Rep. Elliott (Alabama), 3–5.
24. "Federal Aid for Library Service in Rural Areas," House of Representatives, Subcommittee of the Committee on Education and Labor, May 25, 1955, comments by Rep. Young (Nevada), 8–9.
25. Ernest N. Patty, president, University of Alaska, Letter to Ray L. Trautman, March 15, 1955, RLT Materials.
26. Henry W. "Eskie" Clark, Letter to Ray L. Trautman, March 4, 1955, RLT Materials; E. S. Robinson, librarian of Vancouver Public Library, BC, Letter to Ray L. Trautman, March 14, 1955; Patty, Letter to Ray L. Trautman, March 15, 1955; Gov. Frank Heintzlman, Letter to Ray L. Trautman, March 14, 1955; Ralph Dunbar, Letter to Ray L. Trautman, March 25, 1955; D. J. Phelps, Letter to Ray L. Trautman, August 8, 1955, RLT Materials.

27. D. J. Phelps, Letters to Ray L. Trautman, October 5, 1955; August 8, 1955, RLT Materials.
28. D. J. Phelps, Letter to Ray L. Trautman, August 8, 1955.
29. Morin, "Alaska and the Library Services Act," 623.
30. Lindley, *A New Deal for Youth*, 43–44; see also Morin, "Alaska and the Library Services Act," 623.
31. Morin, "Alaska and the Library Services Act," 624.
32. Molly Manning, Interviews with Eric Trautman, February 8, 2022; April 7, 2024.
33. "Profile of a Professor," *Columbia University School of Library Service* (newsletter), March 13, 1967, RLT Materials.
34. "County Soil Unit Begins Program of Tree Planting," *Times Record* (Troy, NY), May 4, 1951, 8.
35. A. F. Amadon, superintendent of tree nurseries, State of New York Conservation Department, Letter to Ray L. Trautman, February 11, 1952, RLT Materials.
36. Molly Manning, Interview with Eric Trautman, March 10, 2022.
37. "*Who's Who in the East*," n.d., Ray L. Trautman bio pasted onto it, RLT Materials.
38. Molly Manning, Interview with Eric Trautman, August 30, 2024.
39. "Profile of a Professor," March 13, 1967.
40. "Library Trustees Accept Program on New Building," *Herald Statesman* (Yonkers, NY), July 25, 1958, 22.
41. J. D. Alger, Letter to Ray L. Trautman, August 18, 1961, RLT Materials.
42. "For Conspicuous Service," certificate from New York State governor to Ray L. Trautman, January 29, 1957, RLT Materials.
43. Gen. G. H. Decker, US Army chief of staff, letter to Ray L. Trautman, January 25, 1961, RLT Materials.
44. Decker, Letter to Ray L. Trautman, January 25, 1961.

## CHAPTER 15

1. Charles Dickens, *David Copperfield*, 53–54.
2. "Institutional Library Service, LS K8209y-Ray Trautman," course syllabus, n.d., RLT Materials.
3. Ray L. Trautman, Letter to Dr. Bernard Hall, December 26, 1961, RLT Materials.
4. Stefan B. Moses, Letter to Alta M. Brown, September 24, 1963, RLT Materials.
5. Dr. Bernard Hall, To Dr. Karl Menninger, "Report on the Menninger Foundation Libraries," September 28, 1962, 1–9, RLT Materials.
6. "A Brief History of the Menninger Foundation," *The Menninger Foundation Report of Progress for the Year from July 1, 1961, to June 30, 1962* (Menninger Foundation, October 1962), i; see also "Karl Menninger, 96, Dies; Leader in U.S. Psychiatry," *New York Times*, July 19, 1990, D19.
7. "Karl Menninger, 96, Dies," D19.
8. Menninger, *The Human Mind*, 3.
9. "Karl Menninger, 96, Dies," D19.
10. Bernard H. Hall, ed., *A Psychiatrist's World: The Selected Papers of Karl Menninger, M.D.* (Viking Press, 1959), xxiii.
11. Hall, *A Psychiatrist's World*, xvi.
12. Lewis F. Wheelock, Letter to Ray L. Trautman, April 1, 1964, RLT Materials; Karl A. Menninger, Letter to Ray L. Trautman, November 2, 1962, RLT Materials.
13. Hall, *A Psychiatrist's World*, xvi.

14. Karl Menninger, *The Crime of Punishment* (Viking Press, 1968).
15. Judith G. Benjamin, Marcia K. Freedman, and Edith F. Lynton, *Pros and Cons: New Roles for Nonprofessionals in Corrections* (US Government Printing Office, 1966), 2.
16. *A Plan to Provide Library Service to People in New York State Institutions*, 4, 6, 17.
17. Application Title VI A, Library Services Construction Act, State Institutional Library Service, submitted to the University of the State of New York, State Education Department, NYS Library Division of Library Development, for project to begin October 1, 1967, RLT Materials; "Warden Tells of Prison Education," *Democrat and Chronicle* (Rochester, NY), August 19, 1964, 54.
18. Randy Schmid, "Milestone Celebrated at Auburn Prison," *Oneonta Star*, November 30, 1967, 11.
19. Schmid, "Milestone Celebrated at Auburn Prison," 11; "Blood and Cheers Mark 150 Years," *Democrat and Chronicle* (Rochester, NY), November 30, 1967, 10.
20. Molly Manning, Interviews with Eric Trautman, July 5, 2022; December 23, 2021.
21. Ray L. Trautman, "A Model Library for Auburn Prison—Supporting Data," memorandum to Marion Vedder, RLT Materials.
22. Trautman, "A Model Library for Auburn Prison."
23. *Proceedings of the Ninety-Fifth Annual Congress of Correction of the American Correctional Association, Boston, Massachusetts August 22-August 26, 1965* (American Correctional Association, 1966), v.
24. Edward B. McMenamin, secretary of the university (Columbia University), Sealed Letter to Whom It May Concern, June 10, 1971, RLT Materials.
25. Price Chenault, "The Illiterate Who Would Be a Reader," *Journal of Correctional Education* 178, no. 3 (July 1965): 5.
26. "Job Corps Opens First Center for Training Underprivileged," *New York Times*, January 16, 1965, 10.
27. Ray L. Trautman, Memo to Dr. Chester Hall, July 17, 1965, RLT Materials.
28. William Steif, "40,000 Dropouts Will Be Taught by System Job Corps Designed," *Evansville Press* (IN), February 11, 1965, 5.
29. "Profile of a Professor," *Columbia University School of Library Service* (newsletter), March 13, 1967, RLT Materials.
30. Stuart, *Stories by Jesse Stuart*, ii.
31. Jesse Stuart, Letter to Ray L. Trautman, June 11, 1968, RLT Materials.
32. "San Francisco Conference," *ALA Bulletin*, July–August 1967, 844.
33. "San Francisco Conference," 843.
34. "Development of Standards and Evaluative Criteria for the Production of Reading Materials for the Blind and Visually Handicapped," project director biography for Ray L. Trautman, RLT Materials.
35. Ray L. Trautman, "Application for Research Report," to the Department of Health, Education, and Welfare; Office of Education, 1969, 8–9, RLT Materials.
36. "Application for Research Report," 7.
37. "Application for Research Report," 4–5.
38. "Application for Research Report," 6.
39. "Application for Research Report," 8.
40. *Production of Reading Materials: Self-Study and Evaluation Guide 1970 Supplement to 1968 Edition* (National Accreditation Council, 1970), 14–16.
41. *Production of Reading Materials*, 27.

42. *Production of Reading Materials*, 35.
43. *Production of Reading Materials*, 35–37.
44. *Production of Reading Materials*, 5.
45. *Production of Reading Materials*, 5.
46. Huesten Collingwood, Letter to Ray L. Trautman, November 25, 1970, RLT Materials.
47. "Institutional Library Service, LS K8209y-Ray Trautman," n.d.
48. Course Evaluation Committee, to Faculty Member, May 28, 1975, RLT Materials.
49. Course Evaluation Committee, to Faculty Member, May 28, 1975, RLT Materials.
50. William J. McGill, Letter to Ray L. Trautman (in green envelope), May 11, 1976, RLT Materials.
51. Terry Belanger, Email to Molly Manning, February 4, 2024.
52. Molly Manning, Interview with Eric Trautman, September 9, 2023.
53. Jesse Stuart, Letter to Ray L. Trautman, December 17, 1966, RLT Materials.
54. Jesse Stuart, Letter to Ray L. Trautman, February 16, 1977, RLT Materials.
55. Jesse Stuart, Letter to Ray L. Trautman, February 18, 1966, RLT Materials.
56. "Author Jesse Stuart in Serious Condition," *Lexington Herald-Leader*, March 23, 1978, 29.
57. Ray L. Trautman, Letter to Jesse Stuart, April 25, 1966, RLT Materials.
58. Manning, Interview with Eric Trautman, December 15, 2022.
59. VITA Test, Volunteer Income Tax Assistance, Department of Treasury, IRS, Ray L. Trautman test, stamped received March 4, 1981, RLT Materials.
60. Joyce L. Robbins, Department of Treasury, IRS, Letter to Ray L. Trautman, June 12, 1981, RLT Materials.
61. Certificate of Death for Ray L. Trautman, January 27, 1982, RLT Materials.

## EPILOGUE

1. *Who's Who*, Trautman, Ray L., 3165, RLT Materials.
2. Boutell, "Authors Are Like People," *New York Post*, August 2, 1945, 23.
3. "Legion of Merit Given R. L. Trautman," 1.
4. "Armed Forces Cultivated the Reading Habit," *Dayton Daily News* (OH), November 15, 1946, 28 (from *Foreign Service Magazine*).
5. "A Soldier's Story," by Abigail Seymour, *US Airways Attaché*, June 2002, 16–17, RLT Materials.
6. *Going Back to Civilian Life* (War and Navy Departments, 1945), 43–45; William Kerwin, "Home Building Is Looming Throughout the Nation; Officials Say Near-Record Housing Output Is Believed Possible This Year," *Chronicle-Tribune* (Marion, IN), March 21, 1954, 9.
7. *A History of the Book in America*, Vol. 5, 73–75; see also Kerwin, "Home Building Is Looming," 9.
8. Molly Manning, Interview with Eric Trautman, July 1, 2024.

# Index

For the benefit of digital users, indexed terms that span two pages (e.g., 52–53) may, on occasion, appear on only one of those pages.